BALLOTS, BOMBS AND BULLETS

The untold story of one man's work to maintain the fair implementation of electoral democracy in Northern Ireland, and in various countries around the world, through the darkest of times.

PAT BRADLEY

Colmcille Press

Regenicity

Published by Colmcille Press 2022 (www.colmcillepress.com), with the grateful support of Regenicity Ltd.

© 2022 in text Pat Bradley.
Edited by Darinagh Boyle and Garbhán Downey.

Front cover, top to bottom:
- Chief Electoral Officer Pat Bradley delivers the result of the 1998 Good Friday Agreement referendum (courtesy *Derry Journal*).
- Pat Bradley announcing the 1984 European Parliamentary Election results at Belfast City Hall (courtesy of Victor Patterson).

Back cover, top to bottom:
- Pat Bradley (on right) in Kyrgyzstan in 2003.
- Bradley (with umbrella) on the 16th century Stari Most (Mostar Bridge) in Bosnia and Herzegovina. The 24m high bridge, connecting the two parts of the divided city, was destroyed in 1993 by Croatian forces under the command of General Slobodan Praltak, who declared that the stones had 'no value'. Praltak was later sentenced by international courts to 20 years imprisonment. The bridge reopened in 2004.
- Bradley meeting with Falintil guerrillas at their secluded mountain camp East Timor in 1999.
- In 1999, the United Nations appointed Bradley, along with Johann Kriegler, a South African human rights lawyer, and Bong-Scuk Sohn, a Korean political scientist, to prepare the groundwork for the referendum which led to East Timor's independence from Indonesia.

The moral right of the author has been asserted.

ISBN 978 1 914009 28 0

All rights reserved. No part of this publication may be reproduced or transmitted in any form or by any means, electronic or mechanical, including photocopy, recording, or any information storage or retrieval system, without permission in writing from the publisher. The book is sold subject to the condition that it shall not, by way of trade or otherwise, be lent, re-sold or otherwise circulated without the publisher's prior consent in any form of binding or cover other than that in which it is published and without a similar condition including this condition being imposed on the subsequent purchaser.

DEDICATION

This book is dedicated to all those who have worked with determination to assist in the creation of true democracy in various parts of the world, and especially those who did so under hazardous conditions.

"One person with a belief is a social power equal to ninety-nine who have only interests."
(John Stewart Mills "Consideration on Representative Government" p.15).

ACKNOWLEDGEMENTS

There are literally hundreds, if not thousands, of people who helped in various ways with this story and this book. They include my dear family, especially Steve, my colleagues and co-workers, my friends, advisors and critics.

To all of you, my heartfelt thanks. It has been my abiding privilege to know you, work with you and serve you.

Pat Bradley, May 2022

CONTENTS

FOREWORD	6
INTRODUCTION	8
CHAPTER 1 *Setting the scene: The modern politics of Northern Ireland*	9
CHAPTER 2 *Joining the Electoral Office*	18
CHAPTER 3 *As Chief Electoral Officer of Northern Ireland*	43
CHAPTER 4 *Electoral Abuse*	65
CHAPTER 5 *As One Door Closes…*	91
CHAPTER 6 *Invitations to advise and operate abroad*	93
CHAPTER 7 *Academic and other conferences attended*	224
CHAPTER 8 *Developing computerisation of STV counting*	233
CHAPTER 9 *A Brief Epilogue*	235
APPENDICES	
1 – Common types of democratic governance	239
2 – Legislation and responsibility for its application	241
3 – Electoral boundaries	244
4 – Voting systems	246
5 – The franchise	248
6 – Voting methods and procedures	250
7 – Counting the votes	257
8 – Permitted expenditure	261

FOREWORD
by Tom Frawley

'It always seems impossible until it's done' – Nelson Mandela

Firstly, in writing this introduction to Pat Bradley's memoir, I want to record what a particular honour I consider it to have been asked by Pat to deliver this piece. Pat is someone I have admired since I became aware of his hugely important role when he was appointed Chief Electoral Officer for Northern Ireland in 1980. In that role, Pat became the guardian of two critical elements of our democratic process: the Electoral Register; and the administration of all public elections, including Local Government, Assembly and Westminster elections.

We, the citizens of Northern Ireland, I believe, often assume – or worse, presume – that the Register of Voters is accurate and up to date, and all we need to do is turn up at the polling station and announcer ourselves to the polling clerks so we can exercise our right to vote, the most fundamental building block of any democratic process.

The guardian of that process in Northern Ireland for many decades was Pat Bradley, yet another outstanding exemplar of the outworkings of the 1947 Education Act which transformed the life chances of so many young people. Pat Bradley's choice of a career as a champion of free and fair elections began when he applied in 1973 for a post in the Derry branch of the NI Electoral Office.

Most of us faced with the unrelenting violence of the 1970s in Northern Ireland, and particularly in Derry, would have had serious misgivings about applying to become Chief Officer in 1980, but not Pat. He understood the critical importance of the office in at least providing the infrastructure for the democratic process that would be essential for any initiative or transition back to a settled society in Northern that one day might be at ease with itself.

It is important to remember that, even during its darkest days, never once did Northern Ireland fail to complete an electoral process. The 70s and early 80s saw many attempts to disrupt and undermine elections. The Electoral Register itself was a contested space with challenges for names of voters to be included and excluded by all sides. Because of the Troubles, the eyes of the world media scrutinised every aspect of these electoral arrangements. 'Vote early and vote often' was the call-sign in news headlines across the globe when elections were being reported. More pressingly, the logistics of even establishing polling booths was contested because what was considered safe and secure for one community was considered unsafe and insecure for the other. In a number of constituencies, bringing in staff and ballot boxes to a polling station was a military operation, involving soldiers and armoured Saracen cars running the gauntlet of bricks, petrol bombs and even, on occasions, gunfire.

Pat Bradley was central to a process to ensure that all of these obstacles were identified, responded to and overcome. Many of these elections were monitored by international experts from the UN, the US Senate, Westminster, the EU and others, and they always passed this scrutiny. Indeed Pat became the go-to person for these international organisations when in the 80s, 90s and 00s, they wanted to run elections in such contested regions as the Balkans, East Timor, the Middle East and many more.

Pat Bradley, for me, warrants our recognition for a life of public service dedicated to the people of Northern Ireland. Throughout our thirty years of intense conflict, he was a beacon, living out through his daily work and achievement that wonderful mantra of Nelson Mandela – 'It always seems impossible until it's done.' How many of our elections, and indeed referendums, must have felt like that for Pat Bradley as he set in motion the challenging logistics for every new electoral cycle, each with its own unique challenges.

This book is important because it provides a bird's-eye view and a personal perspective into the life and times of a senior public servant, who occupied a pivotal role in one of the critical strands of our public life, overseeing a series of election cycles that took us from the reformed Local Government elections of 1973 through Sunningdale, the Forum elections, European elections, Westminster elections, the Good Friday Agreement referendum and the new Assembly elections.

One final dimension of this extraordinary contribution is that Pat Bradley shines through all of this as an outstanding public servant. His dedication brings to mind the inspirational words of Mahatma Gandhi: 'The best way to find yourself is to lose yourself in the service of others.' Interestingly, Pat never alludes to the loneliness of his role, yet he didn't have a political 'sponsor' or mentor. When he made a call or judgement, some saw it as their vindication, others as a concession or favouritism to the other. Every judgement he made could be subject to judicial scrutiny. When the votes were counted and scrutinised and very fine judgements made, there was no plaudits nor endorsements for him. The public who he served so honourably and selflessly assumed, as we always do, that it couldn't be that difficult, it's 'only' administering elections after all.

Beware of what we take for granted. Maybe we should pay particular attention to what happened in the recent US presidential elections and the events of January 6th 2021 at the Capitol in Washington. I would suggest we were very fortunate to have Pat Bradley overseeing the electoral process through the period of our conflict. So for my own part, can I say, thank you, Pat, for a life career dedicated to the service of the public.

You certainly recognised and lived the inspirational words of Condoleezza Rice: 'There is no greater challenge and no greater honour than to be in public service.'

* Tom Frawley is the former Northern Ireland Ombudsman and current Deputy Chair of the NI Policing Board.

INTRODUCTION

I was born and bred in the 'mixed' Bishop Street area of Derry city, and had both Catholic and Protestant friends there. We all got on together, with the exception of a number of short periods each year when tensions arose around particular anniversaries and their associated parades and celebrations. Aside from that we all helped each other despite the otherwise generally hidden 'differences'. Indeed, as my parents advanced in age, they were dependant upon a younger Protestant neighbour who helped them, when necessary, during the times that I was working in Belfast. It was a mutual arrangement – as my father used his experience in bureaucracy to advise that neighbour and his family in the completion of official forms, applications etc. from time to time.

Upon completing our education, my two brothers, sister and I unfortunately had to emigrate to find employment – leaving our parents alone in every sense. It was the same story for all the other siblings within our extended family and for many people across Derry. I retained a strong attachment to Derry, however, and eventually returned, becoming able to assist my parents as they advanced into old age.

Throughout this book I generally refer to Derry, not Londonderry. In more recent decades the choice of name when referring to the city can, to some extent, be viewed as an indicator of one's political views. During my abode both as a child and as a young man, the name commonly applied to the city by both communities was Derry, with Londonderry applied only when referring to formal names of organisation such as The Londonderry Corporation. The name Derry rolls off my tongue automatically without in any way implying any political or religious connotations. However, in my work I did also apply the formal name of Londonderry in documentation. Aside from any political choice or inference, it is not uncommon around the world for places with relatively long names being referred to in an abbreviated form (eg. LA, Jo'Burg).

In my role as Chief Electoral Officer for Northern Ireland any actions or decisions made by me were always done on an impartial basis without fear, bias or rancour – and I believe that I was successful in that regard. In writing this book I have endeavoured to avoid giving my own personal interpretation of major events in Northern Ireland, and have instead used media and official records in the compilation of my descriptions.

During my twenty-six years of involvement in the Northern Ireland electoral process – first as a Deputy Electoral Officer and then as Chief Electoral Officer – I was fortunate to have had the support of dedicated staff, both full-time, part-time and also casuals working during elections. I take this opportunity to pay tribute to them all and to formally thank them. Hopefully they and I have played an important and successful role in the development of the path towards a more peaceful present for Northern Ireland.

CHAPTER 1
Setting the scene: The modern politics of Northern Ireland

THE ISLAND OF IRELAND – LOCATION AND EARLY HISTORY
Ireland's location on the western fringe of Europe has historically given it a degree of protection from invasion. It's only near neighbour is the island of Britain – and particularly Scotland, which at its closest point sits only twelve miles to the north east. Ireland was one of the few places in Europe which escaped the grasp of the Roman Empire. And whilst the Anglo-Normans arrived under Strongbow in 1170 and retained an English presence and influence on the island in the following centuries, the extent of the territory they controlled was limited and they were gradually absorbed into the native population.

Ireland's relative isolation was to alter dramatically in the sixteenth and seventeenth centuries as England, France and Spain wrestled for European dominance and religious supremacy. The Protestant English feared that Catholic Ireland could be used as a base or backdoor for Catholic French or Spanish forces intent on attacking Britain. Securing a firm grip on Ireland became a strategic urgency for the English, and particularly the province of Ulster in the north, the most Gaelic part of the island and stubbornly resistant to English influence. At the end of the sixteenth century England launched a military campaign to secure control of all parts of Ireland, which resulted in the native Irish aristocracy and tribal leaders going into exile in the European mainland in 1603. With the indigenous Irish now bereft of local leadership, England sought to entrench control of the north of the island through a policy of plantation. Significant numbers of Protestants – from England, and particularly Scotland – who were deemed loyal to the English crown were granted land confiscated from the native Irish as an incentive to settle and help pacify Ulster. It was from this point that Irish history began to become polarised along religious lines. The descendants of these settlers saw their destiny inextricably linked with Britain – and a Protestant Britain at that – whilst discrimination and subjugation was used over the Catholic Irish to enshrine minority Protestant dominance and control.

By 1782 Britain felt sufficiently relaxed about its grip over Ireland to establish a separate Irish parliament in Dublin, subservient to the Westminster Parliament. It only lasted until 1800, however, when The Act of Union abolished it to set up the United Kingdom of Great Britain and Ireland. That major constitutional change had been triggered by the 1798 United Irish rebellion. At that time anyone not of the 'established' (i.e. Anglican) church faced varying levels of discrimination in Ireland, including the various other Protestant faiths. This spurred middle-class Ulster Presbyterians to make common cause with their more heavily-discriminated against Catholic neighbours in organising a violent insurrection that was both inspired by, and supplied by, revolutionary France. As well as the Act of Union, that event also led to a cynical redrawing of the religious discrimination laws in Ireland which elevated all Protestants to a more favourable social and economic position above Catholics in a classic 'divide and rule' tactic. That was to remain largely the status quo for Ireland until another armed insurrection in Easter 1916, and the guerrilla War of Independence that followed then heralded huge change.

ONE ISLAND – TWO STATES
Whilst the 1798 United Irishmen rebellion had seen Presbyterians and Catholics unite in a quest for independence from Britain, the divide and rule tactic of leaving the island's majority Catholic population as the butt of discrimination meant that the Easter uprising was very much dominated by that community (with a few notable exceptions). Indeed the Protestant population in the northern counties of the island were determined that they would not become part of any all-Ireland political entity or 'free state', and were willing and ready to themselves resort to armed insurrection to prevent it. The British Government's response was to create two separate states on the island. Approximately 80% of the territory was granted a significant degree of independence within the umbrella of the British Commonwealth ('The Irish Free State'), whilst an area representing six of the nine counties of the ancient province of Ulster was to remain part of the United Kingdom (as Northern Ireland). The latter was to have its own parliament within the United Kingdom but subservient to the Westminster Parliament. By that stage Britain had grown weary of the intractable political problems of the 'Irish question' and unable to resolve them militarily in the face of significant guerrilla warfare. In February 1922 Winston Churchill famously characterised it in relation to the global changes wrought by the First World War:

"As the deluge subsides and the waters fall short, we see the dreary steeples of Fermanagh and Tyrone emerging once again. The integrity of their quarrel is one of the few institutions that have been unaltered in the cataclysm which has swept the world."

Once the new Northern Ireland state was established, Britain left it to its own devices – doubtless grateful to disentangle itself from the centuries-old political complexities and conflicts that its own policies had created. The boundary of the new Northern Ireland had been carved out of the rest of the island to deliver a two-thirds Protestant majority – creating what it was assumed would be a permanent majority in favour of remaining part of the UK. The new unionist dominated parliament in Belfast saw itself very much as "a Protestant parliament for a Protestant people", and from the start denied Catholics equality in jobs, housing, education and voting. Legislation, particularly electoral, was fine-tuned to support that philosophy.

All this resulted in periodic outbreaks of protest and violence over the decades that followed – including a number of armed campaigns by a rump IRA organisation. But all were contained by the overwhelmingly Protestant regular and paramilitary police forces backed by special legislative powers. That was until the 1960s, when a widespread movement arose to demand equality for Catholics. It had taken inspiration from black civil rights protests in America and student demonstrations in France, and had modest demands in terms of equal access to housing and votes. The perpetually paranoid Northern Ireland authorities however viewed them as enemies of the state and responded with overwhelming excessive police reaction. The situation spiralled out of control in only a matter of months at the end of the 1960s, and an unwilling London found itself again forced to engage with Irish affairs to prevent civil war erupting in a number of areas. The British Army was brought onto Northern Irish streets in 1969, and three years later the Northern Ireland Parliament was abolished by London out of recognition that it was part of the problem. Britain begrudgingly resumed direct control over an area that it had largely turned its back on for the previous half century.

ELECTORAL DEMOCRACY IN NORTHERN IRELAND

The Government of Ireland Act, 1920, had established the two separate parliaments for the north and south of Ireland. The Act specified the number of Members to be elected by proportional representation, single transferable vote (STV), to each House of Commons. The Northern Ireland Parliament was to have 52 members, including four university seats. Members were to be elected for a five-year term of office using the existing Westminster constituencies. That parliament was then to elect a senate, also by STV, for an eight-year term with half of its members retiring every four years. The Act also provided that either parliament could revert to the United Kingdom majoritarian first-past-the-post (FPTP) electoral system if it chose, after a period of three years. That meant that the earliest date a return could be made to FPTP would have been June 1924.

The border between the two new entities on the island of Ireland had been hastily and temporarily arranged along long-standing county lines, many of which didn't reflect the reality of economic and social life on the ground. (With the exception of Antrim and Down, the other counties had been formed in and about 1584. The origins of the other two are not clear.) An Irish Boundary Commission was therefore established to determine where the final border should be drawn, and was due to report its recommendations in 1925.

The inaugural Northern Ireland election in May 1921 made history as the first time that all members of a parliament in Europe had been elected under STV. In contrast, wracked by civil war, the southern Free State didn't hold its first election until 1923. The 1921 election in Northern Ireland was, in reality, a plebiscite as to whether or not the territory should be separate from the south, and negotiations for a treaty between the United Kingdom and the new Irish Free State commenced after it. By the end of that year a treaty was signed which gave, *inter alia,* the North the power to dissociate itself from the South and to remain part of the UK, which it immediately chose to exercise.

In 1925 a second parliamentary election took place in the North, this time in an atmosphere in which partition was a reality. As with the 1921 election, the ten constituencies used were those for the Westminster parliamentary elections – with the addition of a constituency for graduates of Queens University, Belfast, giving an overall total of 52 members. The Parliament met in the somewhat unique location of Belfast's present Union Theological College building, known then as the Assembly's College, from 1921 until 1932. That building was and remains the theological college for the Presbyterian Church in Ireland. The Gamble Theological Library there served as the Chamber of the House of Commons whilst the College Chapel housed the Senate. Proceedings transferred to the present Stormont Parliament Building once it opened in 1932. The Northern Ireland Parliament of the period from partition to its abolition in 1972 is generally referred to as 'the old Stormont', to differentiate it from the current and very separate Northern Ireland Assembly which has sat at the Parliament Buildings in Stormont since 1999.

Unionist politicians preferred the first-past-the-post (FPTP) electoral system to STV, and so Stormont utilised the power it had been given to alter the voting system in 1929 (with the sole exception of the Queens University constituency which was to return 4 members). The parliamentary election held that year therefore employed the majoritarian system rather than STV and that continued to be the norm until 1969 for the NI Parliament, and 1972 for local government elections. (An earlier attempt had been made in 1928 to have STV restored to local council elections but it was defeated.) For the Northern Ireland parliamentary elections, 48 single member constituencies were designated the following year, the boundaries of which were of much controversy. It is interesting to speculate whether the pattern and nature of Northern Ireland's political divisions would have assumed a different character, and a less confrontational one, had the PR electoral system been retained. STV tends to assist the participation of minority opinions within the political process, whilst a majoritarian system is usually the preferred choice of dominant groups.

STV had first been introduced in Ireland by the British Government in 1918 at local elections to Sligo Borough Council. Prior to that the borough, later located in the Republic of Ireland under partition, had been placed under the control of commissioners for a number of years due to mismanagement. The British Government then later extended STV to all local government elections in Ireland so as to ensure adequate representation for Catholics in the North and Protestants in the South.

ONE KINGDOM – TWO ELECTORAL APPROACHES

In 1920 Northern Ireland had the same franchise (i.e. voting rights) as the rest of the UK, as electoral laws were at that time uniform across the entire country. The electoral system to be used in Northern Ireland post-partition was guaranteed under the Government of Ireland Act 1920 for a period of three years – after which matters relating to elections to the Northern Ireland Parliament and local councils could be altered by the Northern Ireland Parliament. The 1918 Representation of the People Act (RPA) had prescribed male adult suffrage on the basis of residence and also a qualification based on the occupancy of business premises with rateable valuation of £10 per annum and another based on a university related franchise. Servicemen had a less restrictive residential requirement and could vote at 18. Conscientious objectors were disenfranchised for five years. As regards local government elections that franchise was granted to all owners or tenants, but not to all residents, subject to a residential qualification of six months in the constituency, contiguous borough or county. Women over thirty were enfranchised for Westminster elections if they were local government electors or the wives of such electors. These provisions applied in Northern Ireland at the Westminster elections in 1922, '23-24 and the Stormont elections in 1920 and 1923-24.

The 1928 Representation Act and the Equal Franchise Act of the same year, covering Westminster elections, granted the parliamentary and local government franchise to women on the same terms as men. It has been calculated the change in Northern Ireland resulted in the electorate for Westminster elections being increased by 24.9% overall. Whilst the male electorate increased by 3.3%; the female increase was 55.6%. Women were thus in the majority of electors in every borough and county but two. Again Northern Ireland decided to tailor this change to meet its own perceived circumstances. Thus whilst its own 1928 Representation of the People Act (NI) applied the equalizing of the franchise to Stormont elections it also introduced a company franchise and a three-year residence qualification for local government elections. The intention may well have been to prevent nationalists living near the border coming temporarily into Northern Ireland as residents for sufficient period to register so as to obtain the vote at local government elections, especially in marginal areas.

A further electoral deviation from the rest of the UK was applied when the Westminster Parliament passed another Representation of the People's Act in 1945. Whilst that new law gave Britain a standard qualification for enfranchisement across both local government and parliamentary elections and abolished the ratepayer franchise, the version chosen for adoption in Northern Ireland did neither.

In 1948 the business and university based franchise were abolished elsewhere in the UK but Stormont decided not to adapt that change and retained both the business and university related franchise for the Northern Ireland parliamentary elections, and for local government elections, both the ratepayers' suffrage and the company vote. It has been calculated that by 1961 the retention of the ratepayer suffrage had resulted in only 73.8% of the Northern Ireland adult population having the local government vote. Some six years later it was calculated that some 220,000 of the registered Westminster electors could not vote at the local elections.

Subsequently the UK Speaker's Conference recommended the assimilation of the parliamentary and local government franchise and that occurred under the 1949 RPA in the UK with the exception of Northern Ireland.

The then *modus operandi* of the Stormont Government can be viewed as a device to maintain as strong an electoral base for its supporters as possible, whilst preventing any enhancement of that of opponents.

THE START OF THE TROUBLES

The cessation of the Civil War in the Free State in 1923 saw the IRA largely go into abeyance – in part due to senior members opting for a political route by founding the Fianna Fail party. A small rump of the IRA did continue to carry out occasional activities in the North, including border campaigns in the 1950s and 1960s, but failed to secure much in the way of support from the Catholic community. The situation changed substantially in the late 1960s when the emergence of a peaceful campaign for Catholic civil rights was met with a combination of state suppression and violence from Protestant extremists. The situation soon spiralled into inter-communal violence, and the IRA was hurriedly resurrected – initially to defend besieged Catholic communities in certain parts of the North. The violence escalated and by the start of 1970 the 'Provos' (the commonly applied name to the wing of the IRA involved), began a campaign of bombings, assassinations and ambushes that was to continue until 1994. That resulted in a reported toll of 3,000 fatalities of which 52% were civilian, 32% members of the security forces, and 16% members of paramilitary groups.

In 1971 the Northern Ireland Government introduced internment (detention without trial) in an attempt to contain the situation by taking the ringleaders off the street. But seemingly indiscriminate use of that power only served to fuel Catholic opposition to the state. On Sunday January 30th, 1972 a protest march against internment was held in Derry during which thirteen unarmed civil rights demonstrators were shot dead by soldiers of the British Army's Paratroop Regiment in what became known as 'Bloody Sunday'. That event proved to be a huge recruiting sergeant for the IRA and removed any chance of a peaceful resolution to the continually escalating conflict.

With things spiralling badly out of control, the British Government scrapped the Stormont Government in March 1972 and resumed direct control over Northern Ireland. The move was intended to be a temporary measure – as indicated by the legislation's title of The Northern Ireland (Temporary Provisions) Act – but it was to remain in place for almost three decades. The British Government had come to the conclusion that the Northern Ireland Government was unable to control the situation, and was in many ways itself part of the problem. The Office of Secretary of State for Northern Ireland was set up in lieu of the Northern Ireland Parliament, with a minister appointed by London in charge of Northern Irish affairs.

Local government electoral arrangements had been under consideration for some years in the UK overall. Under direct rule in Northern Ireland the decision was taken to reduce the number of local councils to 26 and the voting method to be used for election to the new councils to be switched to STV. Accordingly the general election planned for NI in 1972 was instead rescheduled to May 1973 to enable staff training and other organisational aspects for the change to the new system. Then in April 1973 an election took place to set up a new Stormont Assembly, also using STV.

THE DEMOGRAPHY OF ULSTER

A number of alternative names are used to describe the jurisdiction that is known as Northern Ireland, and the most commonly used of these amongst unionists is 'Ulster'. That title is an Anglicisation of the old Irish name for the northernmost of the four provinces of Ireland. The original province of Ulster consists of nine counties – including Donegal, which is the most northerly geographically on the island. Under partition three of the province's nine counties – Donegal, Cavan and Monaghan – were awarded to the Free State and so not included in the new Northern Ireland, whilst the remaining six (Armagh, Antrim, Down, Tyrone, Derry and Fermanagh) were. Accordingly it become the custom of many republicans and nationalists to refer to the North as 'the six counties', out of a refusal to even validate the existence or legitimacy of Northern Ireland by utilising its name. The three excluded counties did contain sizeable unionist populations but were majority Catholic and if combined with the rest of the province would have given the entire jurisdiction a 55-45 percent split. That created concern within London and northern unionist leaders, as such a narrow majority for unionists/Protestants could have been eroded over time, thereby reigniting demands for independence again. Donegal, Cavan and Monaghan were therefore excluded on demographic grounds, even though their incorporation into Northern Ireland would have almost halved its current 500 km border, and thereby would have made it easier to manage from a security perspective. As it happened, a sizeable portion of Protestants within those three excluded counties migrated over time into the new Northern Ireland state to live under the rule of their religious and cultural brethren.

Whilst the Northern Ireland state which was created in 1921 had an overall Protestant/unionist majority, it was not evenly distributed across the territory. The three countries in the east of NI (Antrim, Down and Armagh) had at the time, and continue to have now, a strongly unionist population. The three counties in the west (Derry, Tyrone and Fermanagh) had by and large a Catholic majority, with some exceptions with a small number of areas relatively evenly split demographically between the two communities. Whilst Belfast in the east was a staunchly unionist and Protestant town at the time of partition, the second city of Derry/Londonderry in the far north-west was predominantly Catholic and nationalist-leaning. Protestants have had a particularly strong emotional attachment to the city for over three hundred years. Derry was established as a walled settlement in 1618, during the Plantation of Ulster in which settlers from England, Wales and especially Scotland were gifted land confiscated from the native Irish in return for colonising large tracts of the province. The fortification of the city was financed by the merchant companies in the City of London, which led to the city being renamed 'Londonderry' upon the completion of the walls. The episode which secured Londonderry's place in Ulster Protestant hearts and mythology was its famous siege in 1689, in which the city's Protestant community held out against the forces of Catholic King James II for 105 days until the blockade was finally broken by forces loyal to the Protestant King William of Orange en route to claiming the English throne. The siege has been celebrated ever since by the city's Protestant population, and retains a central position within the identity and history of Ulster Protestant population.

On the other hand there is an another vision, particularly on the Catholic side but also in some sections of Protestantism, of the ancient monastic site first founded by Colmcille (Columba) around 546 AD on what was then the Isle of Derry. Colmcille has a very special place in the early history of Derry. In addition the nationalist community has a strong awareness of the general area around Derry having been governed by Irish kingships and chieftainships with tribal history stretching over very many centuries. After the walled settlement had been built, Catholics were forbidden to reside within its walls and, if visiting the site during the day, had to depart before nightfall with a curfew bell sounding to tell them so. When the Northern Ireland state was established ongoing political control of the City Corporation was an absolute article of faith for the unionists. When that was no longer technically possible with the first Catholic controlled Corporation coming into power in 1920 and the appointment of the first Catholic mayor, then gerrymandering of the ward boundaries was employed to regain unionist control.

The term 'gerrymandering' was derived from the efforts of the former Republican Party governor of the US state of Massachusetts, Elbridge Gerry, to draw up a Bill in 1812 to establish a new and convoluted electoral area that was very much to the benefit of his Federalist Party. The resultant map was described by an observer as the shape of a salamander. Another wry observer commented that it was a 'Gerry-mander' rather than a salamander. It thus has become the general term used to describe the manipulation of electoral boundaries to secure disproportionate influence at elections for some party or candidate.

Within the UK the matter of parliamentary electoral boundaries had long been the responsibility of Boundary Commissions. Initially the commissions were appointed, as regards timing, on a somewhat *ad hoc* basis. Then in 1944 the arrangements were set on more fixed periodic reviews by the House of Commons (Redistribution of Seats) Act of that year. A separate Parliamentary Boundaries Commission was to be established for each of the four constituent parts, namely England, Scotland, Wales and Northern Ireland and to meet at prescribed intervals. The Commissions' Periodical Reports are laid before the Westminster Parliament for consideration by both Houses of Parliament. With the establishment of the Northern Ireland Assembly the remit of the Boundary Commission for Northern Ireland was extended under section 28(2) of the Northern Ireland Constitution Act 1973. That required the submission of a Supplementary Report showing the number of members which the Commission recommend should be returned to the Northern Ireland Assembly by each proposed constituency. On the other hand the ward and district boundaries for each district council are a matter to be recommended by a Local Government Boundary Commissioner (Northern Ireland), as set up periodically under the Local Government (Boundaries) Act (Northern Ireland) 1971, to report on the proposed names and boundaries.

THE OUTCOME

After much difficulty and the passage of time, Northern Ireland has moved forward to a more peaceful state but not without ongoing political and economic problems. The British Government legislated for different types of elections as part of its attempts to resolve 'the Northern Ireland problem'. They ranged from constitutional assemblies, conventions and a referendum to the more routine parliamentary and local government elections. The situation has been compounded by the varying religious composition of the population in each of the parliamentary constituencies. A total of 25 elections have been held in the period from the appointment of the first Chief Electoral Officer in 1973 to my retirement, as the third, in 2000 after over twenty year's service in that role and six years before that as a Deputy Electoral Officer.

CHAPTER 2
Joining the Electoral Office

In 1973 I was based in Derry and working for LEDU, the Northern Ireland Local Enterprise Development Unit. I was the area officer for a large territory that stretched over three counties – from Derry city eastwards to the north coast town of Ballycastle, south to Ballymoney, and from there back west all the way to the border town of Castlederg. It involved a lot of travel and often late hours, but it was enjoyable and a continuation of the voluntary efforts I had done as a younger man (with the added advantage of public funding, state involvement and a salary).

The decline in the security situation across the early 1970s made Northern Ireland less attractive to potential inward investment, which resulted in a substantial decline in our workload. Informed sources were suggesting that the Department of Commerce – which had likewise seen its workload decline too – might seek to have LEDU's activities transferred over to its own under-utilised staff. As LEDU was not part of the Civil Service that would probably result in staff like myself facing redundancy. With a family and a mortgage to think about, I therefore decided that the safest option in the circumstances was to find alternative work and leave LEDU before the decision was taken out of our hands.

As luck would have it, I spotted an advert in a newspaper for the post of Deputy Electoral Officer, based in Derry and responsible to the Northern Ireland Chief Electoral Officer (the Chief) for electoral registration and the running of elections. Despite having neither knowledge nor experience of that type of work, I immediately applied. It was the only suitable alternative employment that seemed available in Derry at that time, and I reasoned that few other people in the area would have the kind of knowledge or experience that was required for it either. There was the additional factor that the city's population was primarily nationalist, and it was the sort of job that, for many from that background, would have been unattractive given that it was perceived to be supporting the status quo within Northern Ireland, and also involved facilitating elections to the British Parliament in London at a time when that institution was being boycotted by many nationalists.

I took a different view of the role personally, seeing it instead as an opportunity to ensure that elections were run, and seen to be run, in a fair and equitable manner, and to seek appropriate changes from within. The Derry Electoral Office had only been set up a year or so beforehand and, as I later learnt, its first appointee had resigned after only a brief time in the role. I nonetheless decided to put myself forward. To my mind there was the clear need for society and governance in Northern Ireland to move on from the confrontational attitude that was common to both sides if the jurisdiction was to develop and the steady, intensive drainage of young talent away from the region be reversed. Without that change the economy and the employment sectors would remain at a very low level in contrast to what could and should be attained. At the same time, I did realise that there were those who would not welcome the introduction of fair and effective governance and respect for all. Indeed there was the strong possibility of a negative reaction, or worse, towards those prepared to facilitate a progression forward. I felt that it was time for individuals to stand up for a positive approach despite the potential threats involved. Hence I was pleased to be called for an interview in December 1973, and then somewhat surprised when I got selected. I later learnt that a number of the other applicants had little knowledge or experience of public sector work, and that many of those who were likely to have such experience (i.e. from a unionist background), regarded the post as unattractive due to the political violence within the city. So it may have been the case that I was the only candidate who was both willing and suitable for the role. I was instructed to take up the post on March 1st, 1974. However in early January the Chief telephoned me at home one evening to tell me that I should start almost immediately, as a certain event would probably take place shortly. He was not prepared to explain further but said that he would telephone me at the Derry office on my first day to explain. He also informed me that he had arranged for me to be released immediately from my role at LEDU.

    Immediately prior to taking up the post, a number of events took place that were of particular concern. They included the shooting of a businessman at his home in Derry, the bombing of a supermarket on New Year's Eve, and an Irish police raid on two alleged republican safe houses just across the border in which four men were arrested and six others fled. It was therefore clear that paramilitary activity was increasing locally, and I wondered if my new job would also put me into the firing line. Despite that I felt strongly that the time was right to participate in community service in a positive manner, rather than through routes such as boycotts or extremes like paramilitarism. I therefore accepted the job offer with a determination to make a success of the task and to be seen to operate in an open and equitable manner. Just after I commenced in the post a hijacked helicopter was used in a bomb attack on the police barracks in Strabane (fourteen miles from Derry). A few days after that, seven bombs were found in a vehicle by an army checkpoint on Derry Quay. It was therefore a very difficult time to begin a job that some would view as being supportive of the British State in Derry and Northern Ireland.

THE POLITICAL CONTEXT AT THE TIME OF MY APPOINTMENT

1973 saw the British Government make its first attempt to introduce a self-governing body for Northern Ireland, in which unionists and nationalists were required to share power and work together. Elections were held in June 1973 to form a new 78-member Northern Ireland Assembly, following which a cross-community coalition was formed of the Ulster Unionist Party's pro-Agreement wing (25% of the June vote), the SDLP (22%) and Alliance Party (9%). This arrangement was signed into reality by the British Government in December 1973 in what became known as the Sunningdale Agreement (which has also become the shorthand for this entire first attempt at cross-community power-sharing). On January 1st, 1974 a power-sharing Executive was formed, with the UUP's Brian Faulkner (who had been Prime Minister of NI when Stormont was abolished by London in 1972) as its Chief Executive, and the SDLP's Gerry Fitt as its Deputy. There was strong opposition to power-sharing from the start amongst a sizeable portion of unionism, which was to eventually lead to the new Assembly's downfall after only five months. In January 1974 the cross-party Ulster Unionist Council voted to not participate in the new Assembly. Faulkner was deposed as leader of the UUP by the party's anti-Agreement faction, and replaced by Harry West. West combined the UUP with Ian Paisley's DUP and the Vanguard Unionist Progressive Party to create a new United Ulster Unionist Council. And when the snap general election was called for February 1974 they agreed that only one anti-Sunningdale unionist candidate would run in each of the twelve constituencies.

MY ROLE AS A DEPUTY ELECTORAL OFFICER

Upon arriving for my first day at work, I was greeted by a rather drab and dark office that contained just one other person, my assistant, whose post bore the unusual title of 'clerk-typist'. I had expected that a staff member from headquarters would be there to welcome me, give some introductory guidance and to outline an induction programme. That was not to be, but before I had time to get my bearings within the office the Chief telephoned to finally reveal the reason for my accelerated start date. A UK-wide parliamentary election had been called for four weeks time, and they needed me in place to run the operation for the Londonderry Parliamentary Constituency (Northern Ireland's second biggest city). He directed me towards the bookcase behind my desk, where a copy of the 1948 Representation of the People Act would purportedly tell me everything I needed to do. He wished me all the best, commented that it would be a difficult time for all of us but that we should keep our chins up, and he assured me that he would be convening a staff meeting of the full NI-wide electoral team shortly. And with that our conversation ended and my career in electoral democracy began with a proverbial baptism of fire.

This unusual approach to my appointment was an early introduction to what soon transpired to be a poorly led and therefore somewhat ineffective organisation. I had come to the conclusion that that was probably the likely reason for my predecessor's resignation after only a brief sojourn in the post.

THE PARLIAMENTARY GENERAL ELECTION OF FEBRUARY 28TH, 1974

By 1974 Northern Ireland's Troubles were in their fifth year, and showing no signs of abatement. With 294 deaths that year, it was to prove the third bloodiest in the three decades-long conflict. Elections for high public office can be rough and tumble affairs at the best of times, but in that era in Northern Ireland they were also 'contested' in a very literal sense – with individuals and organisations determined to do whatever they could to frustrate, disrupt or even prevent the entire process. This made elections a greater challenge to organise in NI than in most democracies, and also amplified the consequent level of scrutiny involved – with a ready pool of people prepared to use even the slightest technical error as reason to throw doubt upon the entire process.

Organising the February 1974 General Election was therefore not a game for amateurs, but I was undeniably a complete novice to it all myself. It was clear that I would therefore have to rapidly immerse myself in the role and its requirements – or risk the consequences for my career, the electoral process, and potentially even wider civil order. The 'Representation of the Peoples Act' document that I had been directed to behind my desk offered a good initial outline of what was required, but it was essentially just the equivalent of a recipe. As the proverbial proof of the pudding is always in the eating, there were very many additional steps to navigate between this recipe book and serving up a successfully run election, many of which were not at all clear in advance from that document. The Act referred to a range of job roles that were integral to the physical running of an election – such as presiding officers, poll clerks and counters – so a natural starting point seemed to be to conduct a stock check on where we were with regards these key ingredients. When I asked my assistant to see if we had any staffing lists of those who had fulfilled these roles in previous years, the surprising answer was that there were none. It transpired that up to that point elections had been run by the Clerks of the Crown and Peace, who worked within the Court Service. Their task at elections had been reassigned to the Chief Electoral Officer when that post was established. This coming election, the first under the new system, was to take place in a far from ideal situation for a snap election held in the midst of significant civil and military conflict. However I saw it as a personal test to show that I could be successful in such a challenging situation, and also that I was prepared to stand up to those who opposed or wished to abuse the democratic system.

A quick visit to the local Court House in Derry, where the Clerk of the Crown and Peace was located, only drew another blank. The office had recently been restructured, with all of its old files transferred into storage. I may have had the electoral recipe book, but the ingredients' cupboard was starting to look pretty bare by now. That left the forthcoming staff meeting as my one remaining opportunity to understand the people and processes that had been utilised in previous elections, and to attempt to hit the ground running. Surely that meeting would set me on the right course…?

The meeting took place in a private room in the Strangford Arms Hotel in Newtownards, just east of Belfast. It quickly became clear that not only was my lack of electoral knowledge in good company, but also that I was much more keen to be involved in running the coming election than a number of others who were present. A recent reorganisation of local government in Northern Ireland had resulted in a rationalisation in the number of district councils, so I found myself in the company of a number of persons who had been made redundant from their previous roles as council town clerks (the equivalent of modern-day chief executives). To me they were clearly still unhappy with the situation, and they vigorously indicated that when appointed to their new electoral roles they had been under the clear impression that the Electoral Office's job was to supervise elections, rather than to actually run them. The reality of what they had let themselves in for had finally and rather suddenly dawned upon them during that meeting. However as the starting pistol had already been fired on the snap election, it was too late for them to change their position. There were a few individuals who, like me, had been recruited over the last year or two from a variety of backgrounds. They and I were more subdued than the others, and especially so considering the background of civil strife in the community. They had an added advantage over me in that they had had already been in office for some period, working on the preparation of a new electoral register and the staffing involved.

I gained very little from the meeting and returned to my office bemused both by what had transpired there, and by the general lack of preparedness and suitability of the arrangements for the Derry office – which became increasingly apparent by the day. I realised that I was pretty much on my own. However that just made me all the more determined to rise to the challenge and successfully carry out the task in hand. For example, the electoral office was cramped and tucked away on the third floor of a small former bank branch located in Derry's Shipquay Street, and only accessible via a series of steep concrete staircases from street level. My initial reading of The Representation of the People Act made clear that, just prior to polling day, I would have to prepare ballot boxes for transfer to all the various polling stations within my area. Each box would have to be individually numbered and bundled up with the relevant number of ballot papers, electoral registers, posters, a variety of forms and also the paperwork that needed to be completed by the presiding officers. Also I would have to arrange transportation of these items from my office out to each polling station on the morning of the election, and then from there to the count centre at the close of polls. Quite who decided that a cramped third-floor office accessed by steep stairs would be a suitable place to house the base camp for such crucial activities has remained a mystery to me to this day. It was another example of how poorly thought-through and ill-prepared the organisation, at least for the Derry office, was at that time, for the vital job of ensuring the elections were run well amidst such a febrile atmosphere.

When I was appointed to the post of Deputy there had been no indication at all of an election and the Chief Electoral Officer had promised that I would be given appropriate guidance after I had time to settle into the post. The sudden nature of this snap election obviously changed all that. I did recall one of the few key pieces of information that had been passed on to me – that there was an office equipment store somewhere. When I rang HQ in Belfast to determine its location, I was told that it was near the small village of Bushmills (home to the world famous whiskey distillery) – some 40 miles from my office, in a completely different county and area. The key for the facility was held at a nearby police station and I needed to ring in advance to give notice that I would be collecting it, and then present identification upon my arrival. The next day I drove up to Bushmills to find out quite literally what lay in store there. On arrival at the police station I mentioned my surprise at the choice of location for the store, given how far it was from Derry, and was told that it was located there for security reasons – with the store kept under surveillance.

Perhaps the whole electoral set up wasn't as haphazard as I had initially feared after all? That momentary faith was quickly erased as soon as I travelled the short distance to the facility. Rather than being a 'store' in the sense that I had been expecting, it was instead a very rusty old Nissan-style corrugated metal hut surrounded by thick grass, weeds and bushes. I hacked my way to the door and after a lengthy struggle managed to get the key to do its job in the lock. Whilst battling with the initially unresponsive lock, I looked around at the surroundings and concluded that the reported 'surveillance' can have been nothing more than the occasional brief visual check that the facility hadn't been broken into. When I finally conquered the lock, the door took its begrudging revenge by refusing to open more than just a few inches, no matter how much pressure I applied to it. With the aid of a torch from my car, I could see that bales of printed material in plastic wrapping had fallen from where they were stacked onto the floor immediately in front of the door – and nothing was going to make the opening any wider whilst they were located there. One by one I teased the wrapped bundles out through the small opening and placed them safely next to my car until the cleared space became big enough for me to squeeze through. Upon entry I found what felt like the El Dorado of democracy – ballot boxes, polling booths, stationary, notice of elections. The entire apparatus of what was needed to run an election secreted in a rusty hut amidst scrubland in rural County Antrim. We were finally in business.

BOMBS AND BUSY LIZZIES
Surprisingly for someone who willingly sought out a job running elections amidst a virtual warzone, I had very little actual interest in politics or elections myself prior to becoming Deputy Electoral Officer. In hindsight this general disinterest made me an ideal candidate at a time when impartiality was vital,

and strongly held opinions were commonplace. There were people within Northern Ireland who were vehemently opposed to the holding of elections to any British-run legislature – whether in Westminster or Belfast – and who were prepared to go to extreme lengths in an attempt to halt them. And as soon as I became part of the apparatus that was organising those elections, I began to be considered a target. It didn't take long for that message to be brought home to me first-hand. Shortly after the snap election was announced, I received an anonymous phone call at my office informing me that I would not be allowed to run a parliamentary election in Derry. It had a very calm but determined voice, and the message was clear and sharp but without any reference as to who the call was from – simply that I would not be allowed to run the scheduled election. I responded by stating in a normal tone of voice that I was determined to run elections without fear or favour, and then immediately hung up. Receiving a firmly implied personal threat so early in a new job is one thing, but Derry was my home town so what was even more unsettling was the feeling that the caller's voice was not unknown to me but I could not make any identification.

I decided not to inform anyone of this other than the Belfast head office. I had heard of other such calls that were believed to be from non-credible sources, so I wondered if that was the case on this occasion. Then a day or so afterwards a 200lb bomb was placed in the adjoining building to my offices – located on the same floor and essentially on the other side of the wall from my desk. Someone in the adjoining building discovered the device, so fortunately it was defused before it went off. It was unclear whether it was the act of those determined to impede my work, or just part of the routine bomb attempts that were very common at the time within the city.

Newspaper reports did not mention the specific building in which the bomb had been placed, only the street name, and so I decided it was best to continue not mentioning it to anyone other than my headquarters. The incident did, however, prompt the Chief Electoral Officer to make a rare personal visit from Belfast to see me. His visit lasted no more than 40 minutes or so, during which time he appeared to take more interest in the horticultural plants I had procured for the office, rather than the explosive device that had been planted next door or the actual work we were doing. I knew nothing about household plants and had casually selected a couple of the healthiest looking specimens from a local market in an attempt to brighten up the drab office. When he saw them he smiled broadly, congratulated me on the choice of plants I had made and remarked that they were very appropriate. I learned later that he was a keen gardener, and that the plant varieties were 'Busy Lizzy' and 'Honesty'. With that, he made his way back to Belfast again. I was astonished that he did not stay longer to give me a brief introduction to the job in hand and some reassurance in the circumstances. However he did say that there would be a meeting for all the senior staff at headquarters sometime soon.

LET THE PEOPLE VOTE – BUT WHERE?

Elections obviously require somewhere for a person to vote, and it was my role to determine where polling stations would be located within the constituency that I ran. Public buildings are generally used, with schools the most popular choice, and the Deputy returning officer has the power to requisition them for a day to establish a polling place there. Despite the tension that surrounded elections at that time, the utilisation of their premises for a day to serve as a polling station was often viewed positively by the school community concerned. Common practise was for the school principal to be made presiding officers in charge of the operation at their school, which came with an associated payment. The ordinary teaching staff were happy, as it gave them either an opportunity to be employed as poll clerks for the day or a day off if they preferred. School care-taking staff also got compensated for receiving, storing and assembling the polling screens and other kit. And for the pupils there was the benefit of the school being closed for a day – and unexpectedly so in the case of a snap election. So appointing a new polling station felt like being an electoral Santa Claus for those within the education sector, even if there were others who were less keen.

The law required that a list of polling stations be prepared and published at designated intervals. The same places generally tended to be used from election to election. Sometimes new locations were required however when a previously used facility was no longer available, or where new housing meant that the demands of the polling day operation had outgrown its previous location. This was at a time when the educational divide within Northern Ireland also carried its own political sensitivities. State-run schools catered largely for Protestant pupils and those of other faiths, whilst the voluntary sector was largely Catholic-run and aimed at young people from that background.

That religious divide tended also to be echoed in the composition of a school's staff, and thereby indirectly in the election staffing. It was something that I determined would need addressing slowly over the following number of elections. A more immediate problem was the reaction of some school principals when notified that their premises were to be used on polling day. Some were concerned that their well-maintained premises could be damaged by the constant flow of hundreds of people in and out in all weathers for 15 hours solid, and complained that their premises had been left in a mess after the previous election. Others were mindful that their school was located in an area where the electoral process faced active opposition, and were therefore fearful of a more direct form of damage. A visit to the school in advance usually helped to assuage any concerns, though not always.

On one occasion a recalcitrant principal claimed that it had taken several weeks to get her school back into an acceptable state after the last election, and so informed me categorically that the doors of her facility would remain firmly locked on polling day. I had to remind her politely that this was not a question of choice – that the school was in fact being requisitioned for use in the election, and that entry would regrettably be forced on the morning if so required. It wasn't exactly the type of approach I wished to take, but it was absolutely necessary in the circumstances. People have a legal and democratic right to vote, and facilities must be provided to enable them to fulfil that right. I notified all my staff that they should ensure that they kept a good standard of housekeeping inside the facilities on what would turn out to be a rather wet and miserable polling day.

MY FIRST POLLING DAY – FEBRUARY 28th, 1974

As it transpired, ensuring that floors were kept clean would be the least of the concerns on my first election day. A polling station in the staunchly nationalist Creggan area of Derry came under continued attack from petrol bombs around mid-day. The staff there understandably became very concerned for their safety, and the police advised me that it might be prudent to evacuate them. Shutting down a polling station on election day could have had very negative ramifications however – both by putting a question mark over the result in that constituency, and also by setting a dangerous precedent for disturbances at future elections. I was therefore determined to keep the location open, whilst being sympathetic to the staff's predicament and mindful that voters were also being deterred from going there by the trouble. Accordingly I recruited a volunteer from amongst the casual staff working for me at the election who was prepared to join me in going to the polling station, with a plan of together operating the polling station ourselves once the staff had been evacuated.

Given the circumstances, the only vehicle that could get us safely into the grounds of the polling station was an armoured military Land Rover. Amidst an incoming hail of petrol bombs I asked the driver to reverse us as close as he could to the school's entrance porch, to which he duly obliged – but in the process managed to also accidentally damage the structure. We were able to dismount safely, enter the premises and evacuate the staff into the Land Rover that we had just arrived in. My colleague and I remained on-site to run the polling station as petrol bombs continued to be thrown in our direction outside. Not surprisingly, the fracas resulted in voters being rather thin on the ground.

A short while later I heard a telephone ringing nearby within the building – and as this was the days before mobile phones, I assumed it might be a colleague or the authorities trying to reach me. Instead it turned out to be an irate man complaining that electors couldn't get to the school due to the petrol bombs, with his conclusion being that the polling station should therefore close. My response was twofold. Firstly, to clarify that the petrol bombs were being thrown from the public highway over which I had neither authority nor control, and that he should take that issue up with the police. Secondly, to confirm that if this was his polling station and he had yet to vote, then we would be happy to issue him with a ballot upon his arrival at our location. His response was simply to slam the phone down.

The barrage of petrol bombs did appear to lessen in both intensity and frequency afterwards, however, which enabled voters to begin to reappear as things returned to a more normal state. At the close of the poll the ballot boxes were sealed and taken under the usual armed escort to the count centre, and the job of keeping that polling centre open had been accomplished. There were issues at some other polling stations in Derry on that day, but nothing on a scale to match this. My colleague and I felt very satisfied that we had managed to keep the polling station open and ensured that the ballot boxes were safely delivered to the counting centre. It was illustrative of our determination to do the job we had signed up for, despite the potential problems that could arise.

Earlier on the day of the election I had travelled around various other polling stations to let the staff see that I was immediately available in case of queries or concerns, and also to be visibly present in 'challenging' areas. Army patrols were also out during the day to stop and check cars, and I myself was not spared the detailed searches that they were conducting of vehicles. On one occasion on the main quayside road where an army check point had been set up, I was stopped and a thorough investigation took place of the inside of my car, the boot and even behind the hub caps, to check if anything had been secreted there. As I stood beside the car in clear view of passers-by, some recognised me and made clear from their comments that the situation was a source of some amusement!

An issue also arose in the city's Waterside area that was only averted through some quick thinking. One of the polling stations there was within a school located in a strongly unionist area, but it was also the place where the residents of a nearby Catholic convent were assigned to vote. When the nuns went along to exercise their democratic duty, they were confronted by a very large British flag draped across the entire double-gated entrance to the school. The only way to access the site was therefore to peel back a corner of the flag, which understandably was not something the sisters were inclined to do in front of the crowd that had assembled there. The flag had clearly been put there to intimidate or deter voters of a Catholic or nationalist persuasion, and the nuns complained about the situation to a local councillor, who in turn raised it with me. I decided to investigate the issue with my own eyes, and upon arrival at the school's gates was greeted by the largest flag I had ever seen. Its presence was clearly a problem, but with a large group of young people gathered in the area, any attempt by me to have it removed could have quickly escalated into greater problems. The ideal solution all round was to find a way to persuade them to remove it themselves. The bottom of the huge flag had become stained by flapping around on the wet pavement, and there were reports that a TV crew was in the area to cover the election. I approached a couple of older members within the crowd, who I assumed were the ringleaders, and pointed out that anyone watching on TV would take a dim view of the flag being left trailing on the ground. (Of course, there was no way that a flag of that size could be mounted there without it trailing on the ground.) I advised them that the best solution was therefore to remove the flag before any press or TV crew arrived, which somewhat to my surprise they willingly did. Another potential issue had thankfully been resolved amicably.

All in all my first polling day had proven to be a baptism of fire, but we had managed to keep the show on the road. Derry overall had certainly not been incident-free on that day. A petrol tanker and multiple vehicles had been hijacked, used to block roads and set alight, whilst two shops had also been bombed. Somewhat amusingly a controlled explosion was also carried out on a suspicious vehicle, only for it to transpire that its contents were 400lbs of pork rather than a bomb!

MY FIRST COUNT

For elections in Britain, a key administrative concern after the close of polls seems to be to complete the count as efficiently as possible so that everyone can get home at a reasonable hour on count night. Certain constituencies even engage in a competitive race to see who can declare the first verified result to the country. It's a sport most keenly contested within the North-East of England, where Newcastle pipped record-holders Sunderland to be the first to declare in the 2019 Westminster Election – with an impressive total count time of only 1 hour and 27 minutes. In contrast Northern Ireland has long ploughed a very different furrow when it came to counting the completed ballot papers, with the close of polls seeing ballot boxes sealed and stored securely overnight for a process that never begins until the following morning.

The main reason for this delay in those days was the overall security situation. Ballot boxes had to be accompanied from the individual polling stations to the count centre under armed guard. Some of those ballot boxes would have to travel from remote rural areas, which was not only time consuming but also left them potentially exposed to attack. Even the empty ballot boxes sent out to polling stations before the opening of polls on election day had to have the same police/army escort, with every aspect of the democratic process considered fair game for those seeking to disrupt or halt the event. Throughout Election Day armed police were also present at every polling station. To minimise fraud, Northern Ireland also insisted on the production of identity by anyone looking to cast a vote – something which even to this day is not required in Britain. The security forces therefore had their hands full providing the basic cover required across NI on polling day, let alone being able to provide cover at and for the various counts if they were to be held overnight. The hours of darkness are obviously harder to police than daylight, and there was the added danger that should disturbances break out between opposing supporters in one area, it could quickly escalate and potentially spread to other areas also. So, whilst it put Northern Ireland out of step with the rest of the UK in national elections and guaranteed that we were always the last to declare our results, it was the safest approach to take.

As this was my first election count I kept rehearsing in my mind overnight what had to be done the next day. I was therefore relieved when the count proceeded without a hitch. It wouldn't always prove that way in the years to come, however. I can still recall that during an election some years later, a set of ballot boxes that were travelling a considerable distance to the count centre didn't arrive at the expected time, and were still unaccounted for an hour or more later. The group of army vehicles guarding the convoy transporting the boxes was under the control of an officer who took it upon himself to decide the route that should be taken to the count centre. In some areas it was considered prudent, on security grounds, not to transport the boxes to the count centre along the same route at every single election. The officer in charge of this convoy had therefore decided to take a rather circuitous route, in the process of which he led the convoy down a wrong turn and unwittingly into a staunchly republican neighbourhood. Upon realising his error he had been unwilling to radio-in an update in case the communication was intercepted and their location identified and targeted. Being unaware of the situation, I therefore had to give serious consideration for the first time ever as to what should happen if a set of ballot boxes went missing during an election. Fortunately one of the military scouts sent to search for the convoy managed to locate it, and I was hugely relieved when they finally appeared about an hour later. Even so I was concerned that allegations could be made, if the election result was close, that the boxes had been tampered with. The other concern I had was that the vehicles could have been petrol bombed and the ballot papers destroyed, which would have necessitated the election being re-run.

The February 1974 snap election proved to be a strategic misjudgement by incumbent Prime Minister and leader of the Conservatives, Edward Heath. It saw his party increase its total share of the vote, but it still managed to lose 28 seats; whilst Harold Wilson's Labour opposition won an additional 14 seats to finish with 4 more than the Tories. That made Labour the largest party, but still left them 17 seats short of an overall majority – resulting in the UK's first hung parliament since 1929. When negotiations for a coalition government faltered, Ted Heath resigned as Prime Minister (PM) and was replaced by Harold Wilson at the head of a minority government, (Wilson had been PM until he was unexpectedly ousted in the 1970 election).

In Northern Ireland the election took place in the midst of the Sunningdale power-sharing process, which galvanised unionist opposition to it. The Ulster Unionist Party (UUP), Democratic Unionist Party (DUP) and the Vanguard Unionist Party collectively stood only one anti-Sunningdale unionist candidate in each constituency, which proved to be a successful strategy – with their candidates winning 11 of the 12 seats. The pro-Sunningdale wing of the UUP stood in 7 seats – including sitting MPs Stanley McMaster and Rafton Pounder – but none were successful. The only pro-Sunningdale candidate elected was Gerry Fitt, who retained his West Belfast seat as leader of the new Social Democratic and Labour Party (SDLP). A notable scalp on the nationalist side was the firebrand independent candidate Bernadette McAliskey, who lost her Mid-Ulster seat to Vanguard's John Dunlop. The overall turnout in NI was 68%.

The fact that anti-Sunningdale unionists took almost every seat was a clear illustration of the hard-line shift of unionist sentiment against power-sharing. When it was followed a few months later by the successful Ulster Workers Strike, it led to the inevitable collapse of the Sunningdale Agreement in May 1975.

PREPARING FOR THE NEXT ELECTION – REGISTRATION

The completion of an election count is never the end of the process. A formal Election Return outlining the results had to be completed and forwarded to the Chief Electoral Officer in Belfast, who then transmitted the complete Northern Ireland results on to Westminster. The completed ballot papers from the election had to be sealed and stored securely in case there were any future challenges. All staff, contractors and polling locations also had to be paid for their work. And whilst people often think there is little to be done between elections, in reality it is a process that never really ends.

Having survived my first election with only minimal preparation and no prior experience, I was looking forward to being able to plan properly for future polls – starting with the annual task of preparing a new electoral register and holding electoral hearings regarding it. The extent of the registration area assigned to me overall was far greater than that for the parliamentary election, which only covered the Constituency of Londonderry. My broader registration area now also extended into the Coleraine, Garvagh, Kilrea and Strabane general areas.

By law a new register of electors had to be published annually every September. The starting point in that process was to update the records from the previous year's register, which were held at a Civil Service computer centre located in Belfast. It involved an unwieldy and time consuming process of frequent trips to and from Belfast to transfer amended input forms and bring back the computer printouts containing the updated submissions. The computer was modern technology for its time, but would be considered an unfathomable relic by current standards.

The process for the annual update of the Registrar of Electors went as follows. A household registration form was sent to every known residential address – with the head of household instructed to insert the details of everyone who was entitled to vote there, before returning the form in a pre-paid envelope. Where a completed form was not received from a particular address, an Electoral Registration Assistant (ERAs – employed for a few months each year for this purpose) was sent to canvass that dwelling in an attempt to secure the required information. As the completed household registration forms were received by my office each day, a quick visual scan would be carried out on them before they were collected by the appropriate ERA for that area to enable them to prepare the updated input forms to send to Belfast. From information obtained by the ERAs and elsewhere it was sometimes possible to identify returned forms that bore the names of individuals who were not resident at their stated address and were instead living elsewhere, including across the border in County Donegal. This was not just a matter of electoral fraud, as inclusion on the electoral register also brought with it certain other potential benefits. For example, some couples who in reality were living together endeavoured to use the electoral register to assist in making fraudulent claims for social security benefits on the false premise that they were separated and residing at different addresses. Later, when access to certain schools was enhanced by residency within a particular catchment area, some parents would register themselves on the electoral roll at the address of a relative within that area to enhance the prospects of their child getting into a preferred school (a practise that became known as 'granny-ing'). Banks and lenders also used the electoral register to confirm the address details provided by applicants for mortgages and loans. These bodies had a legal entitlement to receive copies of the electoral roll at a fixed price, which to my mind didn't reflect the intrinsic value of the information being provided to them. So my staff and I had a duty to remain alert to the fact that there would always be some people seeking to game the system, and many reasons for them to try to do so via the electoral roll.

The process of updating the draft register with information from the forms gathered in from both households and ERAs was a rather laborious one in those days. It involved large amounts of paper, and weekly round trips by myself to Belfast with the forms. This information was combined into a new draft register, and placed in libraries and local post offices so that the public could check their details. Recognised political parties were also automatically forwarded the new draft register, which they took great interest in. A specified time-frame existed within which any proposed challenges or amendments to that draft register had to be submitted – which could be in the form of claims for someone else to be included, or objections to a certain name that was already there. This was a quirk in the electoral system in those days, which unsurprisingly attracted much attention from the parties within the hotbed of Northern Ireland's tribal politics.

DEAD MEN CAN'T VOTE
Claims and objections regarding the draft register could be lodged by either ordinary people or by political party agents, and they were considered at the revision hearings that took place just before and after Christmas. The vast majority of the representations made through this process came from the agents of the two main parties operating in Northern Ireland at that time, the Unionist Party, which primarily represented Protestants, and the Nationalist Party which attracted Catholic support. Each party had individual agents covering specific areas who would submit claims and objections regarding their patch and attend the appropriate revision hearing to make their case regarding them. The primary purpose of these agents was to ensure fullest representation of their supporters, including those who did not cooperate with the registration process, or were not

too interested in it. To some extent it was essentially a form of head count. It soon became evident to me that there were mutual rules of engagement between the two parties on this process (though they were not uniformly adhered to in all circumstances or areas), and I suspected that there was a quid pro quo arrangement at times. My suspicion was that prior to the hearings, the various political agents at each hearing, would agree to support some of each other's inaccurate claims so as to get them approved and I was alert to that prospect. At that time the Troubles was still in relative infancy, and both Catholics and Protestants still generally lived in mixed areas across Derry. As a result, the party agents from both sides knew their patch well and had a good understanding of who was living where. As the security situation worsened in Derry over the following years, it resulted in a gradual withdrawal of most of the Protestant population from the majority-Catholic 'city-side' area to the primarily Protestant Waterside area – each on opposite sides of the city's broad River Foyle. The one notable exception to this population drift was the Fountain area, which to this day remains the last majority-Protestant enclave on that side of the river.

I sat in judgement at the revision hearings, listening to the representations made before making a determination on each under a legally prescribed process. I had absolutely no experience of such quasi-judicial hearings, and approached the task initially with some uncertainty. I did, however, have first-hand experience of being on the other side of a Revision Hearing myself some years beforehand when I had returned home from England. A few months after my return I received a notice of objection to the inclusion of my name on the Electoral Register. I had to take time off from work to attend the hearing and was annoyed when it became evident that the objection was based on hearsay. It emerged that the objector had confused me with an elder brother of mine who was residing in London at the time. When I told my father of this experience he explained that the Unionist Party and Nationalist Party had members who watched the 'other side' and accordingly reported on changes within their neighbourhood. This was at a time when Catholics and Protestants lived side by side in many places, and to a much greater extent than they do now. In Derry each of the parties had a paid official who would collate information gathered in this way and lodge claims and objections accordingly. The two sides developed a reasonably good working relationship with each other in that process, and were prepared to recognise when a claim by the other side was genuine or when they'd gotten things wrong themselves.

Anyone who had submitted a claim or an objection, or whose inclusion on the register was being challenged, had to receive by post the details of the hearing to enable them to attend and give evidence. I could require any or all of them to submit their information under oath. The basis for objection had to be stipulated clearly on the letter that was sent out, and a common reason cited was that the person concerned had died in the period following the compilation of the draft register. I felt uncomfortable sending what I regarded as insensitively worded notifications – bluntly stating that the individual had died – to a grieving family, so I instead chose initially to list objections in such cases as simply 'non-eligibility'. Ensuring that the deceased were removed from the register was an important step in minimising impersonation, but I was determined to find a more respectful and sensitive way of handing it.

It was also a task that was not without its difficulties or even comical moments, as the case of a revision hearing in the town of Limavady brought home to me. A political party agent there had lodged an objection to the inclusion of a person on the draft register on the grounds that he had died recently. When I called out the details at the revision hearing, an irate elderly man stood up and exclaimed repeatedly "Who says I'm dead?", and the agent who had submitted the objection melted into his chair. It turned out that the deceased person had been the man's son, who had died shortly after relocating to Scotland. He had exactly the same name as his father, including the same two first names, and when the objector had learned of the death he had assumed that it referred to the older man rather than the son. It had been an honest error on his part, motivated solely by the continual desire of the parties to minimise the risk of impersonation arising from 'the other side'.

Voter fraud was certainly a genuine risk at that time in Northern Ireland (as it arguably still remains), and my favourite anecdote about it concerned Election Day at a polling station in a small rural school in County Derry. The school's headmaster served as presiding officers at the polling station, and knew everybody within the close-knit area. A gentleman presented himself to the presiding officers for a ballot as a particular voter – which prompted the headmaster to get up from his chair, walk over to the man and begin sniffing him theatrically whilst calling out his name. The would-be voter demanded to know what the presiding officers was playing at, to which he was told that he smelled very fresh for a man who had been dead several months! Needless to say the applicant quickly turned on his heels and fled the polling station without further ado.

Eventually I came up with a simple solution that removed almost all potential for impersonation of the dead. I came to an arrangement with the local Registrar of Births, Marriages and Deaths in Derry that they would send me their weekly notification of the deceased. In return I provided them with copies of the Ward Electoral Registers, which was of great assistance to them in precisely identifying the deceased in some cases. At that time many rural areas of Northern Ireland contained houses with no specific address, roads with no formal title, and townlands that contained multiple people with similar names. So the Ward Electoral Register helped the Registrar precisely identify the family of the person whose death was being registered. This local arrangement worked so well that when the Chief Electoral Officer learned of it, he adopted it as the formal process across all of Northern Ireland.

I was particularly determined to ensure that my first revision hearing should take place as far away as possible from my home town of Derry, as I wanted to gain some experience at holding such hearings before doing so in a place where I was well known. Accordingly, my first experience of sitting in judgement was in a rural area at the furthest geographical corner of the territory I covered – namely the village of Garvagh, south of Coleraine. When I arrived at the designated location for the hearing I was greeted by two party agents, one each from the main unionist and nationalist parties. Unbeknownst to myself the area I had picked contained a number of citizens with the same surname and even the same first and second name as my own, so one of the agents was keen to ascertain whether or not I had any relatives in the area (I assured him I did not). I got the sense that both agents were somewhat uncomfortable with the formal manner in which I was carrying out the task at hand, but overall I was pleased with how the hearings went. I also noted that the two agents often worked in collaboration during the hearing, and at its conclusion they approached me to state that the previous practice had normally been for the two of them to meet before the hearing to settle most of the claims and objections amongst themselves, with only a small number then going forward for formal consideration at the hearing. I suspected that there was probably a degree of quid pro quo involved in this practice, which I felt uncomfortable with. I discretely informed them that I would continue to operate an open system which any members of the public in attendance could see was being performed without fear or favour. Despite this, the future hearings at this particular location tended to go well. And feeling encouraged by the experience of running my first hearing, I was also able to approach future ones in a more confident manner.

Once the series of revision hearings concluded each year, the draft register was amended in accordance with the judgements made. It was then published as the formal Register of Electors, and remained in force until the process began all over again the following September.

THE TEMPORARY OFFICE

Having endured and made a success of my first general election with only minimal experience or training, I was conscious of the fact there was much planning to do ahead of the next one. I was also grateful for the fact that there was plenty of time in which to do that preparation, or at least, that's what I thought. General elections in the UK must by law be held no later than once every five years, with the particular timing at the behest of the governing party. In practise this has tended to lead to elections falling at intervals of between four and five years – long enough for the government to get things done and enjoy the benefits of office, whilst not leaving their re-election attempt so late that they became a hostage to fortune and have the date forced upon them. Unfortunately 1974 was to prove a very unusual exception to this trend. The Prime Minister, Labour Leader Harold

Wilson, had out-polled the Conservatives by just 4 seats in the February election but didn't have a majority. Wilson therefore went on to call a second election in October of that year in an attempt to secure a stronger mandate. Like the rest of the country I was of course unaware of his thinking on this in advance, though in hindsight it should have come as no surprise that he would wish to secure a majority at the first opportune moment. In the period after the February 1974 election I therefore focused on getting things into better shape for a poll that convention suggested would probably be another three or more years away.

With the experience still fresh in my mind of running two general elections that year from a rather cramped third floor office on Derry's Shipquay Street, I informed the Chief Electoral Officer that we could not organise another such election from the same premises. Office buildings in Derry had fallen victim to significant bombing at that time, resulting in a shortage of available accommodation. The Chief therefore agreed that I could use a mobile building if a suitable alternative couldn't be found, but advised that if I went down that route then it would have to suffice for the foreseeable future. I was of the opinion that he was essentially warning me of the likelihood that there would be a shortage of any suitable permanent buildings for some considerable time.

After a fruitless search of the city for premises, it became clear that the temporary route was my only option. I did however manage to secure a suitable location on the city's Shipquay Street to replace the Nissan hut arrangement, 40 miles away, where our ballot boxes, polling screens and stationery were stored. And I also identified a location on which to site a new mobile building big enough for our needs at the city's Crown Buildings on Strand Road. On the day the new structure was due to arrive I went along to the site to ensure it met the requirements that I had communicated, and it was a good thing I did. When the structure arrived it was too wide to pass through the double security gates into the site. For obvious reasons the site was well secured, with a strong and high surrounding fence and only one entrance – so there was no alternative way to get it in. I measured the entrance width and contacted the suppliers to see if they could provide a thinner structure which still covered the same area, which fortunately they did – so I arranged a swap via the Civil Service department that had procured the building. The replacement unit was delivered shortly afterwards, meaning that my team and I finally had a suitably sized ground floor office to work from. It was to be of great relief when the second snap Westminster election of 1974 was called just a few months later.

WESTMINSTER ELECTION – OCTOBER 1974

1974's second snap election took place on Thursday 10th October, and did so amidst a security situation that had improved somewhat compared to the previous poll in February. That is not to say that it took place in a period of calm either. There were still barricades in parts of Derry and other towns, vehicles continued to be hijacked and roads blocked, and bus services were often suspended as a result of the buses being hijackers' preferred targets. That, and the earlier parliamentary election that year, signalled a definite change in the overall political scene in Northern Ireland. The days of a simple contest solely between a unionist party and a nationalist party had been well and truly buried by now. At the October election a wide range of parties sought the support of the electorate. Brian Faulkner led the new Ulster Unionist Party, which was in favour of a coalition-based executive in accordance with the Sunningdale Agreement. Enoch Powell, who had stood down as a Conservative Party MP in Wolverhampton for the February 1974 election in opposition to joining the European Economic Community, was elected as an Ulster Unionist MP for South Down. Ian Paisley of the DUP held on to his constituency of North Antrim, whilst the Vanguard Unionist Progressive Party also retained its 3 seats. On the nationalist side, SDLP leader Gerry Fitt held on to his seat in West Belfast, whilst the party took the rather unusual step of not contesting the constituency of Fermanagh-South Tyrone – which enabled the defeat of incumbent Unionist Harry West by Independent Nationalist Frank Maguire. It was the only seat that changed hands in NI in the October 1974 election. This continuation of a plurality of parties being elected indicated that the days of bilateral politics in NI were well and truly over. The voter turnout of 71.3% in Northern Ireland proved to be higher than in February. UK-wide the election also saw Harold Wilson's Labour Party re-elected to form a UK Government with the smallest ever majority of only 3 seats.

A PERMANENT HOME

The temporary office served well for a couple of years during which period I kept watching out for suitable permanent accommodation. Eventually I identified a large Victorian-era house with three storeys over a large basement, located in Derry's Crawford Square – a picturesque street with a communal central garden on the edge of the city centre, in which a number of neighbouring properties had already been converted into commercial premises. The property was vacant at the time so a lease was agreed and we moved in. There was an unexpected event involving army personnel. A number of armed soldiers appeared at the door of the building to announce that they intended to search it for hidden arms or explosives. I explained that I was running the parliamentary election for the Londonderry Constituency, that there were no improper materials in the house, and I had checked all the floors before we moved in. One of the soldiers was particularly aggressive and indicated that they might have to pull up the wooden stairs and floorboards to check for anything that might have been hidden there whilst the building was vacant. I suspected that someone had given the authorities an anonymous tip-off via the confidential hotline to disrupt the election. I noticed one soldier who stood aside from the rest and appeared to be in charge so I approached him, identified myself and indicated my view that someone was deliberately making mischief. I informed him that if I could not meet my statutory obligations then the matter would have to be reported to Parliament. He did not say much but moved to one side, called his soldiers away and they left the scene.

During my tenure as the Deputy Electoral Officer based in Derry from 1974 to 1981, I helped organise a total of six elections – three parliamentary, a Northern Ireland Convention, a local government and a European Assembly Election.

THE NORTHERN IRELAND CONSTITUTIONAL
CONVENTION – 1ST MAY 1975
The power-sharing Sunningdale Agreement and Assembly that was established in 1974 faced vehement opposition from a large portion of unionism right from the start. Amid a flurry of loyalist paramilitary activity (including bombings in Dublin and Monaghan), the Ulster Worker's Council (UWC) organised a strike that brought Northern Ireland to a halt. At that time Protestants comprised the majority of staff employed in key sectors like power stations, ports, shipyards and railways, and the UDA-backed UWC was able to bring society to a halt through its strike. The strike lasted two weeks and led to the collapse of the Sunningdale arrangements and the Northern Ireland Assembly. It also led the British Government to conclude that the people of NI had to find a solution amongst themselves, rather than have one imposed upon them. This resulted in London establishing a Constitutional Convention in 1975 in an attempt to secure from the two communities some form of agreement on how they wished to be governed. After a two-day debate in Westminster in July 1974 and the publication of a White Paper entitled 'The Northern Ireland Constitution', the new body was formally established. It was to use the Single Transferable Vote (STV) system of Proportional Representation to elect 78 members from across NI's 12 Westminster and Assembly constituencies. This was to be my first introduction to the, at times, complicated process of STV. The Government made clear that the Convention was to be purely consultative and would not be a parliament or an assembly – involving no government or executive, no opposition parties, and without having the ability to pass laws. Its task, in the first instance, was just to agree a suitable constitutional arrangement for the governance of Northern Ireland. In addition it was also indicated that the Government would play no part in the proceedings, though the Westminster Parliament would still have the final say on whatever arrangements the Convention agreed upon. This marked a change in tactic by the London Government, following the failure of the post-Sunningdale Assembly that it had played a much more central hand in arranging.

This was a further attempt by the British Government in its endless quest to find a way by which Northern Ireland could be governed through a more inclusive political system that would not only function, but would also assist in ensuring full and proper representation of the overall electorate.

By the start of 1975 the security situation in Derry had improved as a result of a Provisional IRA truce. But it was to prove short lived, as their bombing campaign recommenced on January 28th. Political parties had begun the process of selecting candidates to contest the Convention Election in March, though at that time there was still no indication from Sinn Féin as to whether or not they would stand. The Northern Ireland Office began a public advertising campaign at the end of March to inform the public of the role of the Convention, and stating that the date for the election would be announced shortly. Soon afterwards Sinn Féin called publicly for a boycott of the election – demanding an all-Ireland Convention instead. The Derry Nationalist Party and Derry Labour and Trade Union Party followed up by both announcing that they would not be standing either. Eventually the date for the election was set for May 1st, 1975, and 16 candidates contested the 7 available seats within the Londonderry Constituency. This had been the seventh separate election held in Northern Ireland in two and a quarter years, with an average gap between each poll of only four and a half months (and the longest interval being eight months). Despite this, and the presence of a boycott by some parties, turnout in the Londonderry Constituency was a respectable 70%. In the three other border constituencies (i.e. areas with the highest nationalist populations) the turnout ranged from 60% to 78% – which was well above many constituencies in the east of Northern Ireland where unionists predominated. So remarkably it appeared that election fatigue had yet to set in, even with a boycott in place. The election saw the continuation of the 'United Ulster Unionist Council' (UUUC) arrangement between the UUP, DUP, Vanguard and independents – this time standing as anti-Convention candidates under that unified banner. They eschewed any notion of power-sharing between nationalists and unionists, and wanted a return to the majority rule that had existed before Stormont was abolished in 1972. The UUUC secured a combined 53.8% of the vote in this election, taking 46 of the 78 seats available (a 6-seat majority). Pro-Convention unionists secured only 8.7% of the vote and 6 seats, whilst nationalist parties (the SDLP and Republican Clubs) gained 28.9% and 17 seats (all won by the SDLP). Amongst those elected were figures like Ian Paisley, John Hume, David Trimble, Seamus Mallon, Brian Faulkner and Gerry Fitt. The election count I presided over for the Londonderry Constituency required 12 stages for its 7 successful candidates to pass the quota and be deemed elected, whilst 5 other candidates lost their deposit. The Ulster United Unionist Council obtained 4 of the seats locally, with the SDLP picking up the other 3.

With a majority of Convention seats placed in the hands of unionists that were opposed to it, the body was largely doomed from the start. Instead of securing agreement from the two communities, the Convention instead published a report on November 20th, 1975 that recommended a return to majority rule. As this was unacceptable to the nationalist parties, the report was shelved by London. The Convention was reconvened briefly in February 1976 to make one last attempt at securing cross-community agreement, but it likewise proved fruitless. Whilst the whole Convention exercise can therefore be considered a failure, it was still notable for the fact that it made clear London had no interest in a return to majority rule. London believed that the only way power should be returned to Northern Ireland was if its two communities could find a way of working together politically amongst themselves. The Convention was therefore formally dissolved on March 4th, 1976, and Northern Ireland returned to being ruled directly from London. This therefore reduced slightly the roster of elections that I needed to organise over the next 22 years to just local (council), national (Westminster) and European ones.

COMMON MARKET REFERENDUM – 5 JUNE 1975
On January 1st, 1973 the United Kingdom (along with Denmark and the Republic of Ireland) formally joined the European Economic Community. This move had not been put to a public vote, and was instead enacted solely as the result of an Act of Parliament under the then-Conservative Government. The Labour Party stood for election in 1974 with a manifesto promise to hold a referendum on whether or not the UK should remain within the EEC, which it then duly arranged for June 1975. A Government-issued leaflet entitled 'Britain's New Deal in Europe' was despatched to every household in the UK, in which Prime Minster Harold Wilson laid out the case for the country to remain a member.

The eligible electorate for this referendum was expanded to include all citizens of the Irish Republic who were resident in the UK at the time. That provision had not been granted before, and may perhaps have been driven by a view in the Labour Party that Irish citizens were likely to strongly support membership of the Common Market. The ballot paper contained the following question, to which the elector could indicate their preference for by entering an 'X' into either a Yes or No response box:-

Do you think that the United Kingdom should stay in the European Community (The Common Market)?

The UK was divided into 68 regional counting centres, of which Northern Ireland was one. On the close of poll the votes cast across that region were collated together at each counting centre, with the results forwarded on to the Chief Counting Officer in London who declared the overall result.

Thankfully the referendum passed without incident in Northern Ireland and elsewhere, with all reports indicating that it was quiet. Indeed, there were no signs of any political party campaigning for it on either side, and no agents at the polling stations either, which I found difficult to fathom. The only conclusion I could draw was that the low interest in this referendum among the general population was being mirrored among the political parties too. The turnout for Northern Ireland was relatively low at only 47.4% – versus an overall UK turnout of 64.7%. Whilst the UK result saw the 'Yes' camp secure 67.2% versus a 'No' vote of 32.8%, the outcome was much closer in Northern Ireland – where 'Yes' won by only 52.1%, versus a 47.9% figure for 'No'.

PARLIAMENTARY GENERAL ELECTION – MAY 3RD, 1979
Sinn Féin called for a boycott of this election, which increased the likelihood of the Official Unionist candidate being returned for the Londonderry Constituency. In total five candidates were nominated, with the Official Unionist elected on 49.7%. The runner-up was SDLP candidate Hugh Logue with 30.2%, whilst Irish Independence Party candidate Fergus McAteer finished fourth with 8.6%. Fifteen years earlier his father Eddie had secured 35.9% in the same seat as leader of the Nationalist Party. The SDLP eclipsed the old Nationalist Party across the 1970s, however, and Eddie migrated the remaining support into a new Irish Independence Party in 1978. The 1979 election result confirmed the SDLP as the main contender for the support of nationalist electors at that time.

EUROPEAN PARLIAMENTARY ELECTION – 7TH JUNE 1979
1979 saw the EEC open itself to a popular vote across all its member states, thereby resulting in the first ever election to the European Parliament. Of the 81 seats allocated to the UK and divided amongst its regions, Northern Ireland was to elect three by STV across a single constituency.

This intrigued me as it would constitute a very large volume of ballot papers being transported to, and processed at, a single centralised counting centre. I was even more intrigued when the Chief Electoral Officer asked me if I would organise and run the count. I accepted the challenge, but was somewhat surprised to learn that the count was to be held in Belfast City Hall. It is a majestic building, but lacks a suitably-sized open plan area where the processing of the large number of ballot papers likely to be involved could take place.

I paid a visit to Belfast City Hall to assess the overall space that would be available and to draw up a planned layout for the counting process – involving three separate stages. Stage 1 involved the receipt of the ballot boxes and votes that were cast in each of the 18 Westminster constituencies around Northern Ireland. These would arrive at the Belfast count centre and be counted, but not yet sorted. That would enable the grand total of all votes cast in Northern Ireland to be verified. Stage 2 saw all the ballot papers examined to determine the total number of valid and invalid papers across NI. That would be a lengthier task than the first stage, so would require a much larger floor space to accommodate the required sorting tables. Stage 3 was the largest task, as it involved all of the valid ballot papers being sorted into bundles according to the voter's stated first preference, followed by the allocation of those voting papers to each of the candidates. From there the count progressed, with candidates being either elected or excluded via the re-examination of the ballot papers at each stage to determine the voter's next preference. The count would continue in that manner until three candidates had been declared elected, in a process that involved multiple stages of preferences being reallocated as individual candidates were either elected or 'eliminated'. As an aside, I was uneasy with the use of the term 'eliminated' in the context of Northern Ireland's troubled circumstances at that time, and so preferred to use the term 'excluded'.

Returning from my inspection trip to Belfast City Hall, I sat in my office in Derry to tackle the challenge of how to accommodate the count in the chosen location. In addition to the lack of a space large enough to accommodate the three separate stages of the count, there was also the need to enable candidates' election agents to observe all the stages from an appropriate distance. The three separate rooms available at City Hall would also expend a considerable amount of time and energy in physically moving ballot papers from one hall to the next. I therefore raised the possibility of finding an alternate venue with the Chief Electoral Officer, to which he was very opposed, so I had to find a way to make it work at Belfast City Hall. After much thought, anguish and time I hit upon a workable solution – but it would necessitate a longer period to process the count than it would take at a more suitable location. I estimated that it would require a minimum of two days, but could possibly take up to four, which the Chief didn't seem fazed by when I briefed him.

With the count being run out of a single centre, meetings were held with my fellow Deputy Electoral Officers from the other Electoral Offices across Northern Ireland to determine a combined plan of action, with each of the officers taking responsibility for particular parts of the counting process. The potential problem of how to move hundreds of thousands of ballot papers between the different rooms was solved by a simple suggestion from a colleague – to use supermarket trolleys. Everybody worked together as an efficient team at the count, which proceeded in good order, and the Belfast City Council staff were also extremely helpful. An experienced observer with significant experience in the field of STV counts told me that not only was it the largest STV count carried out at one location anywhere in the world, but that it was also the best he had seen.

Northern Ireland's first European Parliamentary Election attracted very senior politicians as candidates from the various political parties that took part. Membership of that parliament was not only seen as of a significant status in itself, but could also be used to attract substantial financial support for projects within Northern Ireland.

The candidate who commentators regarded most likely to top the poll was Dr Ian Paisley, leader of the Democratic Unionist Party. He was elected at the first stage of the count, with 170,688 votes. Up to that point I had been making the various public announcements within the hall myself as the counting progressed, which the Chief had requested me to do. When it came to the formal announcement of the deemed election of Dr Paisley, I felt that it was a task more suited to the Chief himself, as returning officer – so I went to find him within City Hall. Before I could do so I was approached by Dr Paisley who indicated that after the formal announcement of the result he would like to publicly thank those who had voted for him and also the counting staff. I felt uneasy at this request.

The successful candidates at such a count are only formally declared elected after all the counting stages have been completed and the requisite number of successful candidates identified. The term 'deemed elected' is used at the end of each stage when one or more of the remaining candidates have reached or exceeded the quota. At any stage there could be a request made for a recount. If granted, such a recount could result in either a confirmation of the stated result or the overturn of that result, with either no one deemed elected or possibly a different candidate instead. That was extremely unlikely in the case of Dr Paisley, given the size of his vote. Nevertheless if he were to make a speech at an interim stage, that could set a precedent for all the other candidates to wish to follow suit when they were either deemed elected or excluded. This could not only elongate the already-lengthy count process, but there was the added concern that some speeches could be couched in terms that would be considered antagonistic by the candidates and supporters of other parties present. I was also conscious of the fact that Dr Paisley in particular was noted for the length and robust nature of his speeches. This was the first election in which there was a central count held for all of Northern Ireland, and I was determined for it to proceed without interruption, given that it was unclear how long it would take.

When I asked the Chief to make the announcement his initial preference was for me to do it, but he eventually agreed. He also granted Dr Paisley's wish to make what thankfully turned out to be primarily a few words of thanks, followed by leading his supporters in the singing of a hymn. Fortunately when their time came the other candidates were also suitably brief in their comments. John Hume, the SDLP candidate, came second place on first preference votes with 140,622, and was deemed elected at the 3rd stage. The Official Unionist candidate, John Taylor, then made it over the quota at the 6th stage, having by then accrued a total of 153,466 votes. The overall turnout was 57%, and there were 13,774 spoiled votes out of a total of 572,239 votes cast.

That event reassured me of my ability to carry out large and detailed tasks involving major political figures, and also indicated that the Chief was content to leave me alone to handle such tasks, which reinforced my confidence. It appeared from his approach, that the Chief saw me as a safe pair of hands for such a large Northern Ireland-wide project, which was perhaps an early indication (or even a test) of the fact that I would eventually become his successor.

CHAPTER 3
As Chief Electoral Officer of Northern Ireland

The following year, 1980, saw the Chief Electoral Officer announce to his deputies that he would be retiring after just four years in the post. He had previously served as a Deputy in the Belfast office before being promoted upon the death of the previous/first Chief Electoral Officer. I was privately asked by the retiring Chief Electoral Officer if I would be willing to be appointed to the upcoming vacancy. It was a decision with much to weigh up. On the plus side, the work at that level appeared interesting, challenging and important in the development of a more stable and positive society. Weighed against that was the fact that the security situation had continued to deteriorate, I was settled in Derry and unwilling to relocate to Belfast, and my children were at an important stage in their education and attending very good schools. Having weighed everything up by the time I was formally offered the post, I chose to accept it on the condition that I would remain living in Derry (despite the substantial financial support on offer to relocate to the Belfast area). I would instead stay overnight in Belfast for two days of every week, and commute the 150-mile round trip on the remainder – with stays extended to four nights a week during any election period. Fortunately this proposal proved acceptable to the powers that be, and so in 1981 I was elevated to the role of Chief Electoral Officer

The question of where to base myself in Belfast for overnight stays required some consideration on my part. The post of Chief Electoral Officer was a very visible role, that some considered, part of the State machinery. Whilst I was from a Catholic background, various factors created the possibility that I could be deemed a potential target for either side of Northern Ireland's paramilitary divide. I initially opted for accommodation in Hollywood, a small town five miles from the centre of Belfast, but a world away in terms of its security situation. After a few months I decided to rent accommodation in a part of South Belfast known as 'The Holy Lands' on a longer term arrangement for the days that I was working in Belfast. I chose that area as it had a very transient population (it had a sizeable student population in those days, but has since become a predominantly student area). I was also careful to keep a low profile whilst there.

An obvious question to ask is, who does the Chief Electoral Officer report to? Who is their boss, and does that create any potential issues regarding impartiality? In official terms the post is a non-political independent officer, responsible to the courts and to the UK Parliament. My formal appointment to the post was made by a Warrant issued by the Northern Ireland Secretary of State in his then role as Governor of Northern Ireland (a position that was abolished a few years afterwards.) There was no specified time period or limit for holding the office of Chief Electoral Officer, except that it was dependent upon good behaviour – though I later learned that the obligatory retirement age was the same as that which applied to judges. That made sense administratively, as my monthly pay cheque came via the Judicial Salary Office in London. In short, the role was structured to ensure that it was independent, free of political interference and not contained within the mainstream of the Civil Service. I was keen that the role should be seen in this way by the public, and so emphasised its independence as and when I felt it necessary.

A good example of the independence of the office arose in May 1996 when I found myself challenging a decision made by the then UK Prime Minister, Margaret Thatcher. The context was a debate in parliament on an upcoming Northern Ireland election in which a 'party list' system was to be used for the first time anywhere in the UK.

In response to a query raised during the debate, Thatcher declared that the Chief Electoral Officer would not allow the Democratic Unionist Party (DUP) to use their preferred choice of words as the party's description on the ballot paper. They wanted to be listed as "Democratic Unionists – DUP – Ian Paisley", to capitalise on the electoral appeal of their leader and founder. At that time political parties were not required to be legally registered entities as they are now, and it wasn't unusual for the exact names or description of individual parties submitted for inclusion on the ballot papers to vary from election to election, often to reflect electoral pacts with other parties. Upon studying the legislation I came to the conclusion that the Prime Minister had arrived at a wrong determination on this issue.

Whilst the only parties entitled to stand at the election were listed in part II of Schedule 1 to the 1996 Act, there was no corresponding requirement in law that the name to be given on the ballot paper for each party had to exactly match the details as shown in part II of Schedule 1. That was because part II of Schedule 1 was simply designed to identify parties, and only those parties that could submit lists for that election. It did not prescribe how they should be listed on the ballot paper. Rule 6 stated that a submitted list of candidates standing at the election "*shall be deemed to be valid unless and until the Chief Electoral Officer decides that it is invalid*". I had difficulty seeing how the Democratic

Unionist Party name, if shown on the ballot paper in the format they desired, was not of a party listed in part II of Schedule 1 to the 1996 Act. Not being a lawyer and wanting to be sure of my facts before, in effect, challenging the Prime Minister's interpretation, I sought the opinion of Senior Counsel who agreed with my conclusions. Hence, when the DUP submitted nomination papers with the party name in their preferred format, I accepted it. There was much interest from the media as a result of my decision on this.

A few months later I came across a report of the debate in Parliament on the Northern Ireland (Elections) Bill in Hansard, from May 1st. The following is an extract:

> *Mr* Worthington*: As I say, I hesitate to return to the subject of party names, because the issue caused considerable contention in Committee. In Committee, the Government said that the names could appear on the ballot paper only in the way that is set out in the schedule, but, of course, the law is only what is in the Bill, and I cannot see where the Government get their authority for that in the legislation.*
>
> *All that matters is that "…a party is a party listed in part II of Schedule 1 to the 1996 Act"*
>
> *That is very different from saying that a party has to use exactly the same words. For whatever reason a party might put its name forward in a different way. It would be a bold Electoral Officer who rejected the party on that basis, or sought to change the name by which the party described itself.*

Thankfully this was the one and only time I had to challenge a determination by a Prime Minister, though it does highlight the independence of the Chief Electoral Officer's role. On the other hand challenges against *my* interpretation of, and adherence to, rules proved to be a more common phenomenon, however. Over the years there were many such attempts by some Northern Ireland politicians on issues ranging from the number and location of my area offices to more routine matters such as the processing of absent voting applications at elections. The Secretaries of State in office at the relevant time always respected my status as an independent officer, and thus indicated that it was for me to determine such matters. Indeed the Northern Ireland Secretary in post at one such instance, Sir Patrick Mayhew, wrote to a complainant – the MP for the South Down constituency – to clarify that the Chief Electoral Officer had complete autonomy to carry out his functions in the way he believed best and that in so doing the CEO abided by two fundamental principles. In his letter the Secretary of State (SoS) identified those as (1) That elections in Northern Ireland are, and are seen to be, conducted fairly and impartially and are placed beyond the influence of any political party and (2) That the funds used are employed effectively, efficiency and economically. He went on to say that it was with those two vital objectives in mind that the Chief Electoral Officer always keeps the structure of his office under constant review. He stated that he had every confidence in me and was content that elections in Northern Ireland were being run to a standard that would favourably withstand international comparison and scrutiny. It was good to receive the backing of the NI Secretary in this way.

The electoral organisation that I had inherited when I became Chief was to my mind inappropriately structured, and so over time I made changes to make it more effective and more consistent in decision making and general operations. A good example of that was the introduction of an in-house computer system for use in the preparation of the annual electoral registration system. That replaced the use of an out-of-house Civil Service computer that had previously been utilised for a number of years – requiring much time and travel from the staff in each office to deliver the input from their area, and then for the corresponding amendments to be collected for checking by each of the area offices during the yearly preparation of a new Electoral Register.

Over a few years I reduced the number of regional offices from ten to seven, resulting in much more uniformity and efficiency in decision making. A couple of the remaining offices were also relocated as part of that updating process. The Member of Parliament for South Down, referred to above, took exception to the change and so made representations to the Secretary of State. In the letter of reply he sent to the MP, the SoS emphasised that it would not be appropriate for political parties to be consulted about what were essentially management decisions taken to fulfil statutory duties.

In July 1997 the Northern Ireland Secretary of State established a review in the wake of allegations of widespread malpractice concerning the 30th May 1996 local elections. The purpose of the review was to formulate proposals to improve the integrity of the electoral process, and its report was published in October 1998 and laid before Parliament. There was obviously a possibility that such a review could have been critical of me and my staff team and how we conducted that ballot, so I was relieved when the report gave us a vote of confidence. Its summary recorded "*…the overall conclusion that, given the regulations by which electoral procedures are governed, elections in Northern Ireland are efficiently and fairly administered, often in very difficult circumstances…and that the Review has concluded that much of the credit for the successful administration of elections in Northern Ireland must go to the current Chief Electoral Officer. However the Review believes that this success is often in spite, rather than because, of regulations as they currently stand.*" The review then went on to outline a number of measures that should be considered, which were very much in sync with my own thoughts on necessary changes to the law.

THE HUNGER STRIKES

Northern Ireland suffered a number of particularly challenging periods during the Troubles, and my promotion to the role of Chief Electoral Officer happened to coincide with a major one. The early years of the 1980s saw an increase in polarisation within Northern Ireland, and particularly so during the 1980-81 Hunger Strikes. They were the culmination of a five year campaign by republican prisoners to have 'Special Category Status' (i.e. to be treated essentially as prisoners of war, rather than ordinary criminals). That status had been introduced in 1972 during negotiations on an IRA truce, but was removed by the British Government in 1976. The campaign to have the status restored reached a climax when the prisoner Bobby Sands was elected as the MP for Fermanagh-South Tyrone on an 'anti-H Block' ticket in April 1981, before dying the following month as a result of his hunger strike. A significant outbreak of violence took place after his death, and that pattern continued as and when nine further hunger strikers died over the following months – with the British Government despatching 6,000 additional troops to Northern Ireland. The election of Bobby Sands was to prove an important event in the evolution of politics within Northern Ireland, as it highlighted to the IRA and to Sinn Fein that democratic channels offered potential in the pursuit of their objectives.

THE ROAD IS LONG

During my first year in office as the Chief, I drove from Belfast to Derry several days per week but was tiring of the long mileage involved. I became aware of a number of other people in a similar position to myself who made a daily commute between the two cities. Car sharing amongst us was considered, but was deemed impractical as a result of each of our journeys not starting or ending in proximity. I therefore decided to approach Northern Ireland's public transport company (Ulsterbus) on our collective behalf to see if they would consider introducing a daily mid-week express bus service between Derry and Belfast, at times aimed at commuters. Ulsterbus indicated that they had given the idea some thought previously, and our approach proved to be the catalyst for them to test the demand for such a service. Their initial offering was limited to two departures a day in each direction – from Derry at 06.30 hours and 07.00 hours in the morning, with the return journeys from Belfast at 17.00 and 17.30. So began my nineteen-year acquaintance with the daily bus commute to Belfast – a lifestyle that remains familiar to many public sector employees living in Derry to this day. At very busy times, such as during elections, I stayed overnight in or near Belfast. For the rest of the time my daily routine began with a 4:50 am alarm, followed by a 5:50 am departure for the 30 minute walk to the bus depot in the centre of town. There were no local service buses available at that time of the morning, and I didn't want to risk the potential security threat of driving in and leaving my vehicle parked in a single place all day long, every working day. Accordingly

I walked from home to catch the 6:30 am bus to Belfast in the morning, and caught the 5:30 pm return service to Derry at the end of the working day, capped off with a walk back home again from Foyle Street bus depot.

Over time the number of people making the daily bus commute from Derry to Belfast steadily increased, and many of us became familiar faces to each other. There was an unwritten rule that people would be left to doze off on the morning trip, with social interaction instead confined to the evening return trip. Over time the operating hours of the service expanded to include departures later in the evening from Belfast, which was helpful for the times that I needed to work longer than usual. Those later departures also gave me an opportunity to bank some sleep on board. In a sign that the commuting was taking its toll, during the winter months I would sometimes wake up in a blur during the middle section of such journeys through the very rural Glenshane Pass, and struggled for a few moments in the dark to determine whether I was on my way to or from Belfast. The Glenshane Pass has a brightly illuminated inn located in the middle of nowhere, The Ponderosa, and it would set me right on whether I was coming or going, on the basis of which side of the road it was on as we passed it. That became my daily routine from 1982 until my retirement in the autumn of 2000.

THE ELECTION MERRY-GO-ROUND

During my time as Chief Electoral Officer, I oversaw a total of 19 elections (including one referendum) over a 19-year period. In most years there was an election of some sort, with a number of years having more than one. The largest gap was between the June 1989 European Election and the April 1992 Westminster Elections. The full list of polls that I oversaw is as follows:

ELECTIONS DURING MY TERM AS
CHIEF ELECTORAL OFFICER

1981 May	Local Government Elections
1982 October	Northern Ireland Assembly Elections
1983 June	Westminster Parliamentary General Election
1984 June	European Parliamentary Election
1985 May	Local Government General Election
1986 June	Westminster Parliamentary By-Elections involving 15 constituencies
1987 June	Westminster Parliamentary General Election
1989 May	Local Government General Election
1989 June	European Parliamentary Election
1992 April	Westminster Parliamentary General Election
1993 May	Local Government General Election

1994 June	European Parliamentary Election
1995 June	North Down Constituency – Westminster Parliamentary By-Election
1996 May	The Northern Ireland Elections (Forum Election)
1997 May	Westminster Parliamentary General Election
1997 May	Local Government General Election
1998 May	Northern Ireland Referendum on the Good Friday Agreement
1998 June	Northern Ireland Assembly Election
1999 June	European Parliamentary Election

The first election for me in my new role as CEO was the 1981 Local Government Elections. Whilst I was ultimately responsible for the running of all the elections in Northern Ireland, the town clerk of each district council (nowadays known as chief executive) acted as the deputy returning officer for local elections and as such looked after the routine arrangements for the running of the poll and the count afterwards. Whilst the individual clerk of council was the deputy returning officer for local elections in his or her area, I was the overall Returning Officer with full formal responsibility and directly dealt with matters such as applications for postal and proxy voting.

My role at local elections was therefore primarily one of supervision and oversight – preparing instructions and guidance notes for the clerks on various aspects of running local elections, as well as dealing with any queries or problems that were referred to me and also checking the declared results at the end of the count. It also provided the various political parties with an appeal route via me if they had concerns with any actions taken at the local council elections in a particular area. The timing of my first local elections as Chief Electoral Officer therefore included the period of the 1981 Hunger Strikes, and came only a month after Bobby Sands had been elected as an MP. Despite that success, however, Sinn Féin did not contest the 1981 Local Elections. A number of smaller groups and independents stood and were elected on tickets supporting the hunger strikes – with the Irish Independence Party winning 21 seats, whilst the Irish Republican Socialist Party (IRSP – the political wing of the INLA) and People's Democracy (Trotskyite republicans) won two each. Nine protesting prisoners contested the June 1981 General Election in the Republic, with two of them being elected as TDs (members of Dáil Éireann, the Irish Parliament).

The first election that I ran directly myself as Chief Electoral Officer (rather than council elections where the clerk of each council actually ran the election in their patch under my general oversight) was the poll for the Northern Ireland Assembly on October 20th, 1982. This was a resurrection of British Government attempts in the previous decade to secure cross-community self-government via a structure where moderate nationalist, unionist and unaligned politicians could cooperate in taking decisions on how to run Northern Ireland. London wanted Northern Ireland to govern itself, but at the same time was determined that there would be no return to the system of unionist-dominated majority rule that had existed until it was scrapped in 1972.

Two previous attempts had been made to establish a power-sharing Assembly for Northern Ireland. The first, via the Sunningdale Agreement in 1973, was brought down by the wide-scale Ulster Workers Council strike. A second attempt followed in 1975 via the Constitutional Convention, but it was dissolved after the report created by its unionist-dominated representatives made no provision for power sharing in decision making. Hoping for a third-time-lucky approach the Government issued a White Paper called 'Northern Ireland: a Framework for Devolution' on April 5th, 1982. This was followed by The Northern Ireland Act 1982 on July 23rd, which proposed that a new Assembly be elected on 20th October 1982 via the single transferable vote system.

Northern Ireland's political parties provided a mixed reaction to this development. The unionist parties and cross-community Alliance Party were willing to participate in the election, whilst the SDLP and Sinn Féin confirmed that they too would participate in the vote – but refuse to take their seats if elected. Neither party agreed with the proposed new Assembly, but was clearly concerned that if they didn't stand on an absenteeism ticket then the result would give an inaccurate indication of the support for the new body within the overall population. The Assembly was to comprise of 78 members elected by Proportional Representation. This would be done using the same 12 Westminster constituency boundaries that had been used in the previous attempt to establish an Assembly, rather than the 17 new parliamentary boundaries that had been designated but not yet employed in any election. In its first report on the proposed 17 new Westminster constituencies (published November 23rd, 1981), the Northern Ireland Boundary Commission had recommended that each constituency should return five members. If that was to be employed at the 1982 Assembly Election it would result in a membership of 85 – thus increasing the Assembly's size by seven members. The Westminster Government instead decided that the number of members should remain at 78 – and accordingly chose to utilise the 12 existing parliamentary constituency boundaries, rather than the new 17 boundaries. This was a controversial proposal, as in the years since the 12 constituencies had been drawn up there had been considerable population movement out of Belfast. Some representative adjustments were therefore required to the 12 constituencies, and this was done by varying the number of members elected for each. Constituencies varied from four to ten members, depending on the number of registered electors there, which resulted in a variation of voters per seat from just over 12,000 to just under 15,000. The allocation of the seats was made as follows:

South Antrim	10
North Antrim	8
North Down	8
Armagh	7
Londonderry	7
South Down	7
Belfast East	6
Mid Ulster	6
Belfast North	5
Belfast South	5
Fermanagh-South Tyrone	5
Belfast West	4

The election saw seven different parties elected with the following numbers of seats:

Official Unionist	26
Democratic Unionist	21
Social Democratic and Labour	14
Alliance	10
Sinn Féin	5
Other Unionist	2
Total	78

The SDLP's Deputy Leader and long-standing advocate of non-violent nationalism, Seamus Mallon, was one of the candidates returned for the constituency of Armagh. He had also been elected previously to represent Armagh in both the first power-sharing Assembly in 1973 and the Northern Ireland Constitutional Convention in 1975. In February 1982 he had then been appointed to Seanad Éireann (the Republic's second chamber) by Taoiseach Charles Haughey. That resulted in unionists formally challenging his October 1982 election to the new NI Assembly, as under the law at that time (The Northern Ireland Disqualification Act 1975) no member of a British Parliament or regional Assembly could serve in a legislature outside of the UK or Commonwealth. That election petition was successful, which saw Mallon disqualified and a by-election held – in which his election agent successfully contested the seat in his place. That was the only legal issue that arose among all of the constituencies at the Assembly elections. Mallon resigned from Seanad

Éireann the following month, and went on to be elected as the MP for Newry and Armagh in 1986, a seat he held until 2005. The law that disbarred Mallon was addressed by an amendment in the 1998 Northern Ireland Act, before being dealt with formally via the Disqualifications Act (2000) which extended eligibility to members of the Oireachtas (the Republic of Ireland's legislative bodies) to stand for election to any UK Parliament or Assembly.

The legislative authority of the new Northern Ireland Assembly was described as 'rolling devolution'. In common parlance that was a process in which the Assembly would only receive power if and when it proved that it could run affairs appropriately. Its initial role was therefore simply to scrutinise Northern Ireland Civil Service departments and draft versions of legislation from Westminster, making reports and recommendations on them to the Secretary of State. An Executive would be formed from the Assembly, with no more than 13 members. In accordance with the Northern Ireland Act (1982), powers would then be gradually evolved to the Assembly over time if what was termed an "extraordinary majority" of 70% or more of its members consented – with those powers being withdrawn again if such consent was removed at any future point.

Unfortunately events in the two years prior to the poll – particularly around the hunger strikes – generated widespread scepticism about the likelihood of this new Assembly working. The murder of a census worker in June 1981 as she was conducting door to door visits in Derry added to this, and gave me concerns about those who were doing door to door canvassing for me in the annual preparation of the electoral register. At the Local Elections in May of 1981 there had been tension in various areas. In Newry and Mourne District Council, for example, there had to be a reassignment of an electorate from their usual polling station to one four miles away on security grounds. I took the decision to do so reluctantly after consultations with the deputy returning officer and the police. In the Dungannon Council Area, where tension around the election was high, a number of postal vote applications were identified as forgeries – which led to a temporary suspension in the issuing of postal ballots by the deputy returning officer who referred the matter to me. After consultations and police investigation into a number of the applications, the issuing of postal votes recommenced 24 hours later.

The declared intention of the SDLP and Sinn Fein to not take their seats in the new Assembly essentially deprived the body of nationalist or republican representation, which doomed it to failure in advance. The Belfast Telegraph newspaper editorial on 3rd October commented that the Secretary of State:

> "… *is trying to pretend that the election has changed nothing and that he can proceed with the first stage of the assembly plan without anything being lost*".

The Assembly managed to exist for a period of four years – though the nationalist boycott meant that further powers were never devolved to it. When unionist members insisted on using the Assembly to protest the Anglo-Irish Agreement in 1985, Alliance Party members walked out and initiated a boycott of it. Devoid of either balance or purpose, the Assembly was therefore abolished by Westminster in 1986. It would be ten years before another attempt was made to establish some form of regional government for Northern Ireland again.

THE NORTHERN IRELAND ELECTIONS (FORUM ELECTIONS) – 1996

The 1990s saw a growing desire on all sides to find a route out of conflict for Northern Ireland. Secret back-channel talks between the IRA and representatives of the British Government had restarted in 1990, after MI5 advised that the Provisionals were looking for ways to end their campaign of violence. These contacts continued over the following years, and in 1993 the Government faced severe embarrassment when news of the talks became public – as London had always proclaimed it "wouldn't talk with terrorists". Efforts continued regardless, and by December 1993 in 'The Downing Street Declaration' the British and Irish Governments affirmed the rights of the people of Ireland to self-determination, and stated that Northern Ireland could only join with the Republic of Ireland if a majority of the citizens in each jurisdiction were in favour. That was considered sufficient grounds for the IRA to declare a ceasefire in August 1994, followed by loyalist paramilitary ceasefires in October 1994, which created the space and a more conducive atmosphere for talks to progress.

By February 28th, 1996 a Joint Anglo-Irish communiqué announced the decision that there should be an election to assist the cross-party momentum towards a lasting peace settlement. Such an election would obviously give credence to those elected with large mandates, whilst highlighting which voices commanded only fringe of support, and by so doing would assist in the creation of a more co-operative attitude. This was a new approach to negotiations on the way forward for Northern Ireland. The Prime Minister stated on March 21st that legislation would be introduced for the elections to be held on May 30th. Even before the necessary draft legislation had been submitted to Parliament, the Secretary of State had put my office on election alert by advising me to commence preparations for it.

There were certain tasks I and my office could undertake as part of that process, but without knowing precise details – such as the voting system, the number of constituencies, the boundaries involved etc – our ability to prepare accordingly was somewhat limited. Speculation ran rife amongst the media and political parties over the various formats that would or could be used for the election. Concern was expressed that voters could face the most complicated election in the province's history. Newspapers reported that the DUP was proposing a single Northern Ireland-wide constituency, with voters choosing between parties rather than individual candidates. The Ulster Unionists were reported as favouring a traditional multi-constituency poll, whilst the SDLP's preference was for a party-list system.

The Northern Ireland (Entry to Negotiations, etc) Act 1996 appeared on April 29th, and stated that the purpose of the election was to provide delegates from whom participants in negotiations could be drawn. The new Northern Ireland Forum would therefore be a deliberative body – without legislative, executive or administrative functions, nor any power to determine the conduct, course or outcome of the negotiations. In its schedules the Act provided for five delegates to be returned for each of the Westminster parliamentary constituencies in Northern Ireland, with a further 20 elected for NI as a whole via a regional list system. Political parties had to submit the name of between two and five candidates to stand in any constituency, and if a party was standing in at least three constituencies it was also entitled to submit a list of candidates for the regional Northern Ireland-wide list. A candidate could only be on one or other of a constituency or a regional list, and anyone in prison was disqualified from being on either list. Ballot papers had to show the names of each of the parties for which a constituency list had been submitted for the constituency.

By providing each party leader with a strong influence on the selection and ranking of members on their party's list, and by that list being operated on an NI-wide basis, the system facilitated a possible political compromise in two ways. Firstly, those candidates who were more supportive of their leader and party's stance could be placed at the top of the list, whilst those who were less supportive or even hostile could be ranked in a lower position where they were unlikely to be elected but couldn't claim that they hadn't been put forward as a candidate. Secondly, the fact that the party lists were NI-wide was also important. To paraphrase a comment reportedly made by a very senior Northern Ireland Office official, it was a move driven from a viewpoint that those who are part of the problem have to be part of the solution. Smaller paramilitary groupings, and especially the loyalists, were certainly part of the problem, but were unlikely to secure enough votes in any single constituency to have candidates elected – but their province-wide vote could accumulatively get them representation via the Northern Ireland list. This was also the first election held in Northern Ireland using the 18 Westminster constituencies that had been introduced as a result of the most recent Parliamentary Boundary Commission Review. The Elections (Northern Ireland) Order 1996, SI 1229, made special provision for these 18 new constituencies, as otherwise they wouldn't have come into effect until the next parliamentary general election.

The 110-delegate Forum was therefore to be elected with each of NI's 18 constituencies returning five delegates, with the regional list adding another twenty to the total. Those regional places were filled by the ten parties with the highest NI-wide vote returning two delegates each. Whilst a candidate could be included in both the constituency lists and the regional list, if successful in the direct election they were to be disregarded from the regional list.

When the format for the election was eventually revealed there was opposition from various political parties, including assertions that the regional list system was too complicated for voters to understand. I personally saw merit in the proposed system, and felt it necessary to highlight to the public that the voting method was not as difficult as was being alleged. My opportunity to do so came by means of an interview reported by the Belfast Telegraph newspaper. My punch line was:

> *"This is not difficult. It's very easy as far as the elector is concerned. He or she marks an 'X' against one party's name. It can't be any simpler."*

The period between the Prime Minister's announcement of the election on March 21st and the holding of the poll on May 30th proved extremely busy. In March the Northern Ireland Office had arranged for the distribution of a leaflet to each household – advising them of the deadline for submitting applications for postal or proxy votes, and the documents that would be acceptable for identification at the polling stations. In what was then an innovative step, I set up a special operational unit in my head-office to deal with postal and proxy voting enquiries and requests for application forms.

The deadline for submission of constituency and regional candidate lists was 5pm on Thursday, May 9th, 1996. A total of 926 constituency and 188 regional list candidates were received by that time – with some names appearing on both. I published the lists on May 11th as a 26-page supplement to the official Government 'Belfast Gazette'.

The choice of a party list system in this election was a first for the UK and Ireland. I personally viewed this election as important, but still an initial step in a new overall approach to the peace process, and one that would have to be followed up with a more definitive stage. Accordingly any problems with the operational process of this first stage would not only risk the acceptance of its outcome, but probably also impact on the possibility of moving on to a second stage afterwards. It was therefore vital that it was all conducted properly. To aid in this I issued very detailed guidance to my staff as to the various tasks required for the poll – particularly the counting system – and produced a very detailed step-by-step check list and reporting system to ensure accuracy and consistency between the various count centres.

There was considerable media interest in the election both nationally and internationally, with numerous requests received for information and for access to the counting centres. I arranged for special information packs to be prepared and a number of press briefings were organised. The counting period lasted just over two days, and I also arranged for a special information headquarters to be operated out of Belfast's Maysfield Leisure Centre. It was designed to show the overall results for Northern Ireland various constituencies as they were determined at the various counting centres, and to also collate the regional list result from the figures forwarded by each individual constituency. The results were announced and displayed there to give an overall up-to-date status and was used extensively by the media and by the parties to keep track of the overall results, as well as to clarify any queries raised by the observers. The Maysfield information centre therefore played a useful role and added to the openness of the process. I was very content with the operation of the election overall, and pleased with the role I'd played in it.

After the counting had finished and all the declarations had been made, the allocation of seats for the new Forum was as follows:

NUMBER OF DELEGATES OBTAINED

Party	Constituency List	Regional List	Total
Ulster Unionist Party (UUP)	28	2	30
Democratic Unionist (DUP) – Ian Paisley	22	2	24
Social Democratic and Labour Party (SDLP)	19	2	21
Sinn Fein	15	2	17
Alliance	5	2	7
UK Unionist Party – Robert McCartney	1	2	3
Labour	nil	2	2
Northern Ireland Women's Coalition	nil	2	
Progressive Unionist Party	nil	2	
The Ulster Democratic Party	nil	2	
Total	90	20	110

NORTHERN IRELAND REFERENDUM – MAY 22ND 1998

After two years of often torturous multi-party talks within the Forum, agreement was reached on a proposed way forward for devolution and power-sharing in Northern Ireland. This became known as the Good Friday Agreement or The Belfast Agreement. It was decided to put it to the electorate for their endorsement, both north and south of the border, and a printed copy of the Agreement was sent to every household in Northern Ireland. Given that the Agreement involved removing the territorial claim to NI from the South's Constitution (known as 'Articles 2 and 3'), a referendum was required by law in the Republic before such a change could be enacted to their Constitution.

There was huge interest in the referendum in the months leading up to it – not least from those seeking to vote. My office received numerous letters and phone calls from Northern Irish people living overseas, some of whom had left a considerable time ago, who felt strongly that they should be able to participate in the vote. The legislation was very clear however with regards who was entitled to participate, and it was restricted to parliamentary electors on the Northern Ireland register of electors (except for those registered as overseas electors). Electors had to be 18 years of age or over on the day of the poll. The lead up to the referendum was a very busy time, and the volume of enquiries from those living outside Northern Ireland certainly added considerably to the workload.

Interest was also strong from the media, and not just from within the UK and Ireland. In a press release on May 22nd, I indicated that any media seeking access to the count would have to apply to my office for accreditation and to receive admission passes. I pointed out that as considerable interest was expected, the number of passes may have to be rationed. Little did I realise at the time how considerable the media interest would prove to be. I had originally planned to hold the count in the Nugent Hall – a 2,500 capacity ballroom that was part of the King's Hall complex in south Belfast, and which I had used previously for elections. When the level of interest became clear I switched it to the much larger King's Hall within the complex, to provide more floor space. To facilitate the media at the point that the result would be announced, and to avoid the risk of an unseemly scramble, I arranged to have a fixed camera in position which could be pooled – with a second pool camera in position to provide a continuous 'wall paper' shot of the sorting process during the count. This was important as the nature of the referendum meant that there were no candidates involved, and therefore no political agents to observe the count in detail. The camera therefore provided public scrutiny of the process. In addition I switched the press briefing to the large Europa Hotel in the centre of Belfast to cope with the very large attendance that was now expected from around the world.

Enthusiasm towards the Agreement within political circles was mixed, with the unionist tradition in particular being split. Some were unhappy with the prospect of prisoners being released early, and also the potential presence as they saw it of "terrorists in government".   Whilst it was generally accepted that the referendum was likely to result in a 'Yes' vote overall, there were some concerns that the vote in favour might not be at a scale which would be considered a solid endorsement of the Agreement. Unionist parties, both pro and anti-Agreement held the view that a 'Yes' vote of at least 70% would be required for general acceptance, and so the divide within the unionist population was likely to prove the deciding factor in that respect.

Two weeks before the poll those in the 'No' camp felt that issues around political prisoners would limit the size of the 'Yes' vote to the low-to-middle sixties. The mood changed somewhat in the week before the poll as a result of a concert held in Belfast's Waterfront Hall when U2 singer Bono invited John Hume of the SDLP and David Trimble of the Ulster Unionist Party onto the stage and raised both of their arms together to huge applause. That became an enduring image on television over the following days, and was considered by some to be one of the turning points in the 'Yes' campaign. British Prime Minister Tony Blair also appeared on television with handwritten pledges to the unionists, which he then personally signed in front of the cameras, whilst other major British political leaders also made last minute appearances on the campaign trail. All of this seemed to help create a swing towards the 'Yes' vote.

The design of the ballot paper that was used on Referendum Day was, from a production perspective, very simple. The voter was simply asked to indicate either YES or NO to the question:

Do you support the agreement reached at the multi-party talks on Northern Ireland and set out in command paper 3883?

The polling day arrangements involved a total of 1,228 polling stations at 546 locations throughout Northern Ireland, open from 07.00 hours to 22.00 hours on Friday, May 22nd. The counting of the votes was to take place in the Royal Ulster Agricultural Society's King's Hall in Balmoral, Belfast from 9 am the following morning. Between the close of polls and the commencement of the central count, ballot papers for each constituency were brought to a central location within that constituency for verification that the number of ballot papers in each box matched the number recorded as having being issued for there. After verification the boxes were immediately transported to the King's Hall in Belfast. At the start of the count all ballot papers from the different areas were mixed together and the result compiled for the whole of Northern Ireland. No results would therefore be counted or declared for individual constituencies, to ensure that the focus was on the overall levels of support and opposition to the Agreement rather than the levels in particular areas.

Polling day proved to be busy but nevertheless relatively uneventful. A few areas suffered minor disturbances when the polls closed and ballot boxes were being taken from individual polling stations to the verification centres. In Derry, for example, police were attacked by petrol bombs in two nationalist areas whilst escorting the ballot boxes. In the town of Strabane paint bombs were similarly thrown at the police. Overall there were no reports of any injuries. The various exit polls released after 10 pm predicted a ringing endorsement of between 72% and 73% in support of the Good Friday deal.

Polling day was a very long day for me – much more so than I had expected. It was a hugely important and very high profile referendum – one with people strongly agitating on either side – so it was vital to ensure that everything was done correctly for it. I had an early start to the day at my office around 5 am –

well before the 7 am opening of the polls to check that preparatory arrangements were all working to schedule. Then during the day I made a point of travelling around various polling stations to keep a close eye on proceedings, whilst also keeping in close contact with headquarters by mobile telephone. Thankfully there were no serious problems.

Once polls closed the workload switched to a three-stage checking process with my headquarters. Firstly, close contact was constantly maintained with each of the area offices to check that the ballot boxes were being successfully delivered from each polling place to the relevant verification centre. Secondly, after each verification had been completed, immediate notification was given to headquarters that the verified papers were being despatched from there to the count centre, along with an indication of their expected arrival time. The third and final stage was to check that each batch did actually arrive at the count centre as scheduled, and that all of the deliveries from across NI had been received.

After the close of the poll I went to the main counting centre at the King's Hall to check that the facility was ready for the start of the count the next morning. It became clear that I would not get to bed until well past midnight that night – and then only for a few hours, as I would have to be back at the count centre well in advance of the count commencing at 9 am. The prospect of even just a few hours sleep was a welcome one, however, as I had managed to get only limited shut-eye over the previous 48 hours.

The ballot boxes were due to be stored overnight at the King's Hall under police guard. At the venue that evening the leader of the Democratic Unionist Party, Dr Ian Paisley, approached me to say that he wanted a representative from his party to stay with the ballot boxes whilst they were being stored overnight as he was concerned that the contents of the boxes could somehow be interfered with. He made it clear that he was not inferring that I or my staff would be involved in such action, and instead appeared to be worried about the possibility of dirty tricks being perpetrated by some other source. In reply I pointed out that a representative of mine was due to stay with the boxes continuously throughout the night. This failed to assuage Paisley, so I decided that I would personally stay with the boxes myself. By so doing I was keen to ensure that there were no grounds at all on which the veracity of the result could be challenged or brought into question. Dr Paisley appointed a representative to stay as well, but that individual left half-way through what proved to be a long night. When some of my staff arrived very early in the morning, as arranged, I was able to leave to have a shower and breakfast before returning to the count centre. Despite having had very little sleep over the period, the importance of the event gave me the impetus required to deal with the count and the ensuing media coverage of the result.

The media took great interest in the referendum, and attended en masse. A sea of radio and TV vehicles was encamped all around the grounds of the Kings Hall complex, and reporters and their crews were eager to enter the count centre to secure the best position from which to convey their reports. The count hall had been divided by crush barriers into a number of separate locations, with the largest being the counting area itself. It was apparent from the start that the volume of interest meant that it was going to be difficult to contain the media within their assigned area, despite pooling arrangements having been set up for them.

The Belfast Telegraph newspaper caught the overall atmosphere in its report the following day:

> *"Suddenly from behind the huge white screen stretched across the middle of Belfast's Kings Hall came the sound of a single sorting machine spinning into action. The distinctive whirr of paper on paper, reminiscent of a deck of cards being shuffled and cut, momentarily silenced the TV crews, the reporters and the counting staff. And then the tension, so palpable from first light, eased a fraction again. It was only a dummy run.*
>
> *But there's no mistaking it. Everyone knows the stakes are high. And, when the final hand has been dealt this afternoon, there will be winners and losers. You could see it on the strained faces of the several hundred people roaming like an army of ants over one end of the hall by 9am.*
>
> *Journalists and cameramen from around the world jealously commandeering their spots on the balcony for the best aerial views of the action with lines of counters sitting like nervous exam candidates at their white draped tables waiting for their papers.*
>
> *With just minutes to go to the start of the real count, this mighty amphitheatre was reverberating to the ceaseless banging and hammering of a legion of TV crews putting last minute touches to their set. They had travelled from around the globe to be eye witnesses on this moment in history".*

The Secretary of State for Northern Ireland, Mo Mowlam, was due to arrive just before the announcement of the result. A week or so prior to the count she had forwarded to me the names of some of her staff team whom she wanted to accompany her. The NI political parties were restricted in the number of people they each could bring to the count centre for the announcement of the result. Accordingly I did not see why civil servants should be granted special facilities either, and politely informed the Secretary of State accordingly (I suspect she wasn't pleased). A couple of days before the count she asked if I could confirm the time the result was likely to be announced so she could book it into her diary. It was a difficult thing to judge approximately, let alone precisely, but I made her aware of the likely timeframe anyway. On the morning of the count I was pressed for a more precise timing for the likely declaration of the result as the Secretary of State wanted to adjust her diary for that day. I passed on a more specific educated-guess, which fortunately proved to deviate by only ten minutes or so out from the actual time that the announcement was eventually made.

Counting the ballots ran smoothly across the day, and at 3.10pm I stepped onto the podium to announce the result – accompanied by my senior staff who had worked so hard throughout the process. The media scrambled to be close by, climbing over barriers in the process. I was very aware of the tension within the hall among the anxious politicians and their supporters gathered around the stage where I was to make the announcement.

When it came to the time to announce the result, at the back of my mind there was a concern over the possibility of trouble arising in the hall between the opposing factions – some of whom would obviously be pleased with the result, with others deeply disappointed. Accordingly I decided not to go through the standard procedure of first announcing the number of ballots, spoiled ballots etc before giving the actual result. Instead I decided to proceed straight to the percentage of the votes that each of the two choices on the ballot had obtained – the figures that were widely regarded as the most important, and indeed from a unionist perspective, needed approval of at least 70% to be acceptable. That way I felt the palpable tension would be quickly dissipated and at the same time the acceptability of the result would be clearly indicated. So upon taking the stage I decided to dive straight in and announced "I hereby give notice the percentage vote in the referendum was as follows: 'Yes' – 71.12%…" At that point huge cheers erupted and the hall broke into a chorus of singing, "here we go, here we go, here we go". I soldiered on with the rest of the announcement, but even with the microphone I had to shout to be heard as I announced the 'No' vote as 28.88%, before continuing on with the other statistics that would normally have come before the result. The polling forecasts of a 72 or 73% 'Yes' vote made in the weeks leading up to the vote had proven to be fairly accurate.

Given Northern Ireland's ability to generate a political row out of even the most innocuous of things, the fact that the Good Friday Agreement Referendum passed without incident was in hindsight rather remarkable. Successfully carrying out, as I saw it, the most important event that I was involved with, whether in Northern Ireland or in the various countries in which I operated abroad, felt like the very pinnacle of my career. To deliver such an important, indeed crucial, event without controversy or criticism – with the task solely under my control, and without direct political oversight – did indicate to me that I had attained my goal of providing an effective electoral service that was truly independent. And I feel it also assisted in Northern Ireland's journey along the path to a more inclusive society, and hopefully also, a more cohesive one.

Reaction to the outcome of the referendum varied predictably. British Prime Minister Tony Blair's response was "This is the result we have worked for and wanted. Another giant stride along the path to hope and the future." Northern Ireland Secretary of State Mo Mowlam was of the view "They have chosen the future and they have voted to take control of their own destiny." The Office of the US President, Bill Clinton, commented that "He was calling all the politicians in Ireland with congratulations all weekend. He is not going to walk away with just a job well done send-off. He is very serious about bolstering peace and an economic insurance policy."

Those in the 'No' camp had a different perspective. The leader of the DUP claimed of the 'Yes' campaign: "They bribed and bullied, corrupted and tried dirty tricks and got nowhere." Another leading 'No' campaigner, Robert McCartney, commented: "This referendum is the product of a massive propaganda campaign that would have been illegal in the Republic."

The NI politicians who favoured the result took a very different attitude, as reported in the local media. For example the leader of the SDLP, John Hume, commented "That was a very historic act and you are telling us to lay the foundations for lasting peace and stability, and you did it in great numbers." The Sinn Féin leader, Martin McGuinness, advised: "What I can give is an absolute commitment that Sinn Féin will continue with a peace strategy".

David Trimble, leader of the Ulster Unionist Party, said "It is a very convincing endorsement to have over 71% of the people of Northern Ireland endorse this Agreement. It is not as big a majority of unionists as I would have liked, but a clear majority of them endorsed it. We have taken an important step forward." David Ervine of the fringe Progressive Unionist Party – which had strong links with some of the loyalist paramilitary groups that had previously joined in the ceasefires – commented: "It's a brilliant result. It has to work."

Far from marking a pause in the process, however, the heavy electoral workload continued at pace after the referendum. The date had already been set for a new Northern Ireland Assembly to be elected on June 25th, 1998 which required advertisements with instructions for how people could access postal or proxy votes to be published prior to the referendum date.

NORTHERN IRELAND ASSEMBLY ELECTIONS ON 25 JUNE 1998

The Assembly election was the second key stage in the process of restoring local governance to Northern Ireland. Six members were to be elected from each of the 18 Westminster parliamentary constituencies across Northern Ireland – providing a total Assembly membership of 108. The new Assembly was to be given authority over 'transferred matters', as opposed to 'reserved matters', as defined in the schedules to the 1998 Northern Ireland Act (Reserved matters are those that remained under the control of the UK Government, whilst transferred matters were those that had been delegated to the authority of the Assembly). It was to be one of two "mutually inter-dependent institutions" under the Belfast Agreement (commonly referred to as The Good Friday Agreement). Under that Agreement a new North/South Ministerial Council with the Republic of Ireland was also established to develop consultation, co-operation and decisions on areas of mutual focus across the island of Ireland. All decisions had to be agreed by the two sides, and the First Minister and Deputy First Minister of the Assembly were to act together to nominate ministers to attend the North/South Ministerial Council meetings and then report back to the Assembly at its following meeting.

To balance the north-south body and its involvement of the Republic of Ireland's Government (a concession to nationalists), an 'east-west' dimension was also introduced alongside the NI Assembly and the North-South bodies – through the establishment of a new British-Irish Council. It was a concession to unionists – and contained representatives of the British and Irish Governments, the newly devolved institutions in Northern Ireland, Scotland and Wales, and representatives from the Isle of Man and the various Channel Islands jurisdictions. Finally within Northern Ireland a consultative Civic Forum was also established, containing representatives from business, trade unions and other community sectors, to act as a consultative mechanism for social, economic and cultural issues.

The first election to the new Northern Ireland Assembly delivered the following allocation of seats to each party:

Party	Seats
Ulster Unionist	28
Social Democratic and Labour Party	24
Democratic Unionist Party	20
Sinn Féin	18
Alliance Party	6
UK Unionist	5
Independent Unionist	3
Northern Ireland Women's Coalition	2
Progressive Unionist	2
Total	108

The referendum and Assembly Elections took place only a month apart, and both were keenly observed and crucial to the smooth performance of democratic events moving forwards. I was keenly aware that any criticism of how the referendum and the Assembly elections were run could have had adverse consequences on the overall acceptance of the results. Fortunately both proved to be very successful in operational terms, and I was proud of how the electoral staff involved at all levels had performed. A very senior Northern Ireland Office official later commented to me that the success of the arrangements for both of these electoral events had been crucial to their acceptance. London's 26-year search for a new form of power-sharing devolved administration for Northern Ireland had finally succeeded.

THE HARD MILES

Unfortunately it wasn't to be plain sailing from there onwards, as the newly formed Assembly has suffered multiple crises and periods of hiatus in the years since. The first stumbling block was around decommissioning. Under the terms of the Good Friday Agreement, the participants in the conflict had reaffirmed their commitment to the total disarmament of all paramilitary organisations. In 1997 an independent body was established to oversee this process, by agreement between the British and Irish Governments. The Independent International Commission on Decommissioning (IICD) was a three-person body – chaired by retired Canadian General John de Chastelain, working alongside a Finnish Brigadier and American Ambassador. Its team carried out the very first 'ceremonial' decommissioning of paramilitary weapons, in which a number of sub-machine guns, handguns, ammunition and improvised explosives were destroyed. However, by February 11th, 2000 the Commission had reported that no information had been received from the IRA on when it would commence decommissioning of its arsenal. That led to the Secretary of State suspending the Executive and Assembly and restoring Direct Rule instead. When agreement was subsequently reached on decommissioning, devolution returned to Stormont from 30 May 2001. It was to prove to be just the first in a number of suspensions that the institution has suffered in the years since.

THE 1999 EUROPEAN PARLIAMENTARY ELECTION

With the referendum and the first Assembly Elections taken care of, it was back again to the bread and butter business of the regular cycle of elections. Elections to the European Parliament were next up – scheduled to take place continent-wide every five years, and always in the month of June. The 1999 election was to be the last election I would run as the Chief Electoral Officer of Northern Ireland.

Fortunately it proved to be a rather routine and event-free election, in which the three sitting members (Ian Paisley, John Hume and Jim Nicholson) were all re-elected. The total votes received by each of the candidates in the election were as follows:

Ian Paisley, Democratic Unionist	192,762	(28.4%)
John Hume, Social Democratic and Labour	190,731	(28.1%)
Jim Nicholson, Ulster Unionist	119,507	(17.6%)
Sinn Féin	117,643	(17.3%)
Progressive Unionist	22,494	(3.3%)
UK Unionist	20,283	(3.0%)
Alliance	14,391	(2.1%)
The Natural Law Party	998	(0.2%)

CHAPTER 4
Electoral Abuse

Electoral abuse is as old as the electoral process itself, and exists to varying degrees all over the world. Whilst we most commonly think of it in terms of voter impersonation (or 'personation', as it is known in electoral terminology), every stage of the electoral process can fall prey to abuse – from how electoral candidates are funded in the first place, through to determining which names get to appear on the electoral register. It can also be extremely difficult to eradicate electoral abuse entirely, and it also has a tendency to outmanoeuvre any steps that are taken to stifle it. Whilst writing this book, for example, I came across a newspaper article from 9th November 2018 that was very critical of elections in the US. It gave an example of the gubernatorial election in Georgia, which was won by a tiny overall margin in a State where it is alleged hundreds of thousands of poorer voters had been removed from the register. It outlined how a judge ruled that 34,000 names had been struck off illegally, whilst the decision on a further 53,000 electors was held up until after polling day. One of the explanations given for why certain names were struck off was because on the original registration form they were spelled with a hyphen, whilst on the state records they were not. Even in some long-established democracies, therefore, actual or claimed electoral abuse can be a significant problem (and the US has very many continuing issues around electoral boundaries and registration).

There are a number of primary ways in which electoral abuse usually occurs:

- <u>Personation</u>: The term is widely perceived as applying to the stealing of votes at polling stations, but it has a much broader definition under the legislation – including illegal voting by postal ballot or by proxy.

- <u>Multiple voting</u>: A person may genuinely divide their time between more than one residence, and therefore be legally entitled to be registered to vote at more than one address. How they use those entitlements to vote is the key issue. An offence would arise if the individual used the registrations to vote more than once at the same parliamentary election, as it is an offence to vote more than once anywhere in a Westminster general election. The rules are different for local authority elections, however. It is illegal to vote more than once in the same local government area – but if an individual is registered in more than one council area then s/he can legally vote in both, on the basis of also having residence there. Voting more than once in the same local authority/council area is illegal, however, even if you split your time between more than one residence in the same area.

- <u>Multiple Registration</u>: An individual registered at more than one address, which are not their genuine residences.

- <u>Undue influence</u>: This is defined by the legislation as covering not only the use or threat of force, violence or restraint to induce or compel a person to either vote or to refrain from voting – but also where there is the use of any fraudulent device or technique to obtain the same end. Intimidation of electors would obviously fall under this legislation, as would, for example, using activists to follow those delivering the postal vote mail out, and then calling at the houses concerned to collect the postal ballots (sometimes before the electors had completed them). Over the years I received from time to time complaints about this from both individual electors and from representatives of political parties.

A BRIEF HISTORY OF ELECTORAL ABUSE IN NORTHERN IRELAND

Electoral abuse has existed to varying degrees throughout Northern Ireland's century-long history. At one extreme it was actually baked into the democratic system in certain constituencies through the practise of gerrymandering – particularly in Derry city in the 1960s. At the other, it was also a widespread, low-level and organised practise indulged in by political representatives from both unionist and nationalist camps.

Whilst I was the Deputy Electoral Officer based in Derry, some political agents even admitted to me that personation had been a practice for a very long time. At its most benign level – if a voter was away at election time or otherwise unable to attend, it was considered entirely reasonable for someone else to unofficially vote for them as a substitute. More malignant forms of genuine voter personation – or straight-forward vote stealing – also occurred, though were less common in practise.

In April 1997, the seasoned journalist David McKittrick wrote an article for the Independent newspaper – entitled "In Belfast, they still vote early and often" – in which he lifted the lid on some of the practices that had characterised electoral abuse over previous decades, and contrasted it with more recent practices. McKittrick anecdotally described how former Northern Ireland Prime Minister Terence O'Neill once shook his mother's hand and urged her to 'vote early and often'. And he recounted an election day in the 1960s when his grandmother's parlour was filled with an array of hats and coats that were being used to provide personators with a change of clothing. Whilst commentators from elsewhere might have been embarrassed to recount such family involvement in the low-level subversion of democracy, McKittrick described electoral abuse as:

> *"...part of the culture and regarded as a feature of politics, at most a venial sin and certainly not a mortal one. It ranks on a par with offences such as tax-dodging and distilling poteen in illicit stills".* In his view *"The persistence of irregularity is perhaps hardly surprising, given that for centuries it has been a recognised part of the Irish electoral scene".*

He provided further anecdotes that lent it the air of being almost a sport or a parlour game. Even though the practice was publicly condemned by Northern Irish politicians, McKittrick described how some (including MPs and members of the House of Lords) used to cheerfully recall the way it operated in the old days. It even had its own vocabulary – in which 'plugging' meant to cast someone else's vote, whilst an 'Open Box' was a polling station that was devoid of personation agents. If an open box was 'riddled', it meant that a high number of fake votes had been cast there.

Even though all of this was clearly illegal, unwritten rules of engagement for the conduct of these practices were shared across unionist and nationalist camps. For example – it was considered bad form for a unionist personator to 'plug' a nationalist vote, or vice-versa. Instead personators sought to vote on behalf of those electors within their own 'tribe' who were deemed too apathetic to vote themselves. McKittrick's 1997 article claimed that this rather quaint or 'sporting' form of low-level electoral abuse came to an end in the 1980s when Sinn Féin entered the political arena with a much more wholesale approach to personation.

He quoted former Unionist MP Harold McCusker rather amusingly complaining to the House of Commons that the previous 'honour-code' system of cheating at elections had been destroyed by the advent of this more methodical and organised approach: "In the comparatively recent past there occurred benign personation, practised by both sides, operated by both sides, and with unwritten rules. But that has now changed because Sinn Féin have broken the rules – they have engaged in vote stealing on a massive scale."

The UK Government claimed that as much as 20% of Sinn Fein's tally of 102,000 votes in the 1983 General Election had been obtained by electoral abuse. As a result they tightened the law considerably in NI, requiring voters to produce official identification for the first time. The May 1985 Local

Government Elections were the first held under the requirement that an elector applying at a polling station to vote had to produce one of a number of specified identification documents before being issued with a ballot paper. Those changes appeared to dampen down the alleged level of abuse. However it has never been entirely eliminated, and still occurs across Northern Ireland's political divide. This was evidenced in my report for the year 1989-90, when I identified the use of forged identification documents at the 1987 Parliamentary Election and the 1989 local elections – particularly in the Newry and Mourne, Cookstown, Omagh and Strabane areas.

At times very generalised claims of electoral fraud would be made after an election by one of the parties involved, but without providing specific examples that could be formally investigated. There was the likely possibility that some of these claims made were simply an excuse for the poor performance of that particular party in that election. Abuse was still an issue, however, so it was important that definitive evidence (rather than vague statements) was unearthed to maximise the chances of cases proceeding to the courts – thereby establishing a clearer idea of the actual level of abuse.

In my annual report for the year 1993-94 I reiterated the need to "… reappraise the absent voting provisions and regulations with a view to identifying means by which actual and potential abuse can be more effectively controlled and to facilitate the conviction of those involved in the abuse of the system."

ELECTORAL ABUSE – AS POLITICIANS SAW IT

A debate on electoral fraud in NI took place in the House of Commons chamber on 13th May 1998, in which a number of speakers gave a long term overview of the situation. The following are extracts from Hansard (the UK Parliament's official record):

> Mr William Ross, the Member for East Londonderry, stated that ….*I have been well aware of the dangers of electoral fraud taking place. It is not a new phenomeno*n. *The old catch-phrase, "vote early, vote often", is a testimony to what took place in past years in some elections… However, in those days, electoral fraud was not the danger to the validity of the electoral system and to the democratic system that it has become in recent years. Before the present violence began, a far larger percentage of our population in Northern Ireland lived in mixed communities. The party activists – there were many – therefore had a far greater knowledge of the total population than is now possible. In other words, the ghettoisation of Northern Ireland as a consequence of terrorist violence has increased the difficulties of political organisations in the Province.*
>
> He went on to say… *That means that, whereas in the past the problem was largely confined to very few areas – for example, West Belfast, which was always*

a cockpit of politics – it is now more widespread. Then he referred to a report that I had made to a Select Committee. Describing me rather flatteringly as a man of vast experience in that field, he went on to quote my statement *"… I am referring to the two 1981 by-elections in Fermanagh-South Tyrone where I travelled round the polling stations and I saw organised personation to such a level that I went to the Secretary of State afterwards and said that in my opinion it was totally unacceptable and some change needs to be made to enable a code to be obtained over that particular process".* Those two elections resulted from the death of Frank Maguire, an independent nationalist Member of the House, followed by the election of Bobby Sands, the first hunger striker to die. It was a time of considerable political emotion in Northern Ireland.

The debate in the House of Commons was not confined to personation. Another Northern Ireland MP, Jeffrey Donaldson (Lagan Valley) referred to a number of applications for postal voting that were attested by the same doctor based in the health centre in the town of Omagh. The attestation on each of those forms that the doctor signed stated that the applicant named on each form *"is being treated by me, is receiving care from me in respect of that physical incapacity and that they are likely to continue indefinitely for a period of months. The MP reported that as the applicants did not live within the catchment of the Omagh health centre, and on investigation it was found that they were in fact living in the Mid Tyrone area, the doctor was not in fact treating them.* [Accordingly I had disallowed them.] *He then went on to comment on abuse perpetrated by means of false electoral registration".*

The two MPs referred to above were Ulster Unionist but other parties have also expressed concern over the perceived negative affect of abuse on the veracity of the electoral system. The May 1997 Local Government Election in the Derry City Council area saw the SDLP lose control of the local authority. That prompted former SDLP party chairman, Mark Durkan, to state in the Derry Journal on May 27th, that the party would be delivering a written submission to the Secretary of State demanding a radical overhaul of the Northern Ireland electoral process. He described the poll as being *"…riddled with accusations of electoral abuse and personation",* and stated that other parties had also expressed alarm at the situation. In addition he commented that *"The Chief Electoral Officer has himself raised the issue of abuse of the proxy vote system".* Sinn Féin had taken control of the council, and their party spokesperson Cahal Crumley claimed that the SDLP were using allegations of electoral abuse as a "smokescreen", describing them as *"…a demoralised party trying desperately to explain away our excellent performance in the elections".* Derry DUP Councillor Gregory Campbell agreed that reform of the electoral system was required before the next General Election, but he disagreed with the SDLP's claim that the rise in support for Sinn Féin was due to electoral abuse – commenting *"Undoubtedly there is a sense of movement within the nationalist community to Sinn Féin."*

From its foundation in 1970 until the Hunger Strikes in 1981, the SDLP had been the primary voice of the nationalist community. Across that period Sinn Féin had refused to participate in electoral politics, which they opposed out of a belief that it would legitimise the British system. The sympathy that the Hunger Strikes generated from within the broader nationalist community began to benefit Sinn Féin, however, and encouraged them to see an opportunity to supplant the SDLP. They therefore reversed their policy of not standing in elections – and allegations that they had introduced a more organised and industrial approach towards the long-standing practise of electoral abuse began to arise from the 1983 General Election onwards. This in turn led to pressure from other parties to have the law tightened to address areas that were deemed prone to abuse. This resulted in the Elections (Northern Ireland) Act 1985, which introduced steps to clamp down on personation. One of its key stipulations was that a ballot paper would not be given to a voter at a polling station unless they produced an acceptable form of identification to the presiding officers or a clerk. The list of documents deemed acceptable for this was:-.

- A current driving licence.

- A current British or Irish passport.

- A current book for the payment of allowances, benefits or pensions issued by the Department of Health and Social Services (DHSS) for Northern Ireland

- A medical card issued by the Northern Ireland Central Services Agency for the DHSS.

- A certified copy or extract of an entry of marriage issued by a Registrar General, where the voter producing the copy or extract is a woman married within the period of two years prior to the day of the poll concerned.

The list of acceptable documents was drawn up with the intention that all registered voters should have access to at least one of them. It did not make the administration of elections by my office any easier, however – far from it – but I acknowledged the reasons for the new requirement, so was generally supportive.

The Act also outlined the offences for those involved in presenting false or misleading documentation, and gave the police enhanced powers to search and detain an individual, to search any vehicle in which they suspected documents in contravention of the Act may be found, and also to enter and search any premises and any person found there (where a Resident Magistrate had been satisfied by a complaint on oath in advance). Anyone found guilty of an offence under the Act would be subject to either or both a fine or to imprisonment to a term not exceeding six months.

Prior to the drafting of the Act, I had a number of meetings with the Northern Ireland Office to discuss how safeguards could be introduced to deal with the apparent abuse to the electoral system caused by personation. My preference was for a reasonably simple solution – that would deal with the problem, not deter participation for the general public, and would be reasonably simple to operate at the polling stations. One of the options I considered was for individual registered electors to be issued with a formal Electoral Office ID card – which the elector would sign and present to the presiding officers when requesting a ballot – but it appeared that some of MPs at Westminster were adverse to anything that resembled an ID card. There was also the not-inconsiderable cost of providing and maintaining such a system, whilst the option of using already existing documentation would be practical and not require additional expenditure. The new ID requirement did add to the workload of the staff at both the polling stations and the electoral offices, as well as giving rise to a degree of confusion amongst the general public.

ELECTORAL ABUSE IN BRITAIN
It should be noted that Northern Ireland is not the only part of the UK where electoral abuse exists, and in the course of my job I became aware of what initially appeared to be a rather relaxed attitude towards the issue in Britain. I periodically attended meetings at the Home Office in London, which involved Home Office officials and Electoral Officers from various parts of England – all of which had different organisational arrangements from Northern Ireland – for electoral matters. These meetings were designed to keep the legislation and procedures applying to it under regular review. After attending a number of these meetings it became apparent to me that a very wide variety of approaches were being employed in electoral matters in different areas, rather than a single standardised approach. Northern Ireland was (and remains) the only part of the UK where local authorities were not tasked with running elections. In Britain the Chief Executive of each individual council was responsible for running both the elections and electoral registration within their patch, and they also made the formal announcement of the results and signed the appropriate returns. When I enquired at these meetings about actual or attempted electoral abuse, the officials and other members suggested that little took place. After the first few years of my attendance, however, registration staff from councils in England began to contact me on occasion to enquire about how we dealt with such issues in Northern Ireland – which led me to suspect that it was indeed an issue to some extent there. It became clear that the registration process, in particular, was not conducted with the same degree of rigour and scrutiny that we followed in NI. As the size of an English council's electoral roll was one of the factors used to calculate its level of centralised funding from Government, there was arguably an incentive for councils to do nothing that would result in a reduction

in the total number of registered electors in their area. There appeared to me to be little incentive to take action that might result in such a reduction e.g. removing the deceased, or those who had moved elsewhere. Some council areas even had the practise of routinely carrying over the names of all those registered from year to year for a prolonged period, even though the canvassing process had obtained no information from the households concerned for a considerable period. All of which would unintentionally enhance the potential for abuse. At one stage a London-based law firm (Nicholson Graham & Jones) even set up a specialist elections unit and sent literature to Electoral Officers to advertise their services – including those relating to proxy voting, forged postal votes and personation – as I became aware when I received one of their circulars in April 1996. All of which suggested that the issue was more prevalent than was perhaps being acknowledged.

Perhaps the highest profile example of significant electoral abuse in Britain in modern times took place in London's Westminster Council in the late 1980s. Known as the 'homes for votes' scandal, the Conservative-controlled council was found guilty of socially engineering the population within eight key marginal wards by selling council properties and relocating people it felt would be less likely to vote for their party. The case resulted in a surcharge of £27 million being levied upon the council's leader, Shirley Porter – a sum which then increased to £42 million with interest and further court costs, following repeated attempts by her to challenge the outcome. She left the country for a number of years without making payment, and eventually returned in 2004 under an agreement to make final settlement of £12.3 million. She was also stripped of the title of 'Dame' that had been awarded to her by Prime Minister John Major, for providing his embattled party with a high-profile win in the 1990 council elections.

Many more-mundane examples of electoral abuse in Britain have received media attention over the years. A peculiar case arose at the 1993 local elections in the Eel Brook ward of the London Borough of Hammersmith and Fulham. It involved a Court dispute over whether or not a vital proxy vote cast on behalf of an elderly woman should be allowed to count, after it had been disclosed that a vote had already been cast in her name. In the end the judges ruled that the proxy vote should stand (a decision for which I have been unable to establish any clear rationale), which therefore meant that two votes had been cast under the same single registered name. It also resulted in the two leading candidates in the election finishing on an equal number of votes. The Court ruled that lots should therefore be drawn to decide the winner, which resulted in the candidate who had been deemed unsuccessful prior to the Court case being declared the eventual winner.

Another interesting case arose at the 1993 local elections in the Northfield ward of the London Borough of Hackney. The returning officer launched an inquiry into allegations concerning the veracity of approximately 200 votes. Given that the three successful candidates had been elected by narrow margins, this was potentially enough to have affected the result (though it should be noted that the allegations did not implicate the successful candidates or their agents). Of the 200 votes in question, 114 were proxy – in contrast to the usual 20 or 30 such votes in previous elections. Newspaper reporting of the case at the time also referred to another example of electoral abuse elsewhere in London, where the chairman of the regional agents association of an unnamed political party was found guilty and fined £750 after complaints were lodged that he had falsely obtained proxy forms and used them to his party's advantage. I referred to both these cases in my 1993-4 annual report (presented to Parliament in March 1995) – to illustrate how electoral abuse was not unique to Northern Ireland, and also how a relatively small number of infringements could make a big difference to the result of a specific election. In addition I commented that the potential for abuse was considerable under the present absent voting regulations. I highlighted the fact that applications for postal and proxy voting were generally received at my offices by post, or delivered (at times in bulk) by party agents. In other words it was extremely unusual for Electoral Office staff to actually see the applicant. That was understandable – particularly in the case of those living a distance from the office, or where the application was made on grounds like physical incapacity. It did however facilitate the abuse of the system that was so evident. At the same time the safeguard applied to the voting process at the polling station (specified identification, and the possibility of challenge by a polling agent) did not apply to postal voting. Such abuse was obviously not confined solely to either Northern Ireland or, indeed, to local elections. However – uniquely within the UK, NI had a number of very small local government electorates e.g. Moyle District Council, which existed from 1973 until 2015, had 15 councillors and a total population of only 17,000 residents. That made close results more likely, which therefore magnified the potential for even a small number of fraudulent votes to seriously impact results.

Returning to England for an example of abuse at a parliamentary election, the Devon and Cornwall Constabulary investigated alleged irregularities and possible offences around proxy voting in a part of the St.Ives constituency during the 1997 General Election. After detailed investigation and a referral to the Crown Prosecution Service, it was decided that there was insufficient evidence to obtain a successful prosecution. In my annual report I highlighted the core problem that this pointed to : "In other words the outcome was the same that has been obtained in Northern Ireland in similar circumstances over recent years. That there has been abuse, and offences committed, is beyond doubt – but obtaining the required evidential link is most difficult."

In the 1990s unease began to grow within some quarters in Britain at the manner in which the overall running of elections was performing in what were changing circumstances. This was particularly so on the question of funding for political parties by donations, and especially those from abroad. The Committee on Standards in Public Life was set up in 1994 to examine concerns about the standards of conduct of all holders of public office, and to recommend reforms that were required to ensure the highest standards of probity in public life. It published a total of four reports, and in 1997 its remit was extended:-

> *... to review issues in relation to the funding of political parties, and to make recommendations as to any changes in present arrangements.*

The Government had already announced its intention to ban foreign donations to political parties, and to require the public disclosure of all donations over £5,000. The legislation would also provide for the registration of political parties (although that aspect had not been included in the committee's terms of reference). The committee, known as 'the Neill Committee' after its chairman, Lord Neill of Bladen Q.C., decided to seek written evidence from a very wide range of opinion – not just from political parties but also from people across all walks of life, regardless of whether they were involved in politics or not or were just submitting as ordinary citizens and voters. The Committee then intended to analyse the written submissions and to hold hearings in various parts of the UK to question selected witnesses – with one such hearing arranged to take place in Belfast.

Despite Northern Ireland having earned a reputation for electoral abuse in the 1960s, '70s and '80s, by 2011 the UK's 'Parliamentary, Political and Constitutional Reform Committee' had noted that the tables had turned somewhat:

> "...the clearest trend in patterns of electoral malpractice over the past two decades is that what was once seen as a specifically Northern Ireland problem has since become a specifically English one."

That committee specifically mentioned instances of electoral abuse in a small number of areas in England which had their roots in the south-east Asian cultural tradition of 'Biraderi' (meaning 'brotherhood') – in which the political allegiances of voters are determined primarily by clan and caste, rather than individual ideological preferences. Politics within the London Borough of Tower Hamlets had for some decades been infused with Indian, Pakistani and Bangladeshi cultural traditions, and when a 2007 BBC London programme covered the resignation of the party whip of four councillors there, one of them described the situation as "village politics-based". Reports of similar *Biraderi* practices have also arisen in the Greater Glasgow area, so it extends beyond just England. In contrast, proven examples of significant electoral abuse within

Northern Ireland have been virtually unheard of for some time now – though it is still not unusual for losing candidates or parties to make allegations which they then fail to substantiate.

EASE OF VOTING vs. RISK OF ABUSE
The health, strength and vitality of any democracy can arguably be measured by the extent to which the public engage with the process. In the 1990s concern was growing amongst the powers that be in the UK about a continual decline in voter turnout at elections – prompting discussion about ways to make it easier for people to vote. The 77.7% turnout for the 1992 General Election – in which John Major's Conservative Party won a surprise but narrow majority – marked a high-point in electoral participation in recent decades that has not been bettered since. One suggested way to tackle falling turnout was to make it easier for people to vote by proxy or postal vote. But a 1994 Home Office Working Party urged caution over the risk of electoral fraud that could arise from that:

"A move to absent voting on demand might increase the opportunity for fraudulent applications to be made without the knowledge of the elector. On balance, we consider that the risk of increased fraud outweighs the potential advantage for the electorate of making absent voting available to all"

In short – the belief was that there was a trade off to be made and a balance struck, between the ease of enabling people to access their vote and the risk of that access being abused for fraudulent purposes.

The 1997 General Election saw Tony Blair's Labour Party gain office with a huge majority. Labour has traditionally tended to be more open than the Conservatives to the idea of making it easier to vote – perhaps out of a belief that they would benefit the most from doing so. Blair's Government therefore looked at a range of ways to try to increase turnout. Councils were prompted to ensure that polling stations were located in the most accessible parts of wards, and experiments were held on changes such as weekend polling (trialled in Watford's local elections in 2000) and even polling stations within supermarkets. In 2000 the decision was made to introduce 'postal votes on demand', which represented a major departure from the 1994 Home Office review's interpretation of the risk of electoral malpractice that could arise from that. A simplified procedure for applying to vote by post was also introduced. Prior to that applicants had to have a good reason to justify requesting a postal ballot. The apparent view taken was that none of these changes would significantly increase the risk of abuse. The recommendations therefore came into effect on February 16th, 2000. I was far from impressed with this new approach. To my mind the level of turnout is more likely to reflect the level of interest or even the distaste that the general public has in the political process or the parties involved at any point in time.

Despite this change the turnout at the 2001 General Election fell to 59.4%, which was the lowest participation level since 1918. I, rightly or wrongly, gained the impression there was concern within the body politic that should turnout decline to below 50% the relevance of parliament in making decisions on behalf of society could well be challenged by sections of the public. Even with the introduction of postal voting on demand, turnout did not rise significantly in the 2005 General Election (though there is a view that the changes introduced did at least play a role in preventing the turnout from falling for a third election in a row). Turnout then increased in each of the 2010, 2015 and 2017 General Elections – with a slight fall registered in 2019 (down 1.5 percentage points to 67.3%). No doubt the public interest in elections will vary from time to time depending on a range of considerations. Ironically the more intense the public interest is in any particular election, the higher the potential for electoral abuse is likely to be – resulting in additional workload for the Electoral Offices.

It would appear that politicians in general were more concerned with getting the turnout at elections to a higher level than they were with the adverse consequences this could have upon the probity of the system. I interpreted the situation as politicians being keen to have their public legitimacy enhanced even if it meant an increased risk to the probity of the electoral system. There is an understandable dichotomy in the field of politics at times in which the objectives of the party do not always match exactly the communal needs of society. In this respect I refer to my favourite saying that "Politics is all about access to power." That said, one also has to live in the real world. A good example of that is when in 1997 the then Ulster Unionist leader, David Trimble, publicly criticised me for not holding the May 1997 parliamentary counts immediately after the poll was closed rather than starting at the next morning. He was quoted in the Belfast Telegraph, on 2 May, 1997 saying:

> "*Chief Electoral Officer Pat Bradley came in for fierce criticism today over his failure to operate night-time counts… it was unacceptable the Northern Ireland results trailed in so far behind the rest of the United Kingdom.*
>
> *The first declaration in England was made shortly before 11pm – 10 hours before Ulster counting began. Mr Trimble said: "Why on earth can we not have our election counts carried out with the same expedition?*
>
> *"I feel very strongly about it. I would very much put the responsibility on the chief Electoral Officer.*
>
> *"We could easily have had overnight counts in a large number of constituencies today."*
>
> *"In England last night you had the first result within 45 minutes. Within two hours there was a flood of results. I bet you after two hours in Northern Ireland, they've scarcely even started."*

I could understand Mr Trimble's frustration as there was the possibility of a tight result across the UK in 1997 between the Conservatives and Labour, with the possibility of a government being formed only through the support of a third party. Unionist MPs could then have found themselves in a position to influence such a formation, with discussions likely to have commenced before all the results were finalised. Trimble would understandably have wanted to be a participant in any such discussions, and knowing the actual or likely number of his MPs earlier in the process would have helped in that. After all that is what politics is about. In reality, however, the 1997 General Election saw Labour win by a landslide.

I also felt that Trimble's analysis was not comparing like with like. In contrast to the rest of the UK, the security situation within Northern Ireland required the security forces to be involved in aspects of the electoral process – such as guarding ballot boxes during their delivery to and from each polling station, guarding their transfer to the relevant counting centre after polls closed, and then maintaining an overnight watch over the centres with the ballot boxes inside. In addition every polling station also had to be discretely guarded during the hours of the poll. All of this placed a large call on security force resources at election times, which necessitated them being enhanced to avoid any attempt to use the process to disrupt the normal conduct of society during it. It therefore made no sense to me to compare the relatively straightforward process of counting votes in Britain with the much more complex reality of doing so in NI.

I kept in close contact with the police in the run up to each election, and especially parliamentary elections, to be kept aware of any potential problems that might arise from a security perspective. In so doing I was very aware that the security forces were already stretched throughout the process. It was unlikely that they would have been capable of extending their involvement to enable counting to commence immediately after polls had closed. Even if they could, I was concerned by the potential for serious disruption from competing supporters of various parties gathered at night-time to await the outcomes – particularly in a bitterly divided city like Belfast.

MY OVERALL EXPERIENCE

During my time as the Deputy Electoral Officer based in Derry, the process of electoral registration was identified as an obvious route through which those not eligible for inclusion onto the register could submit false applications. This arose in a variety of ways, as can be illustrated by two specific cases that stand out on my mind. The first concerned a former senior Northern Ireland politician who had left Northern Ireland to work in mainland Europe and rented out his house – but wanted to keep the door open to returning and potentially standing for election again under his former address. He therefore apparently made steps to ensure that he remained entered onto the household registration form that was submitted from his former NI address every year. The other case was of a school teacher who moved from Derry to live across the border in Donegal (parts of which are essentially suburbs of Derry city). He rented out his former home, and I was told he had instructed the tenants there not to submit their own names on the annual electoral registration form for that address. I ensured that the individual concerned, who was not eligible for registration within Northern Ireland, was therefore not included in the electoral register. There was also some abuse around postal voting, which I was able to give particular attention towards identifying and tackling. The scale of personation I had to deal with during my time as Deputy in Derry, however, paled in comparison to that which was to arise later whilst serving as Chief Electoral Officer (CEO) in Belfast. I was only in that role a year or so when a high level of abuse first became apparent to me.

In 1981 two parliamentary by-elections were held in the nationalist-unionist swing constituency of Fermanagh-South Tyrone. As these were free-standing by-elections I was able to pay prolonged visits to a number of the polling stations there during them. From my observation, both within the polling stations and whilst travelling between them, I concluded that personation was occurring on a well-organised level. In addition, large groups of people were gathered at or near to each polling station and their behaviour towards me clearly indicated that my attendance was not welcomed (for example, upon departing some polling stations I had to walk between sections of the group to get back to my car).

After the latter of those two by-elections I advised Secretary of State Humphrey Atkins of the need to introduce some form of identification to ensure that anyone requesting a ballot paper at a polling station was the person they claimed to be. Through his officials, the Secretary of State consulted with the NI political parties on what safeguards should be introduced – but there was reportedly considerable opposition to my proposal (even though some political activists acknowledged that abuse was an issue).

On September 4th, 1981 – just over a year after I'd been appointed CEO, an article appeared in the Belfast Telegraph newspaper highlighting personation as a growing problem. Dr Brian Feeny, a Belfast City councillor, was quoted in the article stating that voters should be required to present identification. He also claimed, however, that presiding officers at polling stations were not as clued up about the rules as the personators were. This touched on an inadequacy in the law at the time around how and by whom suspected personators could be challenged. Polling station staff had no legal entitlement whatsoever to challenge anyone presenting themselves as an elector, beyond asking a set of statutory questions – i.e. whether they had voted before at that election, and whether or not they were the person on the electoral register that they claimed to be. If those questions were answered appropriately, the polling station staff could take no further steps to prevent that person from voting, despite any doubts they may have had. The process for challenging individuals at that time was via an officially appointed polling agent at the relevant polling station. Under the legislation a candidate at the election could appoint an individual (called a polling agent) to observe the process at one, some or all of the polling stations – and s/he could also challenge an elector whom they suspected to be personating. The procedure was that the polling agent asked the presiding officers (the official in charge at the particular ballot box) to put the statutory questions to the applicant. The polling agent could also ask for the applicant to be arrested on suspicion of personation, but that could only be done whilst the person was still inside the polling station.

If the case went to court and was unproven, the individual could pursue damages for wrongful arrest. One such example took place in the County Court in Cookstown following the contest for the Fermanagh-South Tyrone seat in the 1981 General Election. An individual accused of personation had been arrested and held in a police station for four hours. When the case came to court the Judge dismissed it and ruled that the candidate had to bear responsibility for their agent's mistake. They awarded the claimant £100 in damages, but refused to award the costs of the case to them. In contrast, a rather unorthodox example of a successful conviction for personation arose in the 1989 Local Government Election. The alleged personator was arrested and brought before the court – where it was claimed that upon being challenged in the polling station he had torn up the ballot paper he was using and proceeded to eat it. It was also claimed that he tried to dispose of a forged medical card that was in his possession. He was given a two month jail sentence and fined £100.

The role of a polling agent had long ceased to be utilised elsewhere in the UK for a number of years, but remained in operation in Northern Ireland – presumably to deal with the much higher level of abuse that existed here. I introduced a number of measures to assist polling agents in the effective discharge of their duties. They included the following:

- A common polling station scheme and ballot box allocation at all types of elections. Each candidate at an election was given a list of all the polling stations to be used at the election – including the exact location of each, and the number of individual ballot boxes to be employed within each. Some would only have one box, but in the larger urban areas two or more boxes would be necessary.

- That common scheme apportioned the same group of electors to the same ballot box from election to election whether it be a local government, parliamentary or European parliamentary election.

- The printed register of electors clearly shows the composition of each ballot box – the electoral register being sub-divided into blocks of electors, corresponding to their allocation to the ballot boxes for that particular ward. Accordingly the political parties could therefore preplan the selection of political agents, taking into account their local knowledge and experience, long before any election took place. If they had any knowledge of past attempts to abuse the system they could also advise the relevant polling agents so that they were prepared.

Polling agents therefore played an important role for political parties in NI long after they had ceased to do so in Britain – but presented a number of problems when it came to their effective use. It could often be difficult for parties to obtain the services of the desired number of polling agents. They might have the right number overall in most areas, but not where the party had either little support or was less well organised. Of course the tensions, fears and the culture of violence and intimidation that was ongoing within Northern Irish politics at that time also compounded the problem. As polling agents could play a key role in combating personation on election day, in the early 1980s I compiled a booklet to advise them on their role and the legislation that applied to it.

I felt that they were not being fully instructed in their role by their parties, and at times many of them were only last minute appointments. Copies were supplied to the various political parties, and updated from time to time to accommodate changes to legislation and experience gained from each election. At elections copies were also provided at each polling station to be given to the polling agents in attendance there. Over time, however, the tense political atmosphere in Northern Ireland led to a serious drop in the number of individuals willing to act as polling agents. One political activist, who had fought vainly for years to contain personation, suggested that the duty should be transferred from polling agents to polling station presiding officers – a suggestion that I was not inclined to support. To my mind, the appropriate solution to tackling personation was to require the use of a suitable and secure form of identification rather than to tinker with a system that clearly was NOT addressing the problem. It wasn't until the 1985 Elections (Northern Ireland) Act was introduced by the Westminster Parliament that my preferred solution was finally implemented – though even then, only to a limited extent.

LEGISLATION TO TACKLE ELECTORAL ABUSE
1985 saw the introduction of two pieces of legislation that had a significant impact upon the potential for, and practise of, voter personation. In the years prior to that change there had been quite an upsurge in personation in more marginal constituencies in NI – and especially those areas where paramilitaries were most active. It was a problem that I had flagged up in my annual reports to the Westminster Parliament. The 1985 Elections (Northern Ireland) Act was therefore introduced to deal specifically with this issue, and applied only to NI. The Act required voters in Northern Ireland to present one of a number of

specified documents at a polling station before they could be issued with a ballot paper. The list of identification documents that could be used was as follows:

- A current full driver license (not a provisional license).
- A current British or Irish passport.
- A current book for the payment of official allowances, benefits or pensions issued by the Northern Ireland Department of Health and Social Services.
- A medical card issued by the Northern Ireland Central Services Agency for the Health and Social Services
- A certified copy, or extract, of an entry of marriage issued by the Registrar General – where the voter producing the copy or extract is a woman married within a two year period up to the date of the poll concerned. The term " a Registrar General " was defined as meaning the Registrar General for England and Wales, the Registrar General of Births, Deaths and Marriages for Scotland or the Registrar General for Northern Ireland.

Care had been taken in drafting the legislation to ensure that the range of acceptable documents would not exclude any particular social group. For example, anyone below retirement age who didn't drive and didn't go overseas on holidays – would be unlikely to have the first two documents on that list. A medical card, which was available to anyone upon request – was therefore included specifically to cater for such individuals, and the health department made plans to deal with an expected increase in demand for them following the introduction of this new legislation. However, I became concerned that this form of ID was essentially the weak link in the list of approved documents. I obtained specimens of the cards so that I could advise polling station staff of their design and layout. The cards were printed on stiff cardboard and had been issued over a great many years – making the actual cards prone to deterioration over time. I dug out my own medical card, which by that stage had been in my possession for a good number of years, to discover that it was by then in a rather worn state and had faded in colour.

When I visited the government office that issued the medical cards, it also became clear that the colour of card used to produce them had varied over the years. This was understandable for a document that had previously existed solely to convey personal information via a low-cost format/keepsake, but it made medical cards far from being anywhere near as secure or as reliable as the other forms of allowable ID. At some elections following the introduction of this new legislation, I travelled around polling stations in areas considered most likely to experience personation. There I encountered cards that had been presented as proof of ID and which the polling station staff had retained as suspected forgeries. After examining them I came to the same conclusion, and after further investigations (including with the department responsible for issuing the cards) I notified the police. They later reported back that they had raided suspected premises and found a stock of fake medical cards that had clearly come from an unauthorised source.

The question of whether or not an individual medical card submitted at a polling station was genuine or a forgery therefore became a major issue for staff at elections. When I raised the matter with the Northern Ireland Office it became clear that there was a reluctance to remove the medical card from the list of acceptable documents, as for many people it was the only acceptable ID they had access to. I therefore issued very detailed guidance to polling station staff on how to differentiate a false card from a genuine one. It did add considerably to my workload initially, with visits required to various polling stations to check on suspected false cards that had been presented. The various problems that arose also added considerably to both the overall election workload and to the creditability of the process.

The 1985 Act also made it illegal for someone to possess a document with the intention of committing, or enabling another person to commit, the offence of personation at an election. It authorised a police constable, having reasonable grounds, to search and detain a person, search any vehicle, and to seize and retain any suspicious documents found in the course of that search. The Local Government Elections on May 15th, 1985 were the first at which identification was required, and overall the media were of the opinion that the problem of personation had been addressed as a result of the changes. Indeed the Irish News described the practice as "…well and truly buried" in one of its editorials.

Of course the local elections were not as good a 'stress test' of the new process as a parliamentary election would be. The new requirement was also not universally supported within the world of politics. The leader of a major party called for my resignation and that of the Minister concerned. Another politician from a different party claimed that the new requirement had, in effect, disenfranchised genuine electors – which he viewed as a greater evil than personation. My suspicion was that some unionist politicians found themselves torn by these changes – between the need to stop an abuse that was becoming more apparent in Northern Ireland, and their political desire for NI to always be in legislative alignment with the rest of the UK. Unionist parties were generally opposed to Northern Ireland having different electoral requirements than those in the rest of the UK. Their preference seemed to be for the introduction of a UK-wide Identification Card, but that was not a popular idea amongst the public in Britain. On the nationalist side there was concern that such safeguards could unwittingly disenfranchise supporters who might be unwilling or unable to obtain the required documentation.

Operationally I was strongly of the view that measures like this were designed primarily to frustrate the abuse and make it less likely to occur on a wholesale basis. This point was echoed by The UK Standing Advisory Committee on Human Rights when they met with me in 1991 and commented on the inherent challenge between ease of voting and the likelihood of electoral abuse arising from it:

It would be disingenuous to suggest that (some form of identification) … would stamp out personation: it would not be beyond the ability of a determined personator to acquire identification but it might go some way towards making life more difficult for those who seek to organise personation on a large scale. If a serious attempt is to be made to tackle this problem it seems likely that some infringement of the absolute right to vote will be necessary. The danger with demanding some form of identity is that some people may be discouraged from voting.

In addition to the NI-specific Elections Act that year, 1985 also saw a separate UK-wide 'Representation of the People Act' passed by Westminster which involved a number of changes to electoral law – some of which related to abuse. For example – it changed the law regarding the level of evidence that was required to prosecute for personation across the UK. Up until that point a person could only be convicted of personation on the oath of two or more credible witnesses – which was an exception to the general rule of law that a court could act upon the uncollaborated testimony of a single witness. Electoral legislation was therefore amended to bring it more into line with the law in general. Changes were also made, on my suggestion, to create a 'standing list' of absent voters for the first time – which detailed those who were eligible to either vote by post or to appoint a proxy for parliamentary elections. Up to that point electors at local and Assembly elections had to apply for an absent vote at each and every election as and when it was announced. This proved to be a regular source of public confusion – particularly when a parliamentary election was closely followed by another type of election, as many people thought that their application for the first election then covered them both. The change brought in under this legislation meant that once someone had registered for an absent vote, that preference continued for future elections until such a point that they indicated otherwise. I had recommended that the standing list should be applied across all elections – due both to the confusion of electors having to reapply for each election, and also the workload which the old law created for my offices at a very busy time – so I was understandably pleased with this change.

ABUSE OF POSTAL VOTING
I encountered examples of it as far back as the two parliamentary elections held in 1974 in the early days of my Deputy role in Derry. In 1978 I was asked by

the then Chief Electoral Officer to conduct a review into potential abuse in marginal constituencies which had a very high level of applications to vote by post – a large proportion of which were suspicious and appeared to have been the product of application 'factories'. The dubious applications had come from across both sides of NI's political divide. I concluded that the system was open to abuse and was in fact being abused, and I reported that finding to the Chief Electoral Officer – who discussed the matter with the Northern Ireland Office to ascertain if and how, appropriate changes could be made to the legislation.

Shortly after my appointment as Chief Electoral Officer I made a point of visiting all our area offices to personally examine past applications for postal and proxy voting. I was interested in establishing if there were differences in approach between the offices, and especially whether the volume of applications that were received had any impact upon how they were being assessed. Whilst the majority of applications were in good order, it became apparent that some received by a rural electoral office – made on medical grounds, and certified by a doctor – were a cause of concern. Some appeared in batches that had all been completed in the same handwriting, and in many cases the address given for the doctor who had signed each one off was not in the same area as the person applying for the absent vote. Whilst some individuals could understandably need help in completing their application, the volume involved suggested that a less altruistic dynamic was at play. The volume of suspect applications varied from constituency to constituency, and unsurprisingly proved highest in marginal seats where the result had the potential to be close. I wrote to the British Medical Association (BMA) to indicate that the improper certification of applications for a postal or proxy vote by a doctor was an electoral offence, and that under the legislation offenders would also be liable to discipline by the BMA. The BMA in-turn wrote to all their Northern Ireland members to advise them of this fact. That appeared to have the desired effect, and substantially reduced or even stopped the number of bulk applications that were signed by a single medical practitioner.

By the mid-1990s I had grown increasingly concerned by the fact that postal voting abuse was on the rise again in Northern Ireland. In my 1993-4 annual report to Parliament I commented that "… the potential for abuse is considerable. Such abuse strikes at the very heart of the democratic process. It is not confined to one political party or group." Local council elections were particularly prone to their results being influenced by postal vote abuse, as each individual electoral area was much smaller than those for parliamentary elections – so a handful of votes could, and occasionally did, decide the outcome of more than one seat. As always, balanced against this possibility of abuse was the desire to avoid placing unnecessary obstacles in the way of any electors who genuinely needed and qualified for a vote by post.

Events at the 1989 Local Government Elections in Northern Ireland, however, had emphasised the necessity of tightening the legislation around postal applications. During those elections I referred a total of 548 cases of suspected postal vote abuse to the police – mostly in the Mid-Ulster and Newry and Mourne areas. Their investigations obviously took some time, particularly given the volume of cases involved. In the Newry area alone 232 applications were referred to the police for investigation, of which they were able to contact 103 of the electors involved (or a close relation). Of those applications 177 were confirmed to be dubious, whilst only one proved genuine. It was not always possible, however, for the police to contact all of those involved – and some indicated clearly that they were not interested in meeting with the police. For example, of the 123 questionable applications from the Cookstown Council area that the police were able to make contact regarding, 40 were confirmed as dubious and 23 related to genuine electors (though that didn't necessarily mean the applications had been made by the genuine elector concerned). There were also approx 200 suspect applications in the Omagh and Strabane council areas. Meanwhile in Fermanagh a large number of postal voting applications had been submitted on behalf of the residents of a hospital. Of the 55 postal votes that were issued in response, 39 were returned unused – with official confirmation by the consultant geriatrician that the applicants were not actually capable of exercising the franchise. It was therefore clear that concerted and organised attempts had been made to influence the results across multiple council areas in the 1989 Local Government Elections.

The police outlined to me the various difficulties they faced which hindered their ability to investigate such alleged instances of voter fraud. Time was a considerable issue – as the large number of alleged abuses could only be brought to their notice shortly before an election, which was a busy period for them anyway. In addition, whilst electors would usually acknowledge that they had not themselves applied for a postal vote, they would rarely agree to give evidence of that fact in court. No doubt some were fearful of the possible consequences that could arise if they did. Also, the period leading up to elections is also a very busy period for the staff processing applications at the various Electoral Offices, which would realistically increase the likelihood of some instances of postal voting abuse slipping through the net.

The following Local Elections in May 1993 saw a continuation of postal voting abuse. In my annual report to Parliament covering that year I highlighted an incident that arose during a subsequent by-election for a seat in the Derry City Council area, triggered by the resignation of a sitting member. The bye-election was held on 21st October 1993 with 3 candidates standing. Shortly before polling day reports of alleged electoral malpractice via absent voting began to circulate, and these allegations were discussed at the September and October meetings of Derry City Council – with allegations and counter-allegations traded between representatives of the SDLP and Sinn Féin on the council. As polling day approached staff informed me that a number of suspect proxy and postal voting applications had been received at the area office in Derry. After calling to the office myself to meet the Deputy Electoral Officer, I decided to refer some applications to the police for investigation. After the election an analysis of the voting figures showed that the total number of postal and proxy votes included in the count amounted to 200, whilst the successful candidate had not only secured a majority of 553 – but had also won 385 more votes than the other two candidates combined. Furthermore, no reports of alleged electoral abuse had been received on the day from the polling stations. Therefore, whatever level of absent voting abuse occurred had had no material impact upon the result.

On November 16th, 1993 the Council notified me by letter of the contents of two resolutions that had been passed by Council. The first referred to "…the most serious undermining of democracy in the shape of fraud, forgery and personation in the polling booth since the gerrymandering of wards that crucified Derry for generations." It went on to say that the second resolution condemned all electoral fraud and indicated support for any measures that would eliminate fraud, provided that they did not infringe upon individual rights. The matter of possible illegal practices in that election needed to be investigated, but unfortunately the letter I received from the Council was the only indication, let alone evidence, of abuse referred to me at that point – and it arrived a month after polling day. On November 22nd, I responded to the Council Clerk to indicate my concern at any abuse being perpetrated against the electoral system, and informing him that the matter had already been reported to the police. I requested that the councillors, some of whom it would appear from their comments at the Council meeting – had personal knowledge of the events, should assist the police by passing on the appropriate evidence. I then asked the police to contact the councillors concerned, but apparently no actual evidence was obtained as a result of them doing so. It was almost three months later that I came to the conclusion that either there was no hard evidence available to support the allegations, and/or that it had been raised primarily as a cover for poor performance at the polls. Then on February 11th, 1994 a report in the Derry Journal newspaper had a heading which read "RUC PROBE SPARKS NEW ROW". The report highlighted resentment in a strongly republican area at the appearance of the police at individual's addresses to check on the accuracy of applications that had been made under their names.

The May 1993 Local Elections saw similar allegations made in relation to proxy voting in the Dungannon District Council area. Indeed, there was even a call for the election to be postponed there until a police investigation had been completed. When my office contacted a number of electors for whom dubious absent voting applications had been requested, the vast majority stated that they had not requested any such facility and certainly hadn't signed any applications for one, whilst the others proved uncontactable at that time by letter or phone. A comparison between the signatures on the written replies we received versus the original application forms that had been submitted also highlighted a clear difference. However, when the police investigated the matter it was the usual story that the electors invariably declined to repeat or go on the record with their original statement, and so no progress could be made in investigating the cases. As I commented in my annual report to Parliament for the year 1993-94: "Substantive evidence has built up to indicate that some parents are applying for postal or proxy voting facilities in the names of their sons or daughters who are either permanently or temporarily away from home. It is apparent that a number of such applications have been submitted without the knowledge, let alone the consent, of the family member named. It appears that such parents are much more anxious for their children's votes to be cast than the electors themselves are. So much so that, in fact, they submit false applications. It is not always the case that sons and daughters share the same political affiliations as their parents".

Two elections were held in Northern Ireland in 1997 – one for Westminster and the other for local government. In addition the Northern Ireland Forum Elections had been held in May 1996 to provide delegates for the ongoing peace negotiations. At all three of those elections concerns were expressed about absent voting. It was unusual to have three such elections in such close chronological proximity, so I took advantage of that fact to gather all the absent voting applications from them together at my Belfast headquarters to try to identify any dubious submissions. Earlier in March 1996 I had set up a special unit to deal with postal and proxy enquires and application requests for the Northern Ireland Forum Election. Rather than the usual practise of sending out blank forms upon receipt of a request, this time the forms were pre-coded with the electors' name and electoral roll number on them. That enabled the signature on the completed form to be checked against the signature on the original request to ensure both had been signed by the same individual.

The unit dealt with a lot of enquiries and proved to be a useful innovation, so I decided to retain it to assist me in the examination of all absent voting applications received at the three elections across 1996-7. The area offices were asked to forward all the application forms they received to our Belfast headquarters, where they were arranged in alphabetical order within each ward and for each of the three elections. That enabled the applications for individual electors to be easily found and the signatures and reasons given compared across the three different applications/elections. This process of cross-referencing identified many dubious forms from those elections that would otherwise have been considered acceptable if examined in isolation for each individual election – for example, due to signatures being markedly different, or the reasons for an absent ballot varying beyond reason. It was impossible, however, to tell which of the three applications was the genuine one (if indeed any of them were).

I had introduced a number of other changes a few years earlier which also helped in the examination of applications for absent ballots. Up until that point, for example, the annual household electoral canvass had involved a registration form being sent to each known household – which was to be completed and posted back to our offices for inclusion on the electoral register. I decided that the completed forms should instead be collected in-person by our team of canvassers, who would call at each house on up to three separate occasions to do so. If no contact had been made after that, another form would be left to be posted back using Freepost. The canvassers would also look out for any new houses within their area to add to our records, as well as any derelict residential properties.

The number of canvassers we employed during the canvass period was substantially increased to accommodate the extra work this involved. It did have the advantage of obtaining a more accurate register – for example, where a house was clearly not big enough to hold the number of residents that appeared at that address on the existing register. In that instance it would highlight the need to investigate to determine the correct position. In addition to this change, the information we requested from householders on the form was also expanded – to include, for example, their previous address if they had relocated within the last year. That information then flagged up their old address as one to be given special attention to determine the new occupants. If the previous address was outside of the registration area being covered by a particular canvasser, they would pass the information on to whichever of their colleagues was responsible for that area.

By 1997 the Secretary of State for Northern Ireland decided to establish a formal Electoral Review. This was primarily to look into the allegations of widespread malpractice during the May 1996 elections, but also to formulate proposals to improve the integrity of the electoral process overall. The wide-ranging review reported its findings in October 1998 under the title 'Administering Elections in Northern Ireland. (Cm 4081). In addition it examined a number of new initiatives that could be considered in the drive to combat abuse. The report contained 115 pages detailing the conclusions and recommendations, and its summary ended:

The Review has recorded the overall conclusion that, given the regulations by which electoral procedures are governed, elections in Northern Ireland are efficiently and fairly administered, often in very difficult circumstances… that much of the credit for the successful administration of elections in Northern Ireland must go to the current Chief Electoral Officer. However the Review believes that this success is often in spite, rather than because, of regulations as they currently stand.

The review went on to indicate that, although a lack of hard evidence had been presented to it, it still recognised that an unacceptable level of abuse existed. The members of the review body visited my office and inspected the large number of absent voting documents that I had combined from the three elections in 1996 and 1997. They were in no doubt about the apparent level of abuse that had been identified, and of the usefulness of the detection procedures employed. They were clear in their minds that there was no apparent way in which applications for absent votes could be traced back to the original sender if the application was fraudulent and the sender didn't want to be traced.

On a personal basis I was pleased with the review report – not least because of the positive comments it contained regarding my role. The stakes are high in Northern Ireland's intense political atmosphere, with politicians often under considerable pressure and at times tempted to blame electoral setbacks upon others. It was not unusual for myself or my team to find ourselves the targets of procedural criticism from politicians from across the spectrum when things were not going their way electorally. So it was reassuring both personally and professionally to read the following supportive comments within the review:

> *It has been apparent to the review that the Chief Electoral Officer carries out his office with great integrity, energy and skill, his knowledge of electoral law and procedures is second to none. There are problems with the current procedures which make it possible for those who wish to exploit the system to do so. However the Chief Electoral Officer is not responsible for the conditions in Northern Ireland which enabled intimidation to exist or for the shortcomings of the system he operates. The Review has found that the smooth running of both the Referendum and the elections to the New Assembly were in a great part due to the personal dedication and skills of the present Chief Electoral Officer.*

Organising elections is one of those jobs where you almost never receive praise, but are quick to hear about it if people believe you have acted unfairly or injudiciously. The best you can usually hope for therefore is for no feedback at all – because any you do receive will most probably be of a negative nature. It was therefore both unusual and reassuring for my staff and I to have our efforts recognised and praised in this way by an official report. Especially when the consequences could have been very serious indeed during such troubled times if there had been an absence of confidence within Northern Ireland and beyond over how our elections were being managed.

Overall I felt that I had done as much as could be expected (or perhaps even a little bit more) to tackle electoral abuse in the difficult circumstances of that time and with the facilities that were made available to me. However, I was conscious that the role of Chief Electoral Officer was an independent one with only limited oversight, and I felt it important that there be some scrutiny over the operation of my office. Not just in tackling electoral abuse, but in all matters – to determine whether or not I had carried out the post of Chief Electoral Officer appropriately and effectively. I was particularly keen on this, as the reason I joined the Electoral Office originally had been to help in the development of an impartial and effective system that could hopefully knit the two communities closer together. To my mind it was important to have a detailed and impartial review of how I was operating in that regard, so we implemented a process to do so. When those involved in the review came to my office to look at the procedures and practices, I requested the staff to answer all their queries fully and frankly and to identify any areas where they felt matters could have been handled better. I also left the office for the day of their visit so as not to have any indirect influence upon the feedback from the staff.

CHAPTER 5
As One Door Closes…

In 2000 I indicated to the London-based Northern Ireland Office (NIO) my intention to stand down as the CEO. They advised that they would be keen for me to continue in post, and as the time frame for my compulsory retirement was in line with that applying to judges I could have remained in post for much longer. I decided however that I needed a change. There was also an increasing number of invitations to go and advise various states abroad that were evolving into a democratic mode, which was a task I was attracted to. When the NIO accepted that I would not change my mind, a date for my departure was agreed that gave sufficient time to recruit a successor. The advertisement for the job did, I felt, give recognition to the job that I had developed during my tenure in office. It read as follows:

> *This is a high profile post in a sensitive and important area which will require a candidate of the highest calibre to ensure that the organisation retains the confidence of both the public and the Government. The Chief Electoral Officer will have regular dealings with the political parties and the public, Government, various organisations and the media. In addition the appointee will be required to manage and promote the role of the Electoral Office, process its independence, set its strategic direction and ensure that its aims and objectives are met.*

It then went on to explain that the Chief Electoral Officer (CEO) was an independent officer appointed by the Secretary of State and whilst the CEO may delegate functions the persons performing those functions are only acting on behalf of the CEO whose personal responsibility was in no way diminished. The main duties of the office were listed.

Two days before my retirement I published my last official notice. It was the notice of election for the parliamentary by-election for the Westminster Constituency of South Antrim. The notice set the poll, if there was to be a contest, for Thursday, September 21st, 2000. My replacement was, like me, to have an early introduction to elections. Luckily for him it was only a by-election and the actual running would be undertaken by a very experienced employee in the area office involved. Whilst it was only a by-election for him it was bye-bye for me.

On my last day in office on August 31st, 2000 there were media interviews to be done. When I boarded the bus at the end of the day for my trip back home there were photographers recording me going into the bus after having been given a present by the bus station manager who described me as the leading commuter in Northern Ireland. On arrival in Derry there was a repeat performance at the bus station there where I was presented with another travel case. I have to admit that I had mixed emotions then on the way home. It was the end of an important part of my life but also the opportunity to explore further abroad. I had only a few days to pause as I had been invited to attend a conference in Stockholm on September 6-7th, on the lessons to be learnt from elections in Kosovo.

From time to time, afterwards, I would travel to Belfast for various reasons and whilst I sometimes would pass my former office I never paid a visit. I told my staff just before I had retired that I would not call in even if I was close by as I had no desire to intrude into what was now the domain of my successor. I had developed the role into a very personal one and so it was now up to him to determine his approach. I was hoping that it would not be a merely bureaucratic one.

CHAPTER 6
Invitations to advise and operate abroad

The experience I gained running elections in Northern Ireland throughout the Troubles led to me gaining a reputation as someone with solid expertise in both the democratic process and in how it could be utilised within conflict resolution. By chronological fate, it also happened to coincide with the birth of a large number of new nations – particularly via the break up of the Soviet Union. As a result I found myself increasingly in demand across the 1990s from organisations like the United Nations, the European Union and the UK's Foreign and Commonwealth Office, who were all assisting emerging new nations and former conflict zones with the process of transition towards peace, independence and democracy. After decades of a global Cold War, it was clearly in the interests of Western and global organisations like these to ensure that this period of flux and transition led to the establishment of stable entities – and they therefore looked towards people like myself to assist in that process.

At the most basic level of involvement I was sometimes asked to discuss or advise on electoral processes in certain countries – whilst in other instances I was recruited to physically oversee and evaluate the operation of elections there. In total I was involved with almost 30 different nations across Europe, Asia, Africa, Australasia and South America, each of which tended to fall into one of three categories. Some, like Kosovo and East Timor, were brand new nations that had recently emerged following a period of conflict. Others, like South Africa, Cambodia and Bulgaria – were long-established nations that were now democratising themselves. Others still – like Australia and Nigeria, were existing democracies that were interested in learning and applying best practise from elsewhere. I was also involved with a number of countries on a confidential basis, whilst for others my involvement could only be described as minor. That therefore leaves the following 23 countries, listed in alphabetical order, in which I played a significant and public role:

Australia	Hong-Kong	Poland
Armenia	Indonesia	Russia
Bosnia-Herzegovina	Kyrgyzstan	Saudi Arabia
Bulgaria	Kosovo	Sierra Leone
Cambodia	Lebanon	South Africa
East Timor	Malawi	Tajikistan
Georgia	Montenegro	Yemen
Guyana	Nigeria	Macedonia

The visits initially began whilst I was still employed as NI's Chief Electoral Officer, but increased greatly after my retirement in 2000. Some of the invitations to assist came directly from the countries themselves but the usual route was via organisations like the UK's Foreign and Commonwealth Office, European Union, The Organisation for Security and Co-operation in Europe (OSCE), the United Nations and other international organisations.

My first taste of assisting in elections outside of Northern Ireland was for a location that was significantly closer to home, i.e. the Isle of Man, which is a small self-governing British protectorate located in the Irish Sea between England and Ireland. The invitation came via an official phone call requesting that I visit the island to train the designated returning officers there on how to run STV elections. This was my very first introduction into working with electoral organisations outside of Northern Ireland. The Isle of Man's Parliament is known as the Tynwald, and claims to be the oldest surviving legislature in the world. Its lower chamber is called the House of Keys – and up to the point I was asked to assist it had been elected under a majoritarian first-past-the-post system. The 24 members of the chamber were independent of any party – a situation that has changed since with the introduction of political party membership.

A leading member of the parliament had decided that an STV system would be more appropriate, and had either convinced or cajoled his colleagues into agreeing to the change. I accepted the invitation to assist, and spent some time preparing a practise count for the staff to highlight to them the various queries and challenges that were likely to arise. When I arrived at the island's airport I was surprised to find in its shop that one of the minor headlines on the front page of a local newspaper said 'Bradley arrives today', as part of a short article about my trip.

When I was about to start the training session those in attendance made their unhappiness with the task clear. The source of their disgruntlement was the stipulated fee for their electoral role, which I clarified was not something within my remit. Once that hurdle had been successfully overcome, the practice session went well.

Unbeknown to me at the time, that trip turned out to be the first in what was to become a global electoral odyssey which spanned over 25 years in total.

During my period as Chief Electoral Officer of Northern Ireland I obviously had to put my own work as the first and only priority, so the trips increased in both number and length in the years after I retired.

Below I have described some of the more interesting trips.

BULGARIA – ROUND 1

November 10th, 1989 saw the fall of Todor Zhivkov. He had held the top post in the Bulgarian Communist Party for thirty-five years. During his tenure he had attempted to assimilate the 10% Turkish minority: an action that was most unwelcome to the general public. The economy he left behind him was deeply in debt. His departure resulted in a blossoming of many political organisations some of which had been suppressed by the communists when they first took over the country. After his downfall the governmental coalition that emerged was led by the Bulgarian Socialist Party (BSP), a reformed Bulgarian Communist Party. It entered into discussions with the Union of Democratic Forces (UDF) that had been set up by the amalgamation of a number of various groups. It was agreed that an election would be held on June 10th and 17th, 1990 for a constituency assembly having four hundred deputies, half of whom would be elected by absolute majorities in single-member constituencies and the other half by a proportional system based on party lists in twenty-eight multi-member-constituencies. In the single-member constituencies a contestant could only be elected at the poll on June 10th if he/she had obtained more than half of the votes otherwise there would have to be a second poll on June 17th with all candidates participating. At that second stage, if less than half of the eligible turned up to vote, the candidate having the greatest number of votes would be elected.

With the collapse of the Soviet Union the various Western democracies had a keen interest in political developments in Eastern Europe. I was invited to be a member of a UK observer team attending in Bulgaria from June 6th to 20th, 1990 to cover the Bulgarian National Elections on June 10th and 17th, and to report on them. Fortunately it was a particularly quiet period for me in Northern Ireland with an unusual gap in the timing of elections and so I could accept the invitation. We were part of a coordinated operation mounted by the Western economic powers and Japan to determine whether, by the election, Bulgaria could be regarded as a bona fide candidate for democratic status and therefore eligible for economic and technical assistance.

The twelve person observation team was briefed on the political background to the election and also on the arrangements for the holding of the poll. After this detailed briefing we met with key players including the President of the Central Electoral Commission, representatives of the political parties and members of the Public Movement for Free and Democratic Elections. The team also had the opportunity to observe the mass rallies of the two major parties – the Bulgarian Socialist Party (BSP) and the United Democratic Front (UDF) – and to mingle with the participants to observe attitudes. At a BSP rally, whilst in the midst of the large crowd, I heard a voice calling out in English "Hello Mr Bradley". I did not sense that it was a greeting.

Thanks to all those briefings and meetings we were satisfied that we would be able to draw reasonable conclusions from what we would see and hear when we scattered around the country whilst in the process of observing the election and associated events. At a group meeting held on Friday, June 8th the group divided into six teams of two, each group was given a general briefing of the region to be observed. We then departed to various parts of the country, accompanied by an interpreter, to observe the run up to the poll and polling day itself.

The electorate were able to understand the balloting system as a result of pre-election publicity. The local commissions at the polling stations were comprised of members who had been selected collectively by the various political parties and that meant that the members kept a close watching brief on each other.

My colleague and I headed off towards the Black Sea region and on the way across the Danubian Plateau we experienced the attention of a traffic policeman. In theory there was a speed limit on the roads and one that was set at a very low level which none of the local drivers appeared to obey. There was little traffic on the road. Whilst driving on a long straight length of road the car's speed drifted up slightly above the prescribed speed limit. Passing through a small village we noticed a motorcycle policeman watching us but he did not pursue. A few miles further on we came to a small bridge set at right angles to the road and crossing over a single-track railway line. As we slowed down to go over the bridge a traffic policeman appeared from the side of the road waving a red stop disc and so we pulled up.

The policeman stated that as we had being speeding he would fine us the equivalent of $40. Our interpreter questioned how he came to that conclusion and the policeman took him over to a small car that was partially hidden at the side of the road and that bore a speed detector on the roof rack. I thought that the proposed fine was somewhat high, given the economy of the country at that time, and so I bartered with him saying that I would pay in US dollars which seemed to please him. Eventually we settled for $15 after which the interpreter asked how he came to be at that location just as we were passing – there being little traffic on the road. The policeman was quite open in his reply by telling us that his colleague back at the village had radioed him and they agreed to share the fine – they had not been paid for some time and their family would welcome the food that could now be bought. That made us aware of the nature of the economy at that time. In addition I noticed that whilst the road was passing through good agricultural land no farm houses were evident but only the occasional block of flats could be seen. Our interpreter informed us that when the land was collectivised just after the Second World War the inhabitants were all moved into the newly built blocks where they could be more easily monitored.

When we arrived at our designated area we had time to get a general feel of the area and to locate a number of polling stations that we planned to visit the next day. During our contact with the electorate we gained the impression that they had concerns about their future standard of living. At the time there were shortages of life necessities including in particular food and fuel. Many of the elderly citizens we spoke to expressed worry about their future. It appeared that the Socialist Party was claiming that the elderly could well have their state pensions reduced or cancelled if the other parties were to form a government. Under the communist system, pensions and state-arranged holidays were provided for the elderly at the instigation of local party officials. My colleagues and I picked up concern about intimidation but we were not supplied with any specific details. However, on the other hand there were indications of military personnel being pressurised by their officers when they went to vote. Soldiers had to vote at polling stations specifically set up for them only. Overall we were able to attend mass rallies of the parties prior to the poll and by mingling with the participants could observe their attitudes.

Contacts with local residents indicated that they had been reasonably informed of the procedures through the media and that a television transmission on the eve and early morning of the poll had been of great help. On the other hand some team members noted that among the ethnic Turkish population there was both fear and distrust of the system. That was compounded by difficulty experienced in the reconciliation on the electoral registers of their original Muslim names with their new imposed Bulgarian names despite the early publication of the electoral lists.

The general perspective of all the teams was that the election had proceeded in general accord with the legislation but, not surprisingly, there were some irregularities and variations in practice. The electorate were able to understand the balloting system as a result of pre-election publicity. The operations within polling stations did differ very slightly from station to station but no serious, intentional irregularities were observed. The staff manning the polling stations were, in the main, enthusiastic although some gave the impression that they were merely performing a dutiful role. The police did not attend within the polling stations and maintained a low key approach overall.

At the closing of the poll the counting of the votes cast was carried out fairly and in accordance with the electoral regulations at the polling stations we attended during the counting process. Overall the counts were carried out in a good manner although with a few exceptions that probably arose from a misinterpretation of the rules. That is not to say that there was no room for improvement of the overall system but that was not seen as unexpected in the new approach to democracy. There was one particular aspect, however, that caused me concern. Once the count had been completed the details of the votes counted and allocated to each party were entered on a designated form – 'the protocol'. Once completed and signed by the polling station staff, the protocol had then to be forwarded to the regional electoral commission. The protocols were not enclosed in sealed envelopes thus giving rise to the possibility of the entries being altered during transportation. When the protocols were being processed at the regional electoral commissions they were at times the subject of debate – probably because they had not been received in sealed envelopes.

After observing the poll and the counting of the votes cast at each polling station we returned to Sofia on Monday, June 11th. Large groups of UDP supporters had assembled there. The overall count was being processed by computer. Some results of single-mandate elections were announced on Tuesday and the large groups of UDF supporters were becoming restless due to the delay in announcing further results. They seemed to perceive that as suspicious and the party had to be asked to exercise constraint. On the Wednesday the situation in the city improved somewhat and the results of the remaining single-mandate constituencies were announced. Then on Friday the PR results were announced.

During this difficult period I heard reports that the delay in the release of the results was due to problems with the computer system. On the other hand we were aware of rumours that swept around the city on the Monday. They referred to allegations of fraudulent protocols and alterations having been made to genuine protocols. The UDF claimed to have documentary proof of that but our group could not obtain any evidence to support those claims. In addition there were claims that their representatives had been sent away from the computer centre when they found that 20% of the protocols contained erroneous totals. There were also claims that some protocols were received at the Central Electoral Commission after a 20 hour delay. When I checked with the Association for Fair Elections they indicated that they, through their observers, had checked the results for Sofia against the official results and the margin of error found was only 0.1%.

On Tuesday 12th June some results of the single-mandate were announced with the remainder being announced on the following day. On Thursday June 14th, the results of Proportional Representation voting was announced.

The second stage of the election was held on 17th June. As observers we were impressed by the meticulous care taken by the section commissions who made sure that the observers could confirm the authenticity of the results. In some areas voters reported to observers that they were being harassed by socialist officials and there was some evidence of serious intimidation by the armed forces of people working on the election. Strong representations were made immediately to the Regional Commission. There were reports of soldiers being confined to barracks because of how they had voted on June 10th. At this election the completed protocols, in many cases, were transported to the Regional Commission in a car containing a mixed party representation with police supervision.

I gained the impression that the country dwellers were more conservative in their attitude than their fellow citizens living in Sofia and that was reflected in their choice of candidates. We received claims of intimidation but they were, in the main, of a hear-say nature. It appeared that the opposition in the rural areas were not as well organised as the Socialist Party. The opposition, largely due to the rapidity of events and limited resources, had insufficient time to either develop coherent policies that would commend them more widely to people in the country or to organise effective campaigns in each village.

Out of the 400 seats in the Grand National Assembly, the Bulgarian Socialist Party gained 211 seats; the United Democratic Front – 144; the Movement for Rights and Freedom, twenty three; and the Bulgarian Agrarian National Union, sixteen. The Socialists were well organised in the country areas but not so the newer parties. In addition the opposition largely had insufficient time to either develop coherent policies that would commend them more widely to people in the country or to organise effective campaigns in each village. Due to the rapidity of events and limited resources they could not do so. The observer team submitted a memorandum to the president of the Central Electoral Commission listing suggested revisions to the procedures.

We concluded that the election was broadly free and fair. It was not surprising that there were some irregularities considering both the arrangement's complexities and novelty involving both proportional seats in multi-member constituencies and directly elected single-member constituencies. Whilst many of the allegations were without any back up, there were a few that we believed to be true. It is possible that in a close contest they could have affected the result. Nevertheless these elections were a significant step along the road to democracy from the previous mode of governance. The overall assessment on the election was that the general conduct of the polls was broadly satisfactory and that any infringements were not as fundamental and widespread as to justify the conclusion that all the polls were basically fraudulent. The hitherto untried system was relatively sophisticated and so any error could be reasonably accounted for by misunderstandings and differential interpretation of complex rules by thousands of non-professional election staff who had, by necessity, only limited training.

The Grand National Assembly that had been elected, with an expected term of office of eighteen months, was tasked with drafting a democratic constitution. Then fresh elections were to be held.

I returned home pleased that I had been given the opportunity to visit Bulgaria.

BULGARIA – ROUND 2
The Grand National Assembly (GNA) which was elected in June of 1990 had been tasked with the drafting of a democratic constitution. The term for the

GNA was perceived to be eighteen months and the drafting of the Constitution was expected to be completed by then with fresh elections to follow. That timeframe was not to be.

Whilst the Bulgarian Socialist Party (BSP) held 211 of the 400 seats, it did not have the required two third's majority to enact major constitutional legislation. The United Democratic Front (UDF), with its 144 seats, held the balance of power. Eventually the post of President was allotted to the leader of the United Democratic Front as a consensus candidate and a BSP member, the Interior Minister, as Vice-President. Despite that there was the problem that whilst the BSP desired to have a broad coalition the UDR was not so inclined and so the interim government was left in power.

The impasse continued into the autumn and fuel supplies became short. That, coupled with plans being announced for the introduction of both fuel and food rationing, led to street disorder, strikes and demonstrations. In November the interim government resigned. A coalition government was then formed leading on at the start of the new year to, *inter alia*, plans for the passage of a constitution, the re-privatisation of land, both local and national elections and other measures. However little progress was made over the next number of months until the GNA approved a Constitution which was signed on July 11th, 1991. The date of September 29th was set for the combined national and local elections but the President referred the Electoral Law Bill back to the GNA on the grounds that it was in parts unconstitutional. The delay that resulted in the process led to the President's party, the UDF, fragmenting. Another political party, the Movement of Rights and Freedom (MRF), was challenged on the grounds that most of its members were of Turkish origin and that the new Constitution restricted political parties that were based on ethnic origin. It appealed to the Supreme Court but the appeal failed. The MRF indicated that as it was already on the political party register, having fought the 1990 elections, and so it did not have to re-register. The Central Election Commission then decided on that basis to register the party and stayed with that decision despite attempts by others to have it overturned.

The scene was set for the election to the new National Assembly having 200 seats based on thirty-one electoral divisions, with a four-year term of office. Voting was to be by a list system. The allocation of seats to the parties was by the use of the D'Hondt method of proportional representation requiring a four percent threshold. The individuals elected for each electoral division were determined on the particular party's relative voting strength there. In addition there were directly elected members using single member constituencies.

In July 1991 I was again invited to go to Bulgaria to observe elections there. It came at an unusual break in elections in Northern Ireland. There was some uncertainty about the timing of the expected Bulgarian elections and whether the national and local elections would take place on the same day. In August it became apparent that the national elections would take place on October 13th. It was still uncertain if the local elections would occur on the same day. Just before my arrival with three other team members, the four of us forming an advance party, it was confirmed that the local elections would take place on the same day as the national elections. We arrived in Sofia on October 2nd to prepare the ground for the main party arriving on October 9th.

Prior to our departure to Bulgaria the whole observer team had met up at the Foreign and Commonwealth Office in London on September 17th, to receive a thorough briefing followed by a briefing by the Bulgarian Ambassador in London. On arrival in Bulgaria those of us in the advance party met the representatives of the principal parties' and other organisations' main actors including the Prime Minister of the Republic of Bulgaria. On arrival the four of us in the advance team split into two pairs and on Saturday October 5th we departed Sofia for the country with one pair staying overnight in the northern city of Pleven, and the other in the southern city of Plovdiv. The next day we then moved on to Ruse and Smolyen respectively. The intention was to observe preparations and the mood of the people outside Sofia.

The remaining team members arrived in Sofia on October 9th and on Thursday October 10th the whole team was divided into six units. We were assigned drivers and interpreters, and given a general briefing and also a checklist of aspects to examine. The check list was based on that used successfully at the 1990 election. We were then despatched to various locations in and around Sofia to experience the general mood of the people. We were not to observe the election in Sofia but rather in the country areas where the coverage at the 1990 election had been somewhat sparse. The city of Sofia was to be covered by teams formed from embassy staff, both British and Bulgarian, and personnel from other embassies who had agreed to participate as part of the observer team. As team members we were only able to cover a relatively small number of towns and districts.

It was evident that the accuracy of the electoral registers varied from place to place. The queries arising from that slowed down the voting process. Apart from that, the process of voting at two elections on the same day added to the time individual electors took. That was not helped by the considerable number of the staff who were new to the task. From time to time when a query arose they would have to take time to determine the course of action. The count in all the stations visited was carried out in strict accord with the regulations. There were many fewer allegations of intimidation or other wrongdoing than last year. The observers had only cause for concern at two polling stations.

The team concluded, both from our initial impression gained in Sofia and then elsewhere, that the general public atmosphere was much more relaxed than at the previous election. We were able to attend mass rallies of the parties prior to the poll and by mingling with the participants could observe their attitudes.

We got the general impression that the elections would be seen as fairer than last year and that the secrecy of the ballot would be maintained. There seemed to be a freer atmosphere than that attending the last election. And whilst there were some comments on the continuing influence of communism, the fact that people were prepared to talk freely with us whilst others were listening was a good sign. We did receive a number of concerns expressed to us in regards to those Bulgarians who had left the country. Apparently Bulgarians leaving the country had to surrender their internal passports. It was alleged that those passports then fell into the hands of those who unlawfully used them to impersonate the absent voters. The specified beneficiary of this was the BSP and the number of claimed instances was large. This was a very general claim and we received no specific instances.

To vote, the elector would pick a ballot from a range of ballot papers displayed, each indicating a political party, and place it into an envelope which then was in turn to be placed inside the appropriate ballot box. In the municipal elections, if less that half of the voters turned out, then a second round of voting would be required the following week. The names of voters in the electoral register were listed according to residence as opposed to the alphabetical order that had been used at the 1991 elections.

One of my colleagues commented that it was to be a colourful election. At these combined elections the Central Electoral Commission decided to use a colour coding system to differentiate between the two ballot boxes provided at each polling station. The ballot box for the National Assembly election, was to be painted white; and the one for the municipal elections, was to be painted black. In addition there were separate polling booths within each polling station for the two elections. The ballot papers displayed within the polling booth, from which the elector would pick the party he or she wished to vote for, were also colour coded. The BSP's paper was coloured red; the main UDF party's was blue; whilst those for the remaining five parties were white, bearing two or three different coloured stripes.

Queues built up at a number of polling stations leading to some electors leaving before they could vote. However we formed the impression that they were planning to return to vote at a later time. On the other hand there was a problem as regards voting by members of the military. At the 1990 elections they had to vote at polling stations set up in their barracks. This time it was arranged that they would vote alongside the general population and that was to be welcomed. In some instances they were only given a limited time in which to vote resulting in attendance en masse with some having to depart before voting so that they would be back in the barracks on time.

At the conclusion of the poll, the sectional election commission in charge of each polling station determined the number of votes cast and their allocation. That information was then to be entered on a protocol which was to be immediately sent to the relevant district commission who then would send a copy by fax to the Central Electoral Commission where a computer was used to collate all the votes. The use of a fax was designed to speed up the process but also as a safeguard. The actual individual protocols sent to the Central Electoral Commission were each being checked against the faxed copy received earlier.

Because of the combined elections, the sectional and district commissions were given in the order in which the votes were to be counted. The National Assembly votes were to be counted first and then the ballots cast for the members of the municipal council, the municipal mayors and the settlement mayors. The mayors were to be directly elected whilst members of the municipalities were to be elected, on a party list system. To win in the first round a candidate standing for the office of mayor had to receive at least 50% of the votes cast. These changes in the electoral system led to a reduction in the representation of the smaller parties, so much so, that only three – the larger parties – gained any seats at all.

That process was viewed by us as well organised and impartially carried out. On the day following the poll a large crowd of the supporters of one party assembled in Sofia amidst widespread allegations of fraud. It was our view that the difficult situation was not being helped by the delay in announcing the election results. Nevertheless both those assembled in the streets and the authorities displayed good restraint. I got the impression that the delay was at least partially due to problems with the computer system being used to collate the various returns from the polling stations. In this connection we received complaints that some protocols had been handled in to the Central Electoral Commission after twenty hours delay.

Our overall assessment was that, based on the relatively small number of visits that we could make, the poll was free and fair. It was estimated that at least 80% of those entitled to vote did so, even taking into account the varying views expressed by commentators on the accuracy of the registers. The team submitted a report containing recommendations as to how the overall process could be improved for future elections.

HONG KONG

The governance of Hong Kong was due to revert back to Mainland China in 1997. Understandably there was much interest within the colony as to the type of political control that would be introduced after the handover. In addition there had been much concern with the perceived imperfections of the existing system of governance – as that could bode ill as an example for what would succeed it. The existing system was seen in certain quarters as needing a strong commitment to enhance it in the run up to the handover. Indeed the Hong Kong Democratic Foundation's Chairman stated that the Government had not taken the initiative and had shown a lack of commitment to electoral reform and the pace of democracy.

The Hong Kong Democratic Foundation, a moderate political party, saw the need to seek advice on the matter from an outside source and so approached an independent London-based organisation that had been consulted by political and other organisations in many of the newly-formed democracies in Eastern and Central Europe. This organisation's chairman invited me to accompany him on a five day visit to Hong Kong at the end of January 1991. The objective was to examine the administration and monitoring of elections, election rules, preferred electoral systems, the status of political parties, campaign expenses, constituency boundaries and access to the media.

We found Hong Kong a very homogenous society with 98% of the people being Chinese. There was a diverse range of other nationalities and particularly so in the business, commercial and shipping sectors. Indeed in our meetings with various representative bodies of business directors from non-Chinese and non-European backgrounds it became apparent that their main concern was how they could move to and settle in the UK prior to the Communist takeover. We met with a wide range of persons including the Secretary for Home Affairs, officials of the Constitutional Affairs Branch, the Senior Legislative Councillor, various political groups and academics.

The colony had a Legislative Council, membership of which was by appointment from the various businesses, commercial, shipping and union sectors. Political parties were not recognised as such. Instead they were required to be registered as limited companies. At the time in the UK there was no registration of political parties. That may well have been due to the belief that the common law provisions relating to corporate and incorporate bodies was sufficient, aside from the provisions in the electoral law relating to joint candidates.

The registration of electors was in one way quite liberal and in other ways unusual. Seven years residence in Hong Kong qualified an individual to the right to vote whatever his or her origin, subject to an age qualification. The qualifying age for voting was twenty-one. The register of electors was compiled in constituency related sections. The delimitation of electoral constituencies was a matter that needed attention. The entries in the register were in strict alphabetical order of individual names and not on the basis of residence whereby all the eligible members of a family would be shown under the particular address. I wondered whether or not that had some origin in its use for ID or security purposes. It was certainly not a user-friendly methodology.

It was a very busy period meeting with a very wide range of interested individuals and groups some of whom were not favourably viewed by the authorities. In addition we met with media representatives. There was a radio interview that was most unusual in that we could not see the interviewer as he was not present in the interview room. It was, apparently, his custom and practice to sit in a room a couple of floors above whilst carrying out interviews leaving us to hear a somewhat dismembered voice.

We concluded that the best approach in our report would be a detailed description of the key factors of an appropriate and internationally acceptable system of the overall electoral processes, whilst highlighting the deficiencies and unsuitabilities of the existing arrangement.

YEMEN

The Republic of Yemen was formed on May 22nd, 1990 when the Yemen Arab Republic, North Yemen, merged with the Marxist People's Democratic Republic of Yemen, South Yemen. The newly united country had a population estimated between 11 and 14 million. It occupies the strategic south western corner of the Arabian Peninsula. Whilst it had a border agreement with the Sultanate of Oman, the much longer border with Saudi Arabia had remained largely undefined. After World War 1, when the Turkish occupation ended, border treaties were signed including one with Saudi Arabia in 1934 which ceded important areas that historically had been part of Yemen. That particular treaty was due for renewal in 1992, but that did not occur. The Saudis then used the lack of fixed borders to challenge ongoing petroleum exploration and production by Western companies between the 16th and 17th Parallel.

This corner of the Arabian Peninsula has from ancient times served as a transit point to Asia for those coming from the Horn of Africa. The remoteness of Yemen's high mountain ranges from civilisations in the north provided a safe haven for refugees, often Islamic dissidents who settled there down the centuries. Suspicion of the outside world has always been high. Coastal Yemen in the south is different both in its terrain and in its attitude. Far from being suspicious of outsiders, it had engaged in commercial trade since earliest times both by sea and land. Its boats ranged over the Red Sea, the Indian Ocean travelling to Sudan, Ethiopia and Egypt and on to various other lands including India, Indonesia, Persia and Oman. The geographical differences between the two regions are reflected in the religious sector as well. Some 60% of the population are orthodox Muslims whilst the remainder are Shi'ite Zaydi Muslims who ruled North Yemen until 1962.

The two parts of Yemen differ in regards to their political development. The North experienced a period when, for example, there was a time of continued civil war between royalists, helped by Egypt, and republicans and also supported by Jordan and Saudi Arabia. South Yemen experienced a British presence that began in 1839 over the fragmented territory that, with the exception of the colony of Aden, they amalgamated into the Aden Protectorate. In 1963 the colony of Aden was incorporated into the protectorate despite the opposition of its population and the new unit was named the Federation of South Arabia. As in other former colonies, Britain eventually departed.

Down the years since then consideration had been given to unification but it was not until the period between 1988 and 1989 that negotiations began in a determined move. Outside events provided the required impetus. First the end of the Soviet empire had a significant effect on the Marxist regime in Southern Yemen. With the collapse of the Soviet Union their ideological basis collapsed. Secondly, the discovery of the first significant oil deposits on both sides of the shared desert boundary between them provided the incentive for joint exploitation.

Yemen is one of the poorest and weakest countries in the Arab world. Illiteracy is high. It has no permanently flowing rivers. The production of khat, a relative of the coffee tree that produces a leaf chewed daily by most of the northern population for its powerful caffeine stimulant effect, has replaced the growth of coffee that Yemen was famous for and which was a considerable foreign currency earner. Large areas of land that used to grow food for the domestic market have been converted to the growth of khat. Ground water supplies are being exhausted and with quicker acceleration by the introduction of bananas and other crops requiring large amounts of water. Yemenis working in the Arabian Peninsula and especially so in Saudi Arabia provided a major source of hard currency and income through annual remittances. Because Yemen abstained from voting on the UN resolution imposing sanctions on Iraq, Saudi Arabia and other Gulf States expelled hundreds of thousands of Yemeni expatriate workers who returned home unemployed with some of them condemned to living in wretched refugee camps.

The united Republic of Yemen was committed to holding democratic elections by November 22nd, 1992. The Government prepared the election law and associated organisational arrangements. At the beginning of September 1992, the Government desired to have the advice of a pre-election assessment prior to the poll. I was asked to be part of the team.

On reflection it became apparent to the Government that the election would have to be postponed, initially to some date in mid-February but then to Tuesday, April 27th, 1993. The objectives of the team were then broadened on the request and agreement of the Minister of Foreign Affairs. The sectors to be considered were identified as follows:

- Status and role of political parties
- Citizen education and training
- Role of the media
- Election official training
- Election observation

The funding of the five-member mission was shared by the British Foreign and Commonwealth Office, The Westminster Foundation for Democracy and the US International Foundation for Electoral Systems (IFES). The delegation was in country from January 26th to February 1st, 1993.

This was not my first time in Yemen. I had paid a very brief visit there to the provisional referendum held on the Constitution on May 15th and 16th, 1991 accompanied by a fellow-member of the mission being discussed. Our interest was not only to view the referendum but also to meet up with the Marxist Party based in the port of Aden to ascertain its view of the outcome of the unification. To get there we had to travel by car from Sana'a over the Taiz mountains. For security reasons we had to use two cars, with local drivers, with each of us in a separate vehicle. Accordingly if one of the vehicles broke down then the other car could take us both in safety to our destination. If that should happen when we were sharing the one car there was the danger of being left isolated at the side of the road with the danger of being kidnapped.

We left early in the morning. There seemed to be little traffic on the road which had been built by the Chinese some years beforehand. Prior to our departure we had been warned of the number of serious accidents that were a very frequent occurrence on that road and especially towards the top of the pass. I was somewhat puzzled by this as there were absolutely no sign of crashed or damaged vehicles as we drove along. When we reached the pass we stopped to look around and observed a precipitous drop at one side of the road and many wrecked cars and vehicles cluttered below. We were later to learn that the most common time for crashes on the road was the afternoon during which it was the custom and practice for the general public to chew khat.

At the top of the pass the Chinese had built a plinth to commemorate their construction of the road. We stopped to inspect it and whilst so doing I noticed at the back, somewhat hidden in a corner of the base, the outline of a shamrock accompanied by two words in Irish *'Erin go bragh'* meaning in English 'Ireland for ever', that had been deeply etched into the concrete whilst it was still wet. It would appear that there was at least one non-Chinese involved in the construction work or else had been there very shortly after the concrete had been cast.

We arrived in Aden, passing a lagoon having many pink flamingos, and met up with the party officials at their office. After a long discussion we were invited to join with them in a meal at their beach guesthouse. The meal was sumptuous and accompanied by the finest of wine, as evaluated by my colleague who was much better educated in such matters than I. He enjoyed the meal so much that, as we walked back to our cars, he commented that he could easily be converted to our host's political beliefs if that was their routine standard of living! We then drove back to Sana'a.

Returning to the mission currently being described I would refer to an estimate of about five million of the population eligible to register as electors. Those registering for the April 27th Election only amounted to 2.7 million so clearly there was much to be done. Of those registered only some 300,000 were women. The high level of illiteracy clearly made the registration much more difficult as did historic constraints on the role of women. Commendable efforts were being made to involve women fully in the electoral process and that was greatly helped by women themselves who had set up organisations to support their role. In this connection I have pleasant memories of one event in which we were involved. The team and some of the Yemeni officials we met decided to have a meal at one of the most renowned restaurants in the capital, Sana'a. Amongst those we had previously met in our discussions was a very intelligent and highly educated lady who had studied at a couple of high ranking universities in the USA. We were aware that the restaurant was, in practice, confined to male customers. On this occasion we insisted on the lady participating in the meal. This, we were told, was the first time that a female customer had ever been catered for.

Voter registration had commenced at approximately 2,000 centres just over a week before our arrival. Registration was to end on February 19th. At each location there were separate arrangements for men and women. The registration process required a photograph of each person registered to be taken at the centre and then attached to the registration certificate. The majority of women in the former North Yemen wore veils in public and would not remove the veil in public to have a photograph taken. Women told us that they would only be prepared to be photographed without veils by other women. To overcome that issue the registration of women was to be carried out by a committee consisting solely of females including the photographer. However that still left a perceived problem. A copy of each photograph that was retained at the registration centre would be eventually sent on to the principle committee in each constituency where it would be filed with the duplicate certificates. Many women and probably their husbands, fathers, and older brothers did not want those photographs travelling beyond the local centres where they were liable to be seen by men.

We ascertained at an early meeting with the Supreme Election Committee (SEC) that women's committees had been constituted only in the cities of Sana'a, Taiz, Aden and Hodeidah. Whilst those cities did comprise the largest centres of eligible electors the failure to have such committees in most areas of the country was potentially disenfranchising all women in those areas. The SEC indicated that the number of established women's committees was growing daily but we saw the possibility that women's committees might not be established in time and if so a significant percentage of women would be denied the right to register and therefore to vote. We had concerns when we learnt that in some areas, particularly in the Sana'a Governorate, women's registration committees were not in place by the ninth day of registration. Also in one registration centre we were told that they did not expect a women's committee and would only set up one should the demand be great enough.

There was a registration review and revision process whereby the registration lists for each centre would be posted publicly and appeals may be made to have names added or deleted prior to the planned election. This registration process did provide the administrators of the forthcoming election with the necessary information as to the appropriate number of polling stations to be set up and the correct number of ballots and other materials to be sent to each location. The previous information from the 1990 election had been far from satisfactory. There were to be approximately 2000 polling stations to service the 301 constituencies. Each polling station was to have three male and three female supervisory staff. Specific criteria had to be met by the staff – they had to be educated, literate, of good morals, able to deal with problems and not to be resident in the district in which they were to work.

There was one particular aspect of the regulations that we were concerned about. As regards the design of the ballot papers the election law provided little guidance on how the ballot paper was to be designed. The SEC's information plan for media coverage indicated the need for the voter to indicate his/hers choice by writing in the name of the chosen candidate. This would have presented a significant hurdle for the majority of the Yemeni voters who were illiterate. There are methods used in other countries sharing the same problem of illiteracy – but the various options used there were, in practice, not workable in Yemen for specific reasons.

The plan was for an elector to vote at the location at which he/she was registered. On enquiry we found that that would not always be the case. It was determined that there was the need for more voting centres than there were registration centres. At the same time the building/room used for registration over a period of time might not be suitable for the poll to be carried out on one day. It was crucial that voters be informed in advance of where they should go to vote. One provision enabled a voter who lost the registration certificate to vote: if that individual's name appeared on the register, he/she could bring one or more witnesses to the polling station. That had the potential to delay the rate of voters passing through the station. We had concerns about the provision in the legislation regarding assistance being provided to illiterate voters. That enabled the voter to be assisted by someone he or she could trust. A committee member could also assist. However, the latter case could give rise to the suspicion that the member could influence the illiterate voter or misrepresent his/her vote when the name was written in.

The electoral law prescribed that firearms or any other weapons were not to be allowed to be carried within a polling station precinct. That was to be a matter for the security forces. However there was no definition of what constituted a polling station. Clear guides on this would be necessary as would the consideration of the term "weapons" as many Yemeni men traditionally carry a large curved knife, *jambiya*, in their belts and this is seen as a matter of status. The carrying of weapons was the custom and we were not convinced that the bearers would comply with the legislation.

In addition to that experience was added the custom of an Arab country as regards the seating arrangement whereby one sat on a low cushion as opposed to a chair. They did offer me a chair but I declined as I saw it appropriate to follow the custom of my hosts. It did lead to some discomfort and slight difficulty in getting up afterwards. However I could see that my hosts were pleased with my action and also when we had a meal as I had ascertained in advance the appropriate method of handling the food. It was a practice that I followed in the various Arab countries that I then went on to visit.

We had meetings with various sheiks. On one or two occasions our host would suggest that we visit a high point that provided a panoramic view over the whole area. For security reasons we would be provided with a number of armed men to act as our bodyguards. At the time I was quite fit from my hill walking and climbing but was no match for the agility of the small, wiry bodyguards, loaded with a fierce array of weapons and ammunition in bandoliers, who could quickly traverse dry, rocky ground in their flimsy sandals – whilst I struggled to keep up.

I decided to travel to the more remote mountainous areas where I understood that the facilities would be very basic. At one location the designated polling station did not have a roof, merely some remnants of roof beams. However it was both a dry and warm day, typical of the region, and the staff there were quite content. After a short visit I decided to travel on and a short time later there was a very sudden and heavy rain storm and so I decided to retrace my steps to the polling station I had just left where the staff were in the process of arranging a plastic sheet on the roof to enable the poll to continue. They welcomed me with open arms and asked if I would visit them again in a month or so. Apparently it had not rained there for a long time and they saw me as a good look charm that had brought on the rain.

My interpreter was a university lecturer who had badgered me for some time on the need to stop and have some food or refreshments. At this juncture he was not prepared to proceed further without his needs being met. We were in a very thinly populated area in the mountains without sign of any suitable place. He made enquiries of one of the staff in the polling station and was informed that there was a place for refreshment a short distance up the pass. When we got there we found it to be a cave in the side of the hill with a cooking stove. Not only were the facilities primitive but also the hygiene. The only choice available was a type of stew that was bubbling in a pot on the stove. In addition there were masses of flies hovering around and occasionally one would fall into the pot and would be stirred in. Nevertheless my colleague was not discouraged from tucking in whilst I decided to abstain. Down the years I learnt to be prepared to go without food for long periods although I always ensured that I had a plentiful supply of water.

On the return to Sana'a, the mission continued with its meetings with a wide range of state, political and security officials in addition to our ongoing deliberations with the Supreme Elections Committee. We had detailed discussions on all aspects of the electoral process and made a number of suggestions. During the visits to houses and offices of non-governmental officials I was careful to continue with the Arab custom of sitting on a low cushion directly laid on the floor and not on the European type of chair that was offered to me. That was appreciated by the hosts. One other custom was somewhat disconcerting when I first experienced it. On the arrival at the house of a sheik, whilst getting out of the car, a fusillade of rifle shot rang out and for a second or so I wondered if we were being attacked. All the men carried guns and the fusillade was their traditional way of welcoming me.

I was impressed by the beauty of the country, perhaps a little rugged for some visitors' liking but, as one who loved to walk the hills and mountains at home and abroad, it grew on me. On the other hand I did at times have some concerns whist travelling to and from the houses of sheiks. They and senior officials built their homes high up in the hills to take advantage of the cool breezes especially in the hot season. Access was by four-wheel drive vehicles on a rather rough and stony tract with steep vertical drops on one side. The local drivers were well used to the terrain but I did have some concern when departing for Sana'a. Such visits usually took place in the early afternoon. After our discussions the host would offer refreshments and as part of the custom *khat* would be offered to all present. I would place a very small amount in my mouth as I did not want to offend my host but I would not chew it. Instead I would, by sleight of hand, pass it onto a cloth I kept for that purpose. My driver would participate in the chewing with great intent and continue doing so when we were driving down the steep slope on our return to Sana'a!

Prior to my departure from Yemen I was guest of honour at a reception held by the United Nations Development Programme (UNDP) Resident Representative. The international interest in Yemen was apparent by the number of ambassadors in attendance including those from France, India, Italy, Japan, Netherlands, United Kingdom, Turkey and the USA. Senior officers of the Supreme Election Committee also attended and there were some informal discussions. The visit was successful and I then had to prepare a report on my arrival back home.

My next visit took place in February 2001 at the UN's request. Parliamentary elections were scheduled for April 21st, that year. Local council elections on the governorate and districts were to be held on the same day. On the previous April the President of Yemen presented proposed amendments to the Constitution. The most significant of which was an extension of the term of office from four to six years for members of the House of Representatives, to be applied to the sitting members as well, and the President's term of office to be extended from five to seven years. In addition the date of the parliamentary elections would be reset from April 2001 to April 2003. Whilst Parliament concurred a referendum was required for the people of Yemen to confirm the amendments.

The Supreme Elections Committee (SEC) had the task of organising the referendum and also the local elections as Article 80 of the Election Law specified that a referendum on constitutional amendments had to be held simultaneously with any general election scheduled for the same year. The SEC set the provisional date for the referendum and the local general elections as February 20th, and more than two months prior to the parliamentary elections due to be held on April 27th, in case the voters rejected the constitutional amendments.

The election law established the SEC as an independent institution with the seven members appointed by the President of the Republic, selected from a list of fifteen names submitted to him by the parliament and coming from different political perspectives. Their tenure was for four years with a maximum of one reappointment. The current members of the SEC were in their last year of office. A proposed amendment to the electoral law provided for the appointment of a Chief Electoral Officer.

The Electoral Law provided that the SEC appoint a number of committees whose members had to have the approval of two thirds of the SEC's membership subject to the restraint that the members of any committee shall not all belong to the same political party. The committees were:

- Control Committees which were responsible for electoral operations in each of the 20 Governorates and having 180 members.

- Basic Committees responsible for electoral operations in each of the 325 Districts with 975 members

- District Basic Committees responsible for electoral operations in each of 2,073 Registration Constituencies with 6,219 members.

- Polling Station Committees responsible for electoral operations in each of the 22,400 polling stations and comprising 67,200 members.

The combined elections would require a considerable number of staff. The segregation of the sexes at the election accounted for the very large number of staff involved. Training sessions were in the process of being compiled.

The register of voters had been compiled in 1996 and updated through a partial voters' registration in April 1999. The total number of electors registered was just over 5.7 million of which 30% were female. For the referendum voters would have to select one of two choices on the ballot paper – either **YES, for the constitutional amendment, or NO**. The text in Arabic of the proposed amendments amounted to six pages and so a simple choice was all that could be incorporated on the ballot paper.

The local government elections were to be based on governorates. Yemen was comprised of twenty governorates. Each governorate consisted of districts, 325 in total, and the voters in each district would elect by a simple majority one representative to the post of member of the Governorate Local Council. The relevant Local Authority Law provided that each Governorate Local Council be composed of a minimum of fifteen members, including the Governor designated by the President of Yemen.

Each of the 325 districts was in turn divided into a number of local electoral districts according to population total ranging from eighteen districts, up to thirty districts. Voting would be on a simple majority basis. I estimated that the total number of district local council members throughout Yemen would be in the region of 6,825.

The SEC had prepared a budget for the parliamentary elections scheduled for April 27th, 2001. At the time of my visit they were still in the throes of compiling the budget for the combined referendum and the two local elections. A rough estimate had been prepared that amounted to the equivalent of some 18.2 million US$. The SEC had received approximately the equivalent of some 4.85 million US$. No contributions had as yet been received from possible international donors.

Planning was under way for the training of all members of the Election Committees at both governorates and district levels involving approximately 1,154 officials over four days in Sana'a. Those trained would then in turn train the committee members of the local electoral districts and the polling station officials at the provincial level. A procedural manual was to be employed. Regulations had to be compiled covering political campaigning, the nomination of candidates, polling procedures, the counting of votes. Those were then to be included in a simplified manner in the Electoral Manual to be used by the electoral administration at all levels. The manual was to include a full set of examples of forms and protocols. In this connection it was important that the different sectors of the SEC be involved, namely technical, legal, media and public relations, so as to ensure the maximum comprehensiveness of the manual.

The Electoral Law specified that election campaigning would be from the 14th day before the poll until the day before the poll. The SEC was to establish all regulations and rules governing the electoral campaign and exercise direct control over the candidates' campaigning activities. In this connection the media and public relations sections were in the process of updating the existing code of conduct for political parties and/or candidates that had previously been used.

The SEC was required to ensure the operation of a voter/civil education campaign. An initial general plan had already been prepared for consideration by the SEC. Also under consideration were the arrangements for electoral observation including local and international participants. A document outlining the general rules and regulations on observation operation had been prepared and a new accreditation system was being prepared.

There was much to do and advise on. I was asked to extend my mission by two weeks. Having retired from the post of Northern Ireland Chief Electoral Officer I could accommodate the request.

RUSSIA

The collapse of the Soviet Union had certainly given rise to much interest among Western democracies as to the development of democratic politics in the former Soviet states and none more so than in Russia itself. The European Council agreed on a joint report to the European Union's Foreign Ministers on all aspects of the Russian parliamentary elections to be held on December 12th, 1993 after President Yeltsin had issued an invitation for such a mission. He had called the elections following the siege the White House, Moscow's parliament building, on October 3rd – 4th. They were to be the first democratic parliamentary elections in post-communist Russia.

As part of the agreement formulated by the European Council, the Foreign and Commonwealth Office (FCO), asked several organisations to nominate personnel for membership as monitors to report on the elections. I was nominated and informed of my inclusion in the team. The team was comprised of twenty monitors, including eight parliamentarians and also electoral officials, political party agents, academics and legal experts. The terms of reference for the teams were quite wide and included the expression of a view as to whether or not the electoral authorities acted with consistent impartiality, whether political parties and alliances enjoyed freedom of organisation, movement, assembly and expression and whether the electoral rules were scrupulously and even-handedly enforced. In addition the report of the mission was to express a judgement as to whether the elections were free and fair.

The weather forecast for Russia was ominous. The winter snows had come very early and the ambient temperature was dropping fast and was expected to be at least -30 degrees Celsius. We were advised to obtain suitable clothing from the Survival Shop in Euston Railway Station concourse where an account had been opened for each of us. I arrived there and I was fitted out from head to toe. At first I did try to see if I could use the type of mountaineering gear normally used in the wintertime in the UK and further afield. Hill walking and climbing, as I've mentioned, was a favourite hobby of mine. I wondered if it was possible to supplement in more severe climates the protection offered by such gear by using the addition of very heavy duty thermals. The staff in the shop convinced me otherwise.

Disembarking from the airplane at Moscow it was apparent that a thaw was setting in and so my heavy quilted jacket was quickly discarded. It was then on to my hotel which was situated directly on the opposite bank of the river from Red Square. The next morning I woke up to the sound of ice being chipped off the pavements outside the hotel and the nearby streets. I carried out a quick inspection of Red Square wearing normal winter clothing save for a pair of Sorell boots and then went back to the hotel to get ready for the important meeting when we would sit waiting to learn of our assigned areas. I was allocated Kursk. It did sound somewhat familiar to me and I quietly asked my neighbour, a tall, soldierly man, about the location of my area. "Tanks" he replied quietly. Then he stabbed his finger at a spot on a map I had just opened out and remarked, "The biggest tank battle in history." The map clearly showed Kursk in the middle of the Russian Steppes.

The elections had been organised in about ten weeks and involved some 105 million electors in 94,000 polling stations. They were to be the first truly democratic elections in the country. Constituencies varied considerably in geographical size from those in the small high-density Moscow suburbs to the enormous – up to 200 miles across, in sparsely populated rural areas. In addition there were four separate elections to be held simultaneously. These were:

- The State Duma (Lower House) election for 225 constituency seats under the first-past-the-post system
- 225 State Duma seats contested by 13 blocs and allocated by proportional representation
- Two seats in each constituency in the Federation Council (Upper House)
- A referendum on a new constitution

If that was not enough, in some parts of Russia, notably in Moscow and St Petersburg, voters were also to take part in local elections!

The overall responsibility for the conduct of the elections had been given to a new Central Electoral Commission based in Moscow, together with a whole series of constituency and precinct commissions responsible for the elections in individual areas.

The brief period for the organisation of the elections left little or no room for public consultation on relevant matters. For example the boundaries for the 225 constituency seats of the State Duma had to be drawn especially for the election and were decided by the Central Electoral Commission without any public consultation. In addition, due to the shortage of time for preparations, some of the documentation that might have been expected, such as constituency maps, was not easily available.

There were to be two briefing sessions for the team members. The first was on December 2nd, in the Foreign and Commonwealth Office in London and then, on arrival in Moscow. There the twenty members were deployed into ten teams of two and assigned to specific areas for the overseeing of the elections. I was teamed up with a Member of Parliament for the visit to Kursk – formerly, a staunchly communist area that was still regarded as a difficult area. I was told for that very reason I had been assigned there. Accompanied by a Russian speaking official from the FCO, we headed off. It had been the site of a massive tank battle during the Second World War where the Soviets defeat of the Germans marked an about turn in Hitler's plans for his conquest of Russia.

Kursk is on the far western side of Russia next to Ukraine and our trip there required an overnight train journey. There were flights from Moscow to Kursk but we were informed that we would not use them. Apparently there had been instances of aeroplanes loosing one of their engines and crashing. In comparison with some other teams we had a short journey as we could see from the copy of a map we were given showing the locations assigned to the ten teams. The map clearly illustrated the vastness of Russia. During the overnight trip we were supplied with copious amounts of tea and coffee by the woman who was in charge of our carriage. The pull-down bunks in the compartment were far from comfortable and I was unable to sleep much due to the shaking and rolling of the antiquated rail stock.

Our accommodation in Kursk was in a state-owned block of self contained apartments that was available during the Soviet era to party officials travelling into the city from outlying areas to meetings or to report on progress in their districts. Those individuals would cook for themselves using the kitchen in their apartments. In our case we had not brought any provisions with us as we were not aware that we would need to do so. We did manage to get a meal cooked for us by one of the staff in the accommodation but it was quite meagre being a mixture of cooked cabbage and some meat. We went into the town both to get the lie of the land and to buy some provisions. There was a shortage of any reasonable foodstuffs and what we did manage to get was very expensive.

I decided to visit the local government offices to see if they could identify for us any food outlets or restaurants. I presented our credentials that had been issued by the Central Electoral Commission. After some discussions, during which I emphasised that we were members of a mission that had been invited by President Yeltsin, we were enrolled as visitors to the senior officials' staff restaurant. It served meals of excellent quality accompanied by good wines. It was in sharp contrast to the position facing the ordinary citizens. In the restaurant no prices were indicated on the menus and we were told that we could settle up the day we were leaving. Not surprisingly the bills came to a greater amount that we had expected but it was the only viable option for us. A problem remained with our accommodation – heating was almost non-existent.

The general area around Kursk bore a heavy mantle of snow. There was a very strong Communist Party apparatus controlling the area and things could be difficult. It had been agreed that a vehicle and driver/guide would be provided by the local authorities to take us on our travels around the area. The guide did not take kindly to my determination to personally select the villages to be visited and at times would drive us to totally different locations. On visiting a local market and by the use of US dollars, I was able to obtain a good map of the area. That, with the help of a compass that I had brought with me, could enable me to instruct the driver which roads to take. He was far from pleased.

The small, scattered birch forests were immensely beautiful. They looked almost like some scene from a painting with snow on one side of their trunks and moss on the other side. The bare rafters of the stripped roofs of the large and dominating ruined Orthodox churches were evident here and there and still very prominent. We travelled around a lot meeting with people and getting a feel of the area.

On polling day during our visits to polling stations we noted a unique feature at the election. At those locations there were stalls selling foodstuff, alcohol and some items of clothing that were hard to get elsewhere. It became evident that electors coming into to vote entered by one door and after they had voted they followed a one-way system that took them to a different door for exiting. It was on the way out that they passed the stalls selling the various products. By discreet enquiries we learnt that was the standard practice in the past and clearly was designed to attract voters who may not otherwise attend to vote.

THE OVERALL ELECTION RESULTS

The Constitution was narrowly approved by 58% of the voters with a turn out of 55% thus setting in place a presidential system of government, as well as enshrining democratic principles and individual human rights.

In the Duma Election eight of the twelve parties that contested the elections won seats. The details are below. There did not appear to be any plausible working majority. Gaidar's Russia's Choice won 65 seats just one more than Zhirinovsky's Liberal Democrats. The Communists and Agrarians won 48 and 33 seats respectively while other reformist parties won 47 seats. Some 138 deputies were elected under the role of 'Independents' and not many of whom had clear political affiliations. It was reported that about 60 of them were likely to support the reformists and 30 the opposition parties. In the Federation Council (Upper House) supporters of Yeltsin and the Government gained 57 seats. Centralists accounted for 78, Communists 16 and others, unsympathetic to the Government got 19.

State Duma – allocation of seats	Party Lists	Single Mandate Constituencies	Total
Russia' Choice	40	25	65
Liberal Democratic Party	59	5	64
Communist Party	32	16	48
Agrarian Party	21	12	33

Yavlinski-Boldyrev-Lukin Bloc	20	5	25
Russian Unity and Accord (Shakhrai)	18	1	19
Women of Russia	21	2	23
Democratic Party of Russia (Travkin)	14	1	15
Other Parties	-	14	14
Independents	-	138	138
TOTAL	225	219*	444*

* The boycott of elections in Chechnya and Tatarstan left six of the 225 constituency seats unfilled.

Overall the internal observers concluded that the poll was generally fair. The observers noticed within polling stations in many rural areas the social nature of the men and women voters. They all seemed to understand the complicated voting papers. Ballot papers had a bottom box in which the elector could deliberately vote for 'no-one'. After the poll had closed and counting had commenced it was clear that more than a few had done so.

1996 PRESIDENTIAL ELECTION
This election was held on June 16th. Once again I was invited to attend as an observer. This time the invitation came from the Britain-Russia Centre based in London. Prior to departure observers were invited to attend a briefing on June 10th in London.

A year or two beforehand I had visited Moscow on two brief occasions with the Director of the Centre to get a feel for the political situation in the country. At the time the economy was in a particularly difficult situation. There were all types of shortages and Muscovites were in the habit of always carrying at all times a foldable cotton bag just in case they came across some items of food. Any goods at all were often the target as well. If they were not what the individual really wanted they could be bartered for something else that was more relevant. Goods of any type were hard to come by. In addition there were security problems with large gangs operating in the streets as pickpockets. We had the experience of being surrounded in the street by one such gang of young kids but fortunately we were prepared for that possibility and so they were not successful. This time Moscow was to be my area of assignment.

Boris Yeltsin, the incumbent President, ran again. Nine candidates had been successfully nominated. Yeltsin stood as an independent as did Mikhail Gorbachev and three others. Gennady Zyuganov of the Communist Party was a main contender. To be elected as President a candidate had not only to get a bigger vote that any other candidate but, in addition, had to obtain a minimum of least 50% + of all the votes cast otherwise a second round would have to be held. Yeltsin did get more votes than any other candidate but his total was only

35% of all the votes cast and so a second round was necessary. The second round was to take place on July 3rd, and so I departed Moscow on June 19th.

I flew back to Moscow on June 29th. This time my allocated area was Saransk in the Republic of Mordovia. In Russian terms it is geographically close to Kursk. A very experienced English journalist and a member of the staff of the British Embassy in Moscow completed the team.

In the run-off Yeltsin defeated Zyuganov by getting 54.4% of the vote. On the night of the election Zyuganov conceded the race to Yeltsin and congratulated him on his victory. The election took place at a time of tension in the country. It was at the time when there was the war in Chechnya and when, at home, there was widespread dissatisfaction about the payment of pensions and salaries. The campaign by Yeltsin's opponents was seen as ineffective. Yeltsin fell ill during the campaign. It was stated that he was only suffering from a cold/sore throat. When he appeared at the polling station to cast his own vote he appeared "shaky". It became apparent that his health had deteriorated significantly – months after the election it was disclosed that he had had a heart attack.

There were allegations that the election had been rigged. Unfortunately I have been unable to find my records about this second stage of the election or of my visit to Saransk. I still have memories of various events that took place during my several visits to Russia. One of the more memorable was my attendance in the Kremlin of a performance by the Bolshoi Ballet. Another, but less enjoyable, was a visit to a prison in a distant area where, to say the least, the prisoners' accommodation was not much better than a very large dog kennel fronted with heavy netting wire behind which the prisoners were confined. On one occasion in Moscow I was taken out for dinner to a typical Russian restaurant by a senior diplomat. The meal was very enjoyable. Two days later my host informed me that on the evening after our visit there had been a gun attack on the restaurant. It was believed to have been an ongoing dispute between two criminal gangs. The building was riddled with bullets and a number of diners killed. On one visit I stayed at an excellent hotel just straight across the river from Red Square. The receptionist had advised me to be careful when using the lift, to avoid getting out at a certain floor. I was to learn that the floor was the domicile of a Mafia-type group. During my stay the American manager dismissed a staff member whereupon he had a visit from a number of armed men who told him to leave the country or else face the consequences. Wisely the manager departed within a very short time.

MALAWI
President Hastings Banda, then about 96 years of age and a former medical doctor in the UK, had for thirty years ruled Malawi under a one-party state system with his Malawi Congress Party. There was growing opposition in the country and especially in the Northern Provinces. Western donors stopped aid to Malawi

and so in October 1993 Banda gave in to demands that a referendum be held on the introduction of multi-party politics. In doing so he said that he was holding it to prove to the world that only a tiny minority was in favour of multi-party democracy. He was the last of the leaders in sub-Saharan Africa to make any concession to multi-party democracy. He was an absolute dictator who hired and fired ministers, judges and officials at will. It was said that directly or indirectly he owned large areas of the country. There were also reports that he was no longer in total charge and that his wife, much younger than he, had taken overall control.

The UN and the British High Commission organised a number of teams to oversee the electoral registration process in April prior to the referendum to be held on June 14th, 2003. I was invited to participate and arrived on April 13th. After a general induction the various attendees were then given a region to oversee during the registration process. I and two colleagues were asked to go to the Northern Region. We would then split up and each of us would concentrate on a particular district. I stayed in a hotel outside the town of Mzuzu. It became evident that the hotel was owned by the Government and principally used by senior officials.

On my first evening there I decided to have a short stroll around the general area. There I noticed a camp that was identified by a large notice as being a camp for the 'Young Pioneers' and the 'Malawi Youth League'. As it was beginning to get dark I went back to the hotel without exploring further. The activities of the pioneers were to feature in my thoughts over the following days.

As a first stage I decided to meet up with local community leaders to identify any problems they had experienced with the registration process. It became apparent that the Presbyterian and Roman Catholic churches held much influence in the area and were strongly supporting the drive for multi-party democracy. There was a Presbyterian minister who was a leading light in that movement. He was from Scotland but had been in Malawi for many years and had married a local girl. He and others whom I had contacted reported on the real purpose of the Young Pioneers. They were uniformed 'physical persuaders' for Banda. There were reports of citizens being threatened and assaulted by them.

It was important to meet with the Regional Administrator and the Senior Police Officer to make them officially aware of the reports. During our discussions I made it quite clear that a detailed report of our experience of the registration process and the referendum would be submitted to the UN and various governments. It was then time to visit the various registration centres and the overall area, both to see how registration was progressing, and also to meet up with the citizens in general. That required the use of a car and one had been allocated to me from the government regional car pool – as had been agreed as part of the arrangements for the international oversight.

Having observed the areas immediately adjacent to Mzuzu, I decided to travel out to the more remote rural areas to ascertain the events taking place there. My vehicle had a four-wheel drive and hence could cope with the rather rough, un-tarred roads. I travelled for many hours over the next few days. On one occasion I came across a small bush school and the teacher was pleased to explain to his pupils who I was and why I was there. The school had little or no equipment and the teacher used a white, lime-washed wall as a blackboard. I had with me an atlas showing the various parts of Africa and I was pleased to give it to the teacher and then to see the faces of his pupils as they eagerly examined the various maps.

It was fortunate that my vehicle had a four-wheel drive as small streams had to be crossed in my travels. However my good fortune did not last, for when I eventually got back to the hotel, the car was collected by a man who said the vehicle needed a replacement part and would then be returned to me. It was not returned and I suspected that the move was a ploy to constrain my travel in the rural areas.

Instead a standard two-wheel drive vehicle was provided the next morning. That did restrict my ability to travel in some areas. However as there were complaints of problems in a rural area well off a track, I decided to go there, or at least as far as I could. I managed to get somewhat beyond the normal track but then came to a stream that my vehicle could not cross. There was smoke rising a short distance away and I managed to get across the stream using a somewhat precarious makeshift pedestrian foot bridge and came across a number of round, mud-walled, thatched houses. It was a Sunday morning and I saw parents and children very well dressed in basic but very clean clothing apparently on their way to a church service. None spoke English – *Chichewa* being, I understood, their language. I then walked a couple of miles through the bush using pathways that connected various small residential areas and so was able to talk to a few of the locals who could speak some English. Apparently there had been visits there by members of the Young Pioneers seeking to "convince" people to vote against the multi-party option at the referendum.

When I eventually got back to the hotel and went in to dine there were no other guests there. After a short time an elderly European man arrived and sat at a table by himself. A Malawian man came in very shortly afterwards, apparently his driver, but he sat at a different table. The white man came across to have a brief chat with me and I learnt that he had been a coffee farmer for many years. When Malawi became independent he had been so long in Africa that he simply could not face going back to England. When I asked him why there was so much erosion on various hills he replied that the local people had cut down a lot of the coffee trees and other trees and that had led to erosion with heavy seasonal rains causing large land slips.

I interviewed the registration staff and domestic monitors in the various registration centres. I also spoke with district government staff, pressure group representatives and religious leaders about the position in general and also about any disturbances in the villages. In addition my enquiries also included queries about areas that may be susceptible to disturbances or other problems on Referendum Day. The pressure groups identified a number of such locations and also polling places in large schools operated by the Church of Central African Presbyterians, whose Northern Synod was a strong supporter of the multi-party option.

Some campaign meetings had commenced. The major ones I observed were all in support of President Banda's party. They were highly colourful with large groups of women chanting and singing and all wearing special dresses each bearing a large portrait of Banda. These were the *Mbumba*, the faithful female followers of President Banda, the *Life President and Ngwazi (conqueror)*. All around the site of each of the campaign meeting there were tall poles with banners and other publicity materials. It certainly looked like a reflection of a well supported party but, as I was to see in the two weeks prior to the referendum, that was not the case but a rather good propaganda exercise.

There were some problems at the registration process but no worse than at other countries in the process of entering into the democratic mode. After two weeks it was time for me to return to Northern Ireland. I was scheduled to return to Malawi in two weeks time to cover the period in the run up to the referendum and the referendum itself and the counting. Before departing I stressed that the counting process at the referendum should take place at the individual polling stations and that all present at the count should be required to sign multiple copies of the protocol giving the result, one each of which would then be given to all those who signed. That would limit the scope for fraud in contrast to a central count, under the strict control of government appointed officials, where there would be no means of checking the turnout from independent information obtained from each and every polling station.

In June I returned for a two-week period covering the run up to the referendum, polling day itself and three days afterwards. The United Nations Electoral Assistance Secretariat was expecting particular problems in and around the Mzuzu District and asked that I be deployed there. I was the senior district observer for the Mzuzu district of the Northern Region and co-ordinator for the whole of the Northern Region.

Prior to the poll I met with various public officials to clarify the position in relation to the preparations and arrangements being made for the poll. The following illustrate the nature of those discussions.

- **The Police Chief and his senior officers**
  Concerns had been expressed to me by the multi-party activists that the police were using a ploy to restrict certain activists campaigning against the one-party system. They were being arrested and then held afterwards for a period on police bail. During my meeting

I sought assurances that persons on police bail would not be effectively disenfranchised by being required to present themselves at a police station on polling day. Some such persons would have to travel a considerable distance to a nominated police station. I also sought assurances that the police would adapt a constructive role at the referendum and would maintain only the necessary presence in and around polling stations and political rallies.

I had been briefed that the Police Chief had a hard-line reputation. During the meeting I explained that in my report I would have to identify details of improper activities in and about the referendum and the names of those involved. Whilst the Police Chief did not give specific assurances he did appear to be in some discomfort during our conversation. He probably was aware of the clear signs indicating that the referendum was not going the way forecast by Banda. He did promise to refer our meeting to his superiors.

There were no problems reported to me on polling day relating to the police. During my visits to all the polling places in Mzuzu on polling day the police were conspicuous by their absence.

- **The Commander of the Malawian Young Pioneers (MYP) in Mzuzu**
The visit here was to establish the precise role that the MYP were to play during the election period. Assurances were given that the MYP would have no role. They would go to vote in civilian clothes and would then return to their base.

There were no reports of any incidents on polling day involving the MYP. There was an altercation on the day after the poll when a polling official was attacked by some MYP and beaten. He ended up in police custody but I was able to obtain an assurance that he would be released the following day. His release did take place as promised but it was difficult to understand why the apparent victim had been detained and not the alleged attackers.

- **The District Commissioner**
I had been advised that he was viewed in the same light as the Police Chief. He was initially somewhat brash, unforthcoming and, as I discovered later, his preplanning for the referendum did not appear to be as detailed as one would have expected. Through time and after several more visits he became much more co-operative and particularly so on polling day as and when I raised various problems that had been identified. Indeed later on that day

he visited me several times to keep me inform of the corrective steps he had taken. His office was virtually next to my hotel.

- **Representatives of the Malawi Congress Party (MCP) and the multi-party interest groups**
  Visits were made to the individual offices of these groups during the run up to the referendum. The MCP made little comment. The multi-party interest groups did indicate a number of problems they had experienced in the holding of rallies and the alleged pressure applied to their potential supporters. In quite a number of the cases the allegations made were somewhat vague in nature, not directly experienced by the complainants and lacking in specific details.

There was an increase in political campaigning as polling day approached. I came across a number of well organised and colourful election rallies of the MCP. These intrigued me as my travels in the region clearly indicated that there was an overwhelming support for a multi-party system. Accordingly I attended a number of those rallies to see the level of attendance. As indicated above, a feature of the rallies was the attendance of the *Mbumba,* the faithful female followers of President Banda, colourfully dressed and in full voice.

It was evident that there had been a good deal of organisation in the preparation of the venue with many banners mounted on poles held up by large drums with bunting strung across. I decided to observe the scene from a short distance away after the rally had ended. Coaches appeared and all the *Mbumba* boarded and the vehicles then moved off. After an half an hour or so a small fleet of lorries appeared with a gang of men who removed the various poles, bunting and metal drums after which the lorries left in the same direction as the coaches. I had been able to obtain the details of the scheduled election rallies to be held in the general area by the MCP and one was due a couple of hours later on in an area 10 miles or so away. I decided to travel there. On arrival, after parking discretely, I could see the vehicles from the previous site unloading and erecting the various items of display material that had been reclaimed. In addition the *Mbumba* could be seen taking refreshments beside the coaches. There were two particular women who I could identify as having been at the previous rally. Over the next two days there were repeat performances. As there was little support for the MCP čause this was obviously the only way that the pretence of support could be presented.

As regards the referendum there was organisation of a different kind. Packets of the necessary documentation for each polling station were prepared in South Africa and then loaded into two Hercules transport planes and landed in Lilongwe early on Thursday, June 10th from whence they were distributed to over 4,000 polling stations and were in use by 6 am on Monday morning June 14th. This difficult task was achieved by external technical assistance personnel and Malawian civil servants.

The voting process also proceeded remarkably well with long lines existing as early as 5.30 am. As a consequence most polling stations had processed almost all of their assigned voters by 2 pm. Leaders of the multi-party groupings had told their supporters to go early to the poll and then go back home and stay there. I was told that virtually all did that. There were a few instances where MPs or other political figures attempted to campaign and exert influence at the polls but polling officials and those waiting to vote politely but firmly sent them on their way. Observers in all districts noted that a large number of women voted. In many centres there appeared to be more women than men in the lines of those waiting to vote.

On Referendum Day we fielded a total of eighteen teams, each comprising of two to three persons, for the observation of events in the six districts and sub-districts in the Northern Region. I covered the Mzuzu (urban) District and received reports from the various teams on the 167 centres visited overall. Despite the short time that had been available for the distribution of polling station materials the centre had, overall, been well supplied. Where shortages had been identified, the District Commissioner's staff made efforts to augment supplies but the District Commissioner in Mzuzu appeared to be less responsive. He was known as a strong MCP supporter.

In one centre, Rumphi 31, the ballot box reached full capacity at about 3 pm. The boxes in use were small in size. One of the observers took a message to the District Commissioner covering the area, who immediately sent a car to the centre with a second box. One centre in Nkhata Bay District discovered a shortage of ballot papers and was then supplied with additional papers. The same occurred in two centres in Mzuzu where the problem was also remedied. However a more serious situation developed at Kabwafu in the Mzuzu District. One polling station had to close at 1 pm due to the lack of ballot papers when there were still about 100 voters queuing up in line. The staff there claimed that they had informed the Mzuzu District Commissioner of the approaching shortage but that no additional ballot papers had been received. Observers believed that even if more ballots had arrived at a later stage many of the people who had been in the queue had already returned to their homes without voting. The observers estimated that the centre had been short of hundreds of ballot papers.

Many of the teams visiting the polling stations in the morning found that the officials were experiencing some crowd control problems. This was not an unruly or hostile act but rather an eagerness to vote. At one centre in the Karonga District a 'group village headman' stepped in to help organise people. He succeeded in getting them to sit down and the polling station staff then called out the names in the order they appeared on the register and the people came in to vote in that order. All the Northern Region teams agreed that the polling officials were to be commended for the efficient and neutral way in which they worked. The police were also to be commended for their professional conduct on polling day. Voters, whilst determined to vote, were invariably good humoured and patient.

Ballot counting went very well. On my first visit to Malawi I had advised the Electoral Commission to have vote counting carried out at each and every polling station, as opposed to district or regional count centres. In addition I suggested that all present at the counting be asked to sign the official result sheet, the protocol, after which individual copies would be supplied to those in attendance. That would provide better security of the election result and a clearer perspective on the process. On the evening of Referendum Day I was not surprised to find no attendance by pressure group leaders at the District Commissioner's office when I arrived there. They did not need to be there to await the results as they could ascertain them from the compilation of the counting returns from the various polling stations. None of the pressure groups had to rely on the Government for that crucial information.

The District Commissioner was in his office after the counting had taken place at the polling stations. He was overseeing the receipt of the counted ballot boxes for safe storage. I had arranged that I would attend with him so that I could be aware if any boxes had not been safely received. In the early hours of the morning there was a batch of boxes that had not yet arrived. The Commissioner told me not to worry as the lorry may have broken down and would be fixed so that the boxes could then be delivered. He suggested that as it was getting late, I should go back to my hotel, which was close by, and he would stay to receive the boxes. From time to time he would leave the room and I noticed that he held a small radio device. I told him that I would only leave when the missing boxes had been received and checked. It was 4 am before the lorry arrived.

During my oversight of the voter registration process I saw a number of girls being registered who were clearly too young, yet the various interest group monitors did not appear to regard such registrations as inappropriate. There also appeared to be names entered on the electoral registers more than once. There was the clear need for a better organised and more accurate registration process. Any inaccuracies in the registration would have had little effect on the result. In general terms all of the provinces returned very large majorities for multi-party democracies and large majorities also occurred across the Southern Region of the country. Blantyre, the largest city, voted 90% in favour of change. The central provinces, the home of the President and other powerful Ministers, voted the other way. One area voted 95% in favour of one-party rule and two others voted 80%.

An examination of the voter turnout clearly identified that the overall registration process had been seriously flawed. There was little doubt that the bulk of eligible electors had voted, with 3.153 million votes having been cast. In contrast electoral registers contained 4.699 million names. The names of a significant number of persons were registered more than once because the registration officials did not detect the fact that a person's name was already on the register. Some persons may well have deliberately registered a second time in 1993 to ensure that they would not be turned away from the polls by some 'trick' perpetrated by the registration clerks. There had been much suspicion in the minds of multi-party supporters in the run up to the referendum. In the case of the referendum, with the total votes throughout the country being aggregated, such excessive registration would not have as much effect as would be the case with an election for representatives on a constituency basis. The very wide range in the number of electors in the various constituencies would have compounded the matter further. I made recommendations as to the improvements required to the registration process and to the need to have a new constituency boundary review.

There was general agreement among observers that the referendum had, overall, been fairly and effectively run even though there were in some instances, and not unexpectedly, operational problems.

In my report I suggested that the preparation of future registers of electors could be assisted by outside technical assistance and advice. In addition there was the need for a boundary review to ensure, in so far as is practical, a reasonable degree of compatibility as to the number of electors per constituency and especially if the 'X' voting system was to be employed. The use of STV would enable the existing administrative boundaries to be retained by allocating a relevant proportionality of seats to each constituency. The report also referred to the selection of polling stations and the number of electors allocated to individual ballot boxes. The ballot boxes used for the referendum were adequate to accommodate the relatively small-sized ballot paper used at the referendum. In contrast the ballot papers to be used for a consultative or legislative body would, in all probability, require a much larger ballot box.

In Mzuzu, one of the polling places had ten boxes allocated to it. That gave rise to crowd congestion and also required some voters to travel much further than required elsewhere. A review of both the number and location of polling stations would be appropriate. Whilst training manuals had been prepared and detailed training given to the polling station staff, the system for the counting of the ballots had not been as detailed as appropriate – resulting in the counting being both prolonged and somewhat ineffectual due to the lack of detailed guidance. In addition there was the need for the drafting of very specific electoral regulations covering both the count process and ancillary matters.

There was the clear impression gained by all the observers that the multi-party interest groups were mainly united by their opposition to the MCP. Now, with the referendum out of the way it appeared that there was the need for advice and guidance in the operation of the normal type of political activities –

now that the country had shed dictatorial rule. Indeed when I had met with the chairman of a major group on my previous visit in April, he admitted that they had neither plans nor specific ideas as to what they should do should the multi-party groups obtain a clear majority at the referendum. There was the need for outside advisers to assist in the development of a progression to normal political activities. I left Malawi content that the country had reached an important stage in its development.

ARMENIA

The United Nations and the Organisation for Security and Cooperation in Europe (OSCE) agreed to provide international observers at the elections to be held in Armenia in July 1995. This was at a time when democracy was developing within former satellite states of the Soviet Union. International observers were to be deployed across the country.

Armenia has a recorded history of some 3,500 years. Its neighbouring countries include Georgia, Azerbaijan, Turkey and Iran. Control of its territory had oscillated down the centuries from Byzantine, Persian, Mongol or Turkish forces with periods of independence. At the turn of the twentieth century there were about two million Armenians. Then at the start of the First World War the declining Ottoman Empire, under the Young Turks Government, began a persecution of Armenians. This was perceived by many in the outside world as a systematic extermination of 1.5 million Armenians resulting in a remaining population of just 400,000. The Armenian Government has built a memorial to recall what has become known as the Armenian Genocide. During my visit to Armenia I visited that memorial. The Turkish Government has always denied the existence of any such genocide.

In November 1920 the Russians invaded Armenia to install a Soviet Government. In August 1990 Armenia declared its sovereignty but remained in the Soviet Union until its official proclamation of independence on December 26th, 1991 when the Soviet Union ceased to exist. It was then drawn into a bloody war over the mainly Armenian Nagorno-Karabakh region.

There was a very brief period of optimism just after the declaration of independence. Armenians were seen as having a strong idea of their history and their nationalism but, at the same time, were less anti-Russian than those in other liberated post-Soviet states. There seemed to be public cynicism about politics and politicians. Perhaps that could explain, along with low economic development, why there were as many Armenians living outside the country as within the country itself. The diaspora communities in France, the Middle East and the USA continued with their separate political life during the Soviet period and then with the liberation of the country the émigrés were beginning to influence Armenian politics.

In many ways Armenia was somewhat unique within the Soviet Union.

In common with other post-Soviet countries there was a strong nostalgia for the relative economic and social security of the Soviet period and especially so among the elderly. On the other hand Armenian nationalism is a very long established and distinct aspect. It is a very ethnically homogenous state with its inhabitants sharing a common awareness of their history and their place in the world. At the same time there was a better relationship with the Russians than many other post-Soviets states had.

The draft Constitution to be voted on by the electors was considered by the opposition as paving the way for a presidential dictatorship and especially as regards the degree of presidential power and accountability. The opposition in parliament had fought hard against it and by doing so had delayed its publication until very close to the poll leaving the majority of voters with little knowledge of its contents. As regards the parliamentary election to be held, there were 190 seats to be filled of which 40 were to for a single nation-wide proportional constituency and the other 150 seats for individual constituencies on a first-past-the-post basis.

We learnt that, with a few exceptions, the Armenian political parties were relatively small, poorly financed and weak. There were no strong party organisations or clear political manifestos but rather they centred round prominent personalities. One commentator described them as being fluid. For the 1995 election the various parties formed themselves into two blocks or coalitions – pro-government and opposition. The pro-government bloc included the Shamiram Women's Party whose leading lights were largely the wives of senior members of the Government.

For the 1995 elections I was based in the capital, Yerevan. As observers, I and my colleagues had two main objectives in covering both the referendum on the adoption of the Constitution and the elections of Deputies to the National Assembly. First we were to focus on any irregularities in the elections itself and during the campaigning immediately prior to it. The second objective was to identify those aspects of Armenia's emerging democracy that could be developed in advance of further elections. We were able to identify a number of areas where outside assistance could play an important role in such developments.

The elections were to be overseen by the Central Electoral Commission (CEC) that had been set up eighty days before polling day – as laid down in the electoral law. We met with the chairman of the CEC to enquire about the problems that various parties had reported. Twenty-four parties had applied to contest the elections of which the CEC rejected four on the basis that not all of the specified documents had been submitted. A party wishing to stand had to submit a petition bearing between 10,000 to 12,000 signatures. After checking all the petitions, the CEC rejected a further five parties. A total of 570 candidates had been registered to contest the forty party list seats on behalf of the various parties.

The CEC received 2,300 nominations for the 150 single member seats. Their papers were scrutinised by the relevant District Electoral Commissions (DEC) resulting in a total of 827 (none from the pro-government parties) being rejected – leaving 1,473 validly nominated candidates. We enquired about one case which a party had, in the courts, challenged the CEC's decision to exclude it from the contest. The court case had been scheduled for June 29th, but the CEC legal representative had not attended and as a result the case was rescheduled to after the election. The chairman explained that the lawyer concerned had suffered bereavement and so was unable to attend court on the day in question. It was obvious that there were a number of ongoing problems throughout the period of the election and that the CEC was receiving a lot of enquiries about the various aspects of electoral law.

We did get the impression of an air of public cynicism about the election and especially by those who could recall the suspension of the ARF (Armenian Revolutionary Federation or Dashnak) Party in December 1994. We met with the Dashnak Party, as well as other parties, and were informed that the party had been suspended as a result of allegations by the Government of involvement in terrorist activities and drug smuggling. Their case was before the courts. As a result of the party's suspension all their property, publications and assets were seized by the authorities. The two senior members that we met were going to stand in the election as 'independents' and they estimated that up to thirty of their supporters would also stand under that banner. They also said that their nominee for the Yerevan District, the former Head of Organisation of the party, had been intimidated into withdrawing his candidacy after threats had been made to his family by the authorities. They also claimed that the judiciary and certain senior officials were "controlled" by the authorities. All the other opposition parties we met with were strongly opposed to the new Constitution. They wished to have a proper parliamentary system as opposed to the proposed presidential one. It appeared that they were reinforced in that conclusion by their view of the incumbent president.

Following on from our meetings with political parties we then met with members of the media including some foreign press representatives such as the French press and the BBC's Armenian World Service correspondent. They also agreed that the debate between the opposition and the Government was a debate between advocates of parliamentary and presidential government. During our discussions it became evident that the Armenian press was somewhat polarised and politicised and not as inclined to balance in reporting as we had hoped. The sales figures for newspapers were very low due to their cost and irregular supply. TV and radio stations were in the hands of the state and were the major source of news in the country.

The European Media Monitoring Unit had a team in the country since June 12th, and had being monitoring all the media since then. We met up with the head of the unit who made it clear that the Government and its supporters had a considerable advantage in the media field. At the same time he indicated that the figures for TV, radio and newspapers were all very modest. He saw the need to increase debate on TV, the need to give time to the opposition and the need for greater balance. On the positive side he pointed to the establishment of an independent Press Club and the arrival of a new cable TV station that already had many subscribers and a more balanced approach to news coverage.

I had a vehicle and driver provided along with an interpreter. I travelled around the polling stations in the greater Yerevan area. My impressions matched those of the colleagues I spoke to. At the polling stations minor violations of the regulations were noted, the majority of which were seen to be taking place because of inexperience or unfamiliarity with the law rather than any deliberate intention to compromise the integrity of the process. We all came to the conclusion, based on the sample of polling stations visited, that although there were imperfections in the process itself, the voting and counting of votes were in general in accordance with the prescribed electoral law.

Our concerns were more centred on the events in the pre-election period and especially on the six-month ban on the activities of an entire political party thus removing a major opposition voice from the electoral process. Any action taken should have been against the individuals accused of crimes instead of a very broad brush approach. In addition the need for adequate training of election staff coupled with standardised procedures were obvious matters for attention prior to any further elections. The compilation of the voters list required much better attention so as to avoid the inclusion of large numbers of voters who were no longer resident at the stated addresses. It was also evident that the organisation of the system by local officials was not up to the required standard. The overall voter turnout was only 54.3% – an indication of the need to more fully develop the concept of democracy. Overall the elections were certainly not up to international standards and so could not be labelled as free and fair – at best free.

REPUBLIC OF GEORGIA

In the summer of 1995 I was asked to be the technical adviser to the Republic of Georgia's Central Electoral Commission during the preparations for the joint presidential and parliamentary elections due in November of that year. My role included attendance at the meetings of the Central Electoral Commission (CEC) at which I had an interpreter from the university. Understandably the CEC wanted my role to be established on an official and legal basis and so we had a formal contract that specified that I would be paid a nominal sum of $1. One of my tasks was to carry out a needs assessment of the Central Electoral Commission to identify how assistance could be obtained from the various international bodies that were interested in the development of the democratic system in the country. The sectors involved included computers, communications and technical expertise. Then I acted as the co-ordinator in the provision of such assistance. At the same time the European Union asked me to assist their delegation based in the capital of Georgia, Tbilisi. The population of Georgia was estimated at 5.5 million including some 233,000 internally displaced persons.

On March 31st, 1991 a referendum had been held on Georgian independence and the official results indicated that over 90% of the electorate had voted and that 99% of those had voted for independence. This was at the time when the Soviet Union was beginning to fragment. Zviad Gamsakhurdia was elected President on May 26th, 1991. On the same day local elections were held using STV. It was a test for the use of STV at national elections. The chairman of the Central Electoral Commission had stated that the system "had proved very easy to handle". He reported that 200 counters had been trained, identified as mainly physicists and mathematicians, who then briefed the 2000 local election commissions involved. Each district elected between three and five seats depending on the size of the population. In the count calculations a somewhat simplified version was used that did not include the calculation of surpluses to decimal places. It still took ten days to complete the counts.

By the end of that year Gamsakhurdia had alienated key elements of his previous support and was ousted by force in January of the following year. A lengthy debate then followed as to which type of voting system should be employed in the proposed election for a national assembly. The 1921 Constitution of Independent Georgia had prescribed the use of a list system but under an election held in October 1990 it was stated that one list had secured a dominant position even through it only obtained a minority of the votes. An interim State Council was set up involving some fifty parties and it established the Central Election Commission. Not surprisingly there was much debate about a suitable system. Indeed one party, Democratic Choice for Georgia, put forward eight different systems. Some parties preferred STV. In the end STV was adopted on May 21st, 1992. There then followed a change of mind that was led, to some extent, by Eduard Shevardnadze, the former Soviet Union Foreign Minister. (It is interesting to note the role played by Georgians in the running of the former Soviet Union. Shevardnadze was a Georgian and so were a number of other members of the Supreme Soviet including not least Stalin and Beria. It was appropriate to visit Gori and see the house in which it is claimed that Stalin had been born, I have outlined my experience there a little further on.)

It was finally agreed that there would be 84 single member seats elected by simple majority but with the provision that there would be a run-off if no candidate reached more than 50% of the votes cast. In addition 150 seats would be elected from ten regional lists with the number of seats for each being determined by population size.

As there was a much welcomed gap in elections that year in Northern Ireland, with only a parliamentary by-election in North Down in mid-June, I was able to use a good amount of outstanding leave and time-off-in-lieu to attend Georgia for a total of six weeks. Very brief visits took place during the months of August, September and October. That resulted in me having to do plenty of homework at the weekends when I returned home, and particularly so in reviewing the meetings with the Electoral Commission. However I did get back to Tbilisi for a couple of days in November to assess the result of the election. There was the need for a second round in November which I could not attend due to work requirements in Belfast.

At the start of August 1995 I booked my flight to Frankfurt to connect with an Air Georgia flight to Tbilisi. When I had asked my travel agent to book that flight he phoned me back to say that there were no records of such an airline. I knew differently as the EU delegation in Georgia had advised me to book on that flight which they used frequently. The travel agent then ascertained that it was a new airline having only one aeroplane and so did not qualify for inclusion in the ABTA list of airlines: to be so listed an airline had to have a minimum of three planes. Eventually, after much effort by the travel agent, I was supplied with the required ticket.

Arriving in the Frankfurt terminal I sought out the check-in desk for Air Georgia. After walking up and down the length of the terminal a number of times I could not find the check-in desk. I stopped at a number of the desks of several airlines to see if they could direct me. They were all unaware of the existence of that airline. Then I saw a pair of policemen patrolling the terminal and went over and enquired of them. Fortunately they both spoke English – my German being non-existent. They were very helpful, indeed intrigued, and radioed to enquire for me. Their contact could not help and so they said that they would walk the length of the terminal with me to see if they could find the check-in desk. When they had failed to do so they then enquired of the staff at a number of the major airline check-in desks but to no avail until after a good number of such enquiries a person had a recollection of occasionally seeing an individual dressed in civilian clothes carrying a notice board which he would hang on the hooks above a vacant desk. That proved to be Air Georgia.

I ensured that I was there promptly when it came to the indicated time stated on my ticket for checking in. When I approached to check in I was told that as the plane was full up I could not travel. I pointed out, to no avail, that I held a ticket that had been issued some weeks beforehand. Then I used my ace card by pointing out that I had been invited to help in the presidential election at which Shevardnadze, the former Soviet Foreign Minister, was standing and I asked the attendant for his name so that I could inform Mr Shevardnadze of the person who had denied me transportation and preventing me from assisting at the election. My check-in immediately took place and I awaited the departure. Then another passenger arrived, a Georgian I understood, and we had a conversation. When the plane had not arrived an hour after the stated departure time, I asked him to enquire. Apparently the plane had departed late from the airport in America and was not expected for another half-hour.

When I boarded the plane and took my seat I noticed that one male passenger had got out of the seat he had being occupying on the flight from the USA. The seat was immediately taken by another person and so he was left standing as all the other seats had been occupied. My companion from the check-in desk had informed me that a lot of the passengers were part of a large family group residing in the USA travelling back to Georgia to attend a wedding. The man left standing had been a late addition to the wedding party and apparently had paid money to the crew to allow him to travel onwards even though the second stage from Frankfurt had been fully booked. When the plane proceeded to take off, he stood behind a row of seats at the very back of the aircraft whilst the cabin crew proceeded to check that all the other passengers were wearing their seat belts.

I found Georgia a pleasant place although there were serious problems as regards security and stability. I did a number of trips to several parts of the country and especially to those whose leaders were inclined to distance themselves from Tbilisi, the capital. In particular I visited the main regional centres. My purpose was to become acquainted with the various parts of the country, its customs and political culture. I was made welcome in the various areas, wined and dined after our discussions. The meals were held in a typical Georgian restaurant with each party of diners having its own room and the host leaving the toasting etc, as is the custom, to a designated individual termed the *Tamada*. He proposed the numerous toasts and associated matters. Vodka and Georgian wine was consumed in abundance but I had to be careful as I had a speech to give and intended to continue with my travels the next day.

Then there was Gori the birthplace of Joseph Stalin, where his memory was still sacred with the small house reputed to be his birthplace being preserved for public presentation and also nearby the railway carriage he was reported to have used in his travels around the Soviet Union during his long reign. In the general area there were numerous busts and statues of Stalin unlike the other regions where there appeared to have been a purge of such displays. Indeed my colleague on that trip, a sitting Labour Member of Westminster Parliament, had the habit of stopping and asking me to photograph him in front of each statue and bust of Stalin. Apparently his constituency was a marginal one and he wanted to use the photographs as a means of encouraging left wing supporters in his constituency to come out and vote for him at the next election.

During some of my car trips I was not so much regaled with Georgian history, but rather with quotations from Shakespeare – my interpreter, Zurab, was a senior academic who was an *aficionado* of Shakespeare and always keen to quote extensively, in English, from his works. On one trip I travelled to Tskhinvali in the southern part of South Ossetia – North Ossetia was outside the country's borders, being in the Russian Federation. Then I travelled northwards within South Ossetia where many tall watchtowers were very evident all over the countryside. I learned that blood feuds were still very much in operation in the area. Apparently the origins of many of the various feuds went back for generations and the current inhabitants were often unsure as to what exactly had initiated them. Mount Elbrus, the highest mountain in Europe, was located there sharing the border with Russia. During the Second World War when the Nazis had overrun that part of Russia they sent a special squad of mountaineers to plant the swastika on the summit. It is reported that a sole, renowned Georgian mountaineer climbed to the summit to remove the flag. Fortunately I had an interpreter with me who was well skilled in handling the local people but we still felt it appropriate to retreat back out of the district. When I had decided to travel to that area it was suggested that I take an armed guard. To me that was more likely to draw particular attention and also I did not feel that one guard would have been able to repel a determined onslaught by a band of attackers.

My next trip was to Kutaisi and then on to Sukhumi in the Abkhaz region on the shores of the Black Sea. This lies alongside the Russian border and very near to the Russian city of Sochi, a very popular seaside resort to this day for Russians. Another trip was down to the southern part of the Black Sea to Adzhar with its regional capital of Batumi. The area was run by a politician who seemed to me to be running a personal fiefdom. In addition to running the region he also had his own leading football team with a large stadium and I was invited to attend one of the matches there.

One of the purposes of my trips was to meet up with representatives of the various parties to ascertain their concerns and views on the electoral arrangements – an aspect that I wished to discuss with and advise the Central Electoral Commission on at its meetings in Tbilisi. There was general concern about the availability of suitable staff at the forthcoming elections. During my trip I came across some members of an international body who were also travelling around. To my intense surprise one of them indicated to me that staffing was not really a problem. He had discussed it with one of the major parties who would be contesting the elections and they said that they could supply a list of suitable polling station staff!

When a senior member of the international mission in Tbilisi learnt that I was next planning to travel to the far south of the country, a well known wine growing area where many of the inhabitants are of Greek descent, he asked that I try and obtain two crates of wine for him. That I managed to do with one crate being a dry white called *Gurjaani* and the other crate being a dry red called *Mukuzani*. I tasted samples of both of those wines prior to my purchase and found them to be very pleasant. Some days later, I attended a dinner at the main hotel in Tbilisi, the Metechi Palace. I noticed the price on the wine list was exceedingly enhanced from the price I paid even allowing for corkage and a substantial profit margin. During that meal I had a discussion with an American who explained that he was in the country to evaluate the potential for exporting the wine even though it was known not to travel well. He had identified a process by which certain aspects of the wine causing the problem could be removed by filtration – I took this to be by the use of sintered glass filters. He was, I felt, just one of the many outsiders seeking to take advantage of the opportunities that were available.

I had the opportunity to visit an historic Orthodox church situated in a beautiful site at the junction of two rivers. It reinforced my knowledge of the turbulent history of Georgia. The country had gone through long periods of occupation by outside forces and this was reflected in the approved religion at each such stage. The inside walls of churches would then be repainted and adorned with relevant murals. During my visit I met up with some university researchers who had one small section of a wall carefully stripped back to reveal different layers of paint. One layer revealed evidence of the Russian Orthodox Church, another the Armenian Orthodox Church, another its use as a mosque when the Ottoman Empire was the ruling power and then the Georgian Orthodox Church after it had broken away from the Armenian Church.

After my various trips it was always good to get back to Tbilisi. I had managed to rent an apartment there to cover the three month period during which I would only be in the country for a week each month. The main hotel was pleasant but expensive and I could not be guaranteed accommodation there for the several and variable brief periods involved. The apartment I rented was the home of a family but I was assured that they would move out to stay with other family members during my three-month rental period. I was to find that when I was out of the apartment, even during my stays in the country, they still used the flat both to cook and to wash.

When I was not attending the Election Commission meetings I had office accommodation in the European Union Embassy. At lunch time I would attend one of the cafés on the main street of Tbilisi, Rustaveli Avenue. Through time I became a customer of one particular café and grew fond of certain Georgian dishes and especially a cheese pie called *khachapuri*. My host had introduced it to me pointing out it was a delicious snack that for centuries had graced every Georgian dinner table. I was not too keen on the idea when I found out that it was capped by a raw egg. Not wishing to cause any offence by refusing I sampled it. Then I grew to like it immensely. One day at the office one of the staff, who knew of my fondness for the dish, asked if I had read the English language newspaper published that day. It carried a small article headed 'Cheese delicacy baked in the morgue.' The report indicated that the head of Georgia's railways had been arrested on charges of massive fraud for selling off large chunks of rolling stock to Russia and had also hired out the dissection room, having marble topped tables, of a public morgue to a business baking puff pastry *khachapuri* which were then sold at a nearby central market. I immediately lost my appetite for that type of pastry. It was not the only example of the 'free market' that I came across. For example a French acquaintance told me of the opportunity to get a very cheap Lada four-wheel drive vehicle. He had bought one from the army and explained how I could also go about doing that. He was going to use his vehicle in the country and then get it back to France. Somehow or other the idea did not appeal to me even if a suitable and cost effective means of getting it home to Ireland could be arranged.

A day or two after I had returned to Belfast from one trip I came back to my office from an official meeting in Belfast when my secretary then enquired of me if the people in Georgia were nervous? A bomb had blown up Shevardnadze's car parked outside the parliament building in Tbilisi, his driver had been killed and he himself slightly injured. Apparently the European Union ambassador was concerned that the news of that might put me off returning to the country. My secretary informed the ambassador that I was out at a meeting but that she would inform me of his phone call when I returned. She did so with the comment that the people there must be nervous as, after all, there was only one bomb involved in comparison to many bombs going off on the one day in Belfast.

During my time in Georgia, when the CEC was not in session, I had meetings at the various Western embassies in an effort to obtain financial and other assistance for the CEC who were having difficulty getting the necessary funding and equipment required to run the election. In particular there was the difficulty of recruiting appropriate staff because the salary that could be offered was far too low. In addition there was a legal constraint on the source of expenses that could be paid in connection with the election – Article 30 of the relevant legislation required that expenditure at elections could only be charged to the state budget. That precluded funding that could be directly made available from the international community. Clearly, in the circumstances, there was the need to have the law amended to permit such funding.

Not only was there a problem of finance, but in other aspects as well. Each autumn and winter there was an energy crisis. Even if the energy was ongoing, the electricity lines in mountain regions were frequently brought down by snow and wind. The date of the election had been set for November 5th. In addition there was the need to have a dependable two-way contact between the CEC and District Commissions and between the latter and the Precinct Commissions. I ascertained that the CEC had ten computers of which seven were the old '286' models. The relevant software had been stolen and it was reported that the finance to replace it was not available. In addition there was the need to have a back-up electricity system such as an UPS, batteries or a generator that would automatically trip on when necessary. I was able to get computers supplied through the German

Embassy. The German ambassador was very helpful and sought meetings with me to see how the position was developing. In addition it was possible to have the CEC move into part of the old parliament buildings as opposed to the unsuitable basement accommodation that had previously been in use.

I also met with senior Government officials and especially the Chef de Cabinet to stress the need for the CEC to be seen to be independent of the Government and the various political parties. He agreed to arrange for me to meet the various political parties to put that message across. I also stressed the need for a new CEC to be established as quickly as possible to demonstrate the commitment to the November elections as the existing *ad hoc* Commission did not have a chairman (he had died two years earlier) and such an absence was not a good signal. He agreed and stated that a new Commission would be formed very shortly and also that the appropriate legislation would be passed "in a day or two". Next I met with the European Union's advisor to the parliamentary library to get a feel on the position between the parties there and also for him to discreetly make them aware of my presence and purpose.

Other meetings took place with the Parliamentary Legal Committee to discuss various aspects of the electoral law, with the Speaker of Parliament, the Foreign Minister, the Deputy Prime Minister, and many other officials. In addition I met with national minorities, journalists, NGOs etc on an ongoing basis. On one occasion I had a live interview with the main radio station discussing the importance of free and fair elections.

On each of my periodic trips back home via London I would allocate some hours so that I could call at the Foreign and Commonwealth Office in London to establish what, if any, assistance could be supplied to assist in the development of democracy in Georgia. One very small, but in Georgian eyes a significant step, was the organising of a visit to the Westminster Parliament and its senior officials by the Georgian Parliamentary Speaker. In advance of that I forwarded an English translation of the Election Law of Georgia that I had commissioned, along with some of my handwritten notes, as the official translation would not have been available for a good number of weeks. In addition the UK Government was seeking to encourage the European Union to further advance the assistance they were already giving. Each time I would supply an updated needs assessment to identify the priority of each activity and also background details of the CEC's plans to assist in optimising the timing of any available assistance.

My role did not include the oversight of the elections but rather assisting the CEC before, during and after the elections in addressing any problems or difficulties. There were numerous international observers supplied by various European countries and also by the USA. That did add to the work load of the CEC as such observers had to be accredited by it. Most observers were from countries that were members of the Organisation on Security and Co-operation in Europe (OSCE). I identified the specific technical and material needs required. The OSCE Head of Mission would then inform me of whichever of those were being offered by member states. Hence I could identify which were still outstanding and have those details recirculated for further consideration by member states. That greatly helped in the avoidance of any duplication of effort.

It was a busy but also an interesting period. I did not observe any part of the actual electoral process on the ground. Rather my role was to attend the various CEC meetings to advise and suggest solutions to any problems as and when they arose. That included events prior to the elections, during them and at the counting process afterwards. There were, by necessity, times when I had to be back in Northern Ireland to carry out work duties. Even so I could keep in contact from my home through the use of my fax machine and computer. I used up all the outstanding annual leave that I had accrued in anticipation of a long and highly anticipated holiday. On reflection my sojourns in Georgia made up for that.

As I had not observed the elections on the ground I feel that it would be inappropriate for me to comment on their fairness and effectiveness. On the other hand the international organisations that had, and particularly those having had numerous observers on the ground, reported that they were a good entrée to the democratic process. Of course there were areas for some concern but I left Georgia with the hope that the process would grow and develop to the benefit of all.

THE REPUBLIC OF SOUTH AFRICA
The first contact I had as regards South Africa, was an invitation from Trevor Huddleston, the President of the Anti-Apartheid Movement, to attend a one-day seminar on March 15th, 1993 in London on the role of the international community in promoting free and fair elections in South Africa. The programme was to range over a wide number of relevant issues and I was eager to attend. Unfortunately other matters arose at the same time and thus precluded my attendance.

In the following May I was contacted by the Deputy Chairman of The Council of the Republic of South Africa. – a permanent body which advised the State President on matters of public interests and served as arbitrator whenever there was disagreement among the Houses of Parliament over draft legislation. He was on a visit to the United Kingdom and he wanted to have a discussion with me. We agreed a date on which he would fly into Belfast City Airport where I would pick him up and also the official who would accompany him. It was to be a one day visit.

A colleague and I went to the airport where we met up with the two South Africans. Whilst we were travelling back to my office the two passengers appeared to be looking around a lot and spoke briefly to each other in Afrikaans. I later realised that they were somewhat surprised at the basic amenities at the airport. It had previously been used by the Short and Harland Aircraft Company solely as a test base for the new aircraft they produced and from where they were then flown out for delivery to customers. The firm decided to convert it into a civil airport but at that time it was still in a somewhat under developed state in comparison to regional airports elsewhere. In the following years it was further developed to a very good standard.

We discussed the existing electoral arrangements in Northern Ireland. I understood from documentation I had obtained that the President's Council was in the process of compiling a report on decision-making and conflict resolution mechanisms and techniques in constitutional systems, including mechanisms and techniques for the furtherance of consensus and the resolution of disputes. Our meeting was cordial. We had a break for lunch, when I took them out to a local hotel. Afterwards, back in the office, further discussions followed and we then drove them to Belfast International Airport for the return flight they had booked to London.

The deputy chairman later wrote to me expressing his appreciation of the meeting. A short time later he asked me to go out and visit South Africa. I could not do so at that time. In addition I did not want to go out in circumstances that might not appear to be impartial. I wrote commenting on the various electoral aspects that would be desirable in the furtherance of democracy in the country.

That visit gave rise to an interest in the affairs of South Africa and how the Republic came about, especially as Britain had held sway over the area for a good number of years. I saw such information as important in perceiving how change was likely to come about from the then existing apartheid regime. My researches did highlight the way by which Europeans had managed to take control of such a large country. In addition I had an ongoing interest in how other countries in various parts of the world had attained the changeover from authoritarian government.

I learnt that the Dutch were the early colonists and had experienced, as would be expected, resistance from the native tribes and especially the Xhosa in the seventeenth and eighteenth centuries. There was in effect, down the years, a long series of frontier wars. Some historians have placed much stress on the role that this frontier tradition played in the making of modern South Africa with the racist attitudes and ideologies of twentieth century white South Africa. At the same time I was aware from films and books of the British involvement in South Africa and its battles with the Boers who were contesting the imperial efforts and had a successful reclamation of the British annexed Transvaal. They were subsequently defeated in the South African war of 1899-1902. However to attain that outcome the British had to employ a scorched-earth policy and interned large numbers of civilians in 'concentration camps'. Then in 1910 the South African Union was established with a white minority exercising power through a centralised state having a unified defence force, a single police force and a centralised bureaucracy. A few years earlier, 1906 to be exact, the defeat of the Bambatha Rebellion resulted in a change of African resistance to a political and constitutional form with the formation in 1912 of the Native National Congress that later became the African National Congress (ANC).

At the start of the twentieth century there were instances of rebellion and violent resistance from within the white minority. There was the rebellion of 1914, the Rand or Miners' Strike of 1922 and during World War Two reaction from the right wing *Ossewabrandwag,* coupled with the additional failing of relations with the English-speaking South Africans and the British authorities. In 1948 the Afrikaner-based National Party came into power leading to the Government placing a network of statues to separate the races spatially and socially. In the 1960s the apartheid system was perfected and enforced. The massacre at Sharpeville in 1960 led on, with other events, to the ANC moving away from the politics of protests and non-violence and seeing political violence as a necessary evil.

There was conflict at times within the non-white communities as, for example the Durban riots of 1949 involving clashes between Zulus and Indians resulting in massive destruction and slaughter. Even within the black population there was an ongoing power struggle between the ANC, its allies and the Inkatha Freedom Party (IFP), led by Chief Buthelezi, but also involving 'warlords' and endemic factional feuds apparently beyond the control of any political leadership. Indeed the violence by the IFP continued right on until very close to the 1994 election. Just two weeks before the poll, Lord Carrington and Henry Kissinger arrived in Johannesburg to enter into mediation between the ANC and Buthelezi to attain a political formula that would persuade the latter to call off his supporter's violent campaign against the election. A detailed analysis of the role of violence within South Africa would require in itself a large tome.

The change over to a democracy can be seen as emanating from FW de Klerk's famous address on February 2nd, 1990 in which he signalled the transition from apartheid to a democratic progression coupled with the release of Nelson Mandela, the return of exiles and various other reforms. Within the Afrikaners there was a divide between the arch-conservatives, the *verkramptes,* wishing to purify the *volk* and the more liberal Afrikaners, the *verligtes,* and that had a significant bearing in the lead into the negotiated transition. Even de Klerk's predecessor, President P W Botha, who was more inclined to the arch-conservative viewpoint, had in 1986 declared that apartheid could not be maintained. It took a *verligte* of the calibre of de Klerk to recognise the need for real change in South Africa.

The various embassies, particularly the British, German and American, helped to overcome tensions between the Government and ANC officials. Sanctions began to disappear in 1992 with particular significance for the whites of being able to participate in the cricket World Cup in Australia. There then followed rugby tours and the opening of embassies not just elsewhere in the continent of Africa but throughout the world. Later on the Nobel Peace Prize was awarded to de Klerk and Nelson Mandela.

About the same time an unusual partnership evolved between some black ethnic leaders and conservative Afrikaners which further complicated an already complicated situation. The leaders of the four 'independent' and six self-governing 'homelands' had an interest in the continuance of the status quo. They each had their own administrators, army and police officials and so, especially in the case of Chief Mangosuthu Gatsha Buthelezi of KwaZulu, did not wish to lose a guaranteed power base. I found my research interesting but not of any direct relevance to me at that time but that was to change. (Originally homelands were set up in the mid-twentieth century as a device of the Apartheid Government to enforce segregation and effectively exclude black people from the SA political system.)

Within South Africa the Transitional Executive Council (TEC) had been set up to administer the country during the period of negotiation and implementation of the new South African state. It had a number of subordinate committees including a negotiating council as well as one covering law and order, stability and security, whilst others involved defence, intelligence, regional and local government including traditional authorities, finance, and foreign affairs. On December 7th, 1993 the TEC invited the European Union, the United Nations, the Commonwealth and the Organisation of African Unity to observe South Africa's first fully democratic election. Subsequently in January 1994 the European Union, in the process of setting up their Election Unit in South Africa, invited me to attend as Election Advisor to the unit. I accepted the offer on the basis that I would attend on a number of short visits. During my attendances there the Independent Electoral Commission (IEC) invited me to act as an adviser to them also. Between May 1993 and May 1996 only one election, a European Parliamentary Election, was to take place in Northern Ireland and so I was able to attend in South Africa from time to time. When I was back in Northern Ireland I was able to keep up to date with affairs through the use at home of my fax machine and computer.

The objectives of the European Election Unit included:

- To consult with the Independent Electoral Commission (IEC) on the nature and scale of the European Union's support for the election process.

- To make available advice and if requested technical assistance in the planning and running of the electoral process including, support for training of the IEC personnel and election officials.

- To provide support for the mobilisation and co-ordination of local NGOs.

- To advise and where requested to provide support for the monitoring of the security forces responsible for the electoral process.

- To advise and where requested to provide support for the monitoring of the media.

The unit was headed up by Jacob de Ruiter, a former Minister of Justice and Minister of Defence of the Netherlands, Professor of Law and for five years the Procurator-General of the Court of Appeal, Amsterdam.

I was particularly involved in advice to the IEC's Election Administration Directorate on the production of manuals for election officials, voter registration, staffing, devolution of authority, the locating and management of polling stations and the training of officials.

At the end of January 1994 I flew out to South Africa for the first time. This was the start of three visits that I was to make. During that first visit I was to experience some of the tensions within South Africa. Our office was a suite within the Carlton Towers, a multi-rise building, in the centre of Johannesburg. The lower floors were assigned to a hotel and the upper floors to offices. When I arrived at the entrance I saw an armed guard just inside the entrance doors. On checking into the office on one of the upper floors I was advised to be careful when entering and leaving the building. Those doing so ran the risk of being robbed at gun or knife point. The security guard had firm instructions that he was not on any account to leave his post on the inside of the building. If he saw a robbery under way outside he was to radio the main police station nearby and police officers would be immediately despatched to the scene. Any actual or would-be thieves captured would be given a lengthy prison sentence. The robbers adapted a technique that became widely known. If the victim immediately handed over money or valuables he or she would not be harmed. On the other hand if there was any delay or refusal to do so the individual would be stabbed. In either event the robber would in most cases be able to escape before the police arrived. Over time a number of our colleagues were robbed as they arrived or left the building.

I made arrangements for the hire of a car as I would need one to visit various places. It was crucial to have the vehicle parked in a secure location. My vehicle was to be parked in a very secure car park located nearby but many, many feet below ground level in what I assumed had been a former gold mine. Next I attended a bank to open an account so that I could access Rands. I had arranged in advance accommodation in a hotel in the district of Rosebank. That was a relatively secure area located in the northern suburbs of Johannesburg. It was pleasant but after a number of days I decided that I would prefer an apartment. Luckily enough I was able to find an apartment in a modern block located in the nearby suburb of Melrose North in which I could stay for short periods. The management would accommodate my other visits as and when I contacted them from home in advance of each of the specific visits to the country.

I obtained the name and address of a contact who, it was suggested, could inform me of the existing political tensions within his community and so I arranged to meet him at his home. Whilst driving to the meeting I took a wrong turn off the motorway and ended up in a cul-de-sac in a run-down industrial estate. Whilst turning my car around to get back to the main road I saw a group of machete-armed men running towards me and just managed to get away from them. That caused me to obtain large scale maps of the various areas so that I could be better informed as to the exact routes to be taken in future. I was later to learn that the official South African maps did not give the full picture during my work in connection with the locating of polling stations involving the names of some towns I could not locate on the maps. They were black squatter towns and they were not shown on the official maps.

A few days later there was some good news in relation to participation in the forthcoming election. The leader of Ciskei, Oupa Gqozo, decided, after all, that he would participate in the election. There had been much discontent within his Civil Service as to job security should Ciskei fail to participate in the elections, As a result Gqozo decided to join the Transitional Executive Council. That in turn gave rise to pressure on the leader of Bophuthatswana (Bop), Lucas Mangope, by his civil servants and the residents in general. Over a number of weeks that pressure built up. The civil servants went on strike and thousands of the residents took to the streets to protest at Mangope's refusal to participate in the elections. The 'Homeland' police and army gave their support to the protest.

On March 11th white right-wingers, organised by General Viljoen leader of the Afrikaner Volksfront (AVF) and former commander of the South African Defence Force (SADF), responded to a plea by the Bop authorities for help. Some 4,000 heavily armed, khaki-clad white right-wingers poured into Mmabatho, the Bop capital. Five hundred or so of the far-right Afrikaner Weerstandsbeweging (AWB) were involved in this incursion. Instead of obeying orders to guard vital installations, the AWB members carried out a sortie into the town, firing random shots. Several black citizens were killed. Orders from General Viljoen to withdraw were ignored. There had been and remained differences within the Afrikaner right wing. One section regarded participation in the elections as not an option leaving violent resistance as the only alternative. Subsequent to the events in Bop those under General Constand Viljoen came to the view that participation in the elections was a means of demonstrating Afrikaner support for a *volkstaat*.

That afternoon the Bop Defence Force drove the AWB out of town. Sixty civilians were killed in the crossfire. Three AWB members were killed in the battle. TV pictures of their bodies were shown on television around the world. That evening the TEC, meeting in Pretoria, asked the SADF to restore order and two co-administrators were appointed in place of Lucas Mangope. It was evident that the elections could now go ahead there.

At the time I was involved in the planning of training for election observers. I though it would be advisable to pay a visit to the homeland to see what damage had been caused to those facilities that might be required to run the poll there. When I indicated my intention to do so it was then agreed that a small mission would travel to Bop comprising six persons, two persons each from the EU election unit and two each from two other international missions. I travelled along with a colleague in one car. The group left the Carlton Towers at 6 am and travelled non-stop to Mmabatho.

Our first appointment was with the former RSA ambassador now acting as Bop Administrator who was optimistic about the prospect of holding peaceful elections there. He saw the overall security position as having stabilised but, nevertheless, still somewhat volatile. There were specific areas where there was still some public unrest. He said that the Bop police had good relations with the South African Police (SAP). Then over lunch with two senior IEC officials we indicated the need to identify suitable offices in Bop for election monitoring purposes. We inspected several potential buildings that could be so employed including one that had previously been used as a convent.

After lunch we had a lengthy meeting with representatives of several lawyers' committees including Lawyers for Human Rights, Black Lawyers, Anti-Repression and University Lawyers. They had concerns about voter education, the issue of voter identification cards and various other matters including the need for the role of the chiefs to be fully recognised. I enquired about the advisability of having observers in Bop and they confirmed the need to have them in both the town and rural areas.

Before departing Bop my colleague and I had a walk around the part of the town that suffered much damage when the rioters opposing Mangope's rule had burned down property owned by him and his extended family. As was my practice when travelling abroad in such circumstances I had brought with me a high visibility vest marked 'International Observer'. After walking around for a short time I realised that I had forgotten to put it on and then did so. We spent some time on our tour before going into a hotel for refreshments. There we were approached by two civilians who turned out to be warrant officers in the Bop police. They had apparently seen us earlier and wondered who we were and had watched us. A short time later when they saw that I had put on the high visibility vest they decided to approach us at a suitable time and place. Our visit to the hotel gave them the opportunity to do so. They stated that they had been involved in the "rebellion" by the police and that one of them had to go on the run for a day or two afterwards. We had a general discussion on the overall political scene. The two officers believed that the central area of Bop was now stable and generally free of racial and political tension. They felt that there was still the possibility of some tension with the South African Defence Force (SADF) and the South African Police. Before we left for our return to Johannesburg we paid a quick visit to Mafikeng. There I saw the war memorial raised to pay tribute to the British soldiers who had died on service there and also, nearby, a much smaller memorial to the "Black Boys" who had likewise perished.

Just over two weeks later there was another period of violence that again highlighted the strains between factions within a racial group. This time it was in the middle of Johannesburg and within sound and partial view of my office in the Carlton Tower. Just after General Viljoen had committed his newly formed Freedom Front to participate in the election, following on from the events in Bop, the IFP then changed its strategy. It emphasised the role of the Zulu monarch, King Goodwill Zwelithini and Zulu nationalism in general. A Zulu kingdom became a prerequisite for participation in the elections. The ANC entered into discussions with the Zulu monarch and Chief Buthelezi to see how those demands could be met.

On March 28th thousands of Zulus marched through the streets of Johannesburg to show their support for their king. Shooting broke out in two areas of the city including at the ANC's head office. In the ensuing violence 31 people were killed and hundreds were injured. I could clearly hear the gunfire and from my high vantage point could occasionally see armed figures fleetingly running between buildings. Both sides argued as to which was responsible for starting the shooting. It was reported that the ANC denied the police access to Shell House to search for weapons after reports of snipers firing from the offices of the ANC.

There then followed a meeting between De Klerk, King Zwelithini and Chief Buthelezi to discuss the escalation of violence and especially so in Natal. In addition the white right-wing elements opposed to participation in the elections were threatening serious disruption, countrywide, in protest against the forthcoming elections. The election period then seemed likely to experience a violent and turbulent period in at least some regions, not least in KwaZulu/Natal.

On April 19th, Chief Buthelezi made an unexpected move by announcing IFP's intention to participate in the elections. His announcement had been made after the Government and the ANC had offered a package of compromises including recognition within the Interim Constitution of the Zulu monarch as a king, with constitutional powers within the province of KwaZulu. On April 25th, parliament had convened to provide for the institution, role, authority and status of a traditional monarch in KwaZula/Natal. The name of Natal Province had been changed to KwaZulu/Natal some 6 months previously.

The announcement by Buthelezi was much welcomed but did give rise to a potential problem in relation to the ballot papers. For security and other reason it had been decided to have the ballot papers printed outside Africa. The contract was awarded to a London firm renowned for its security arrangements. This was at a time when Buthelezi was openly stating that he, and hence Bop, would not take part in the elections unless and until his demands had been met. This was seen by many, including myself, as a ploy to effectively stop the elections or to delay the elections until a later date if and when his demands had been met. The date of the elections was regarded as fixed and all the other participants were working to that time frame. Before Buthelezi's announcement the time had arrived when the ballot papers needed to be ordered if they were to be available on polling day and so they were ordered with the proof bearing the details of those who were to participate. That by itself would have sent a clear message to Buthelezi of the determination to proceed with the elections as planned.

The 80 million ballot papers, covering both the national election and the nine provincial elections, were then printed and flown to South Africa by plane. It took several large planes to carry them. A four-colour process was used in the printing showing for each party not just its name but also its initials and symbol together with a photograph of the party leader. Once in South Africa there was the considerable task of transferring them to the thirty-nine various provincial and sub-provisional warehouses.

Buthelezi's decision for his party, IFP, to contest the election posed a serious technical problem for the IEC regarding the ballot papers. They were already printed and did not bear any reference to the IFP. After much deliberation it was agreed that a special IPF 'sticker' would be added to the bottom of each ballot paper. This required the need to print, within South Africa, and distribute stickers for affixing to all ballot papers –a significant logistical operation. In addition there was the need to cater for those voting abroad. There was no time to send the IFP stickers to the polling stations in most of the countries involved and so voters for that party were allowed to write in the party name. The IEC had decided that a foreign voting station should be provided at each location outside the country where there were estimated to be 50 or more eligible voters. There were 187 locations in 78 countries selected as foreign voting stations and 92,268 votes were cast in them.

With the participation of the IFP the level of potential violence in and about the election was somewhat lowered. There were attempts by the extreme white right-wingers to upset the electoral arrangements. On the eve of the election a spate of bombings rocked South Africa and the police reacted swiftly by arresting 31 right-wingers in connection with the bombings. There was a final bomb attack at the former Jan Smuts International Airport (now O.R. Tambo International Airport) but there were no further incidents after that. The police seemed to have isolated the perpetrators of the attacks.

In general the security climate within the country improved greatly, almost overnight, in the run up to the poll. The previous security problems in KwaZulu/Natal diminished and the frequent clashes in East Rand between IFP and ANC supporters eased. Concerns remained about the remaining potential for violence during the election period and also the capacity of the South African Police to manage security during the period. That led up to the request for outside police officers to assist the IEC. The European Union was asked to provide such officers as were other international bodies. The concerns proved to be unfulfilled as the election week saw one of the lowest levels of violence for some years. The following figures indicate that and also illustrate the background in the run up to the evolving process leading to the various negotiations.

Level of deaths from political violence

Year	Deaths
1989	2001
1990	2582
1991	3499
1992	4398

The 1601 deaths from political violence in the first four months of 1994 were concentrated in KwaZulu/Natal with 971 and the PWV with 507. The weekly figures during the same period suggest that the election was a turning point in political violence.

Weekly totals	PWV	Natal	Other	Total
30 March – 5 April	12	85	1	98
6 April – 12 April	24	75	4	103
13 April – 19 April	32	51	4	87
20 April – 25 April	51	20	-	71
26 April – 3 May	20	32	-	52
4 May – 10 May	11	25	3	39

This was in no small measure due to the efforts of the security forces and not least the South African Police, whose arrest of the alleged architects of the right-wing bombing campaign, within days of its commencement, demonstrated the security forces' resolve to achieve a climate that facilitated free and fair elections.

The European Election Unit was to participate in the provision of election observers of which up to 4,000 from various international bodies were expected to attend. There was the need to have a training course for EU participants and reasonably close to their individual areas of assignment. In addition there would be the need to have drivers and interpreters available for them during the period of their assignment. Accordingly I spent some time seeking the design and the provision of those requirements. That involved contact with potential contractors.

The EU election unit did have a Joint Operations Unit as regards logistical support for the observers. As and when such observers arrived and were assigned to specific areas they would report back indicating relevant details on how the preparations for the elections were progressing. The election unit could then advise the IEC as and when specific problems were indicated. In addition information during the actual poll and the counting process would be vital to the unit in evaluating the fairness or otherwise of the elections. I saw the need to have one experienced individual to be responsible for analysing the reports being received from the observers and prioritising those for special attention. That would not only provide important information on the electoral process but also ensure that corrective action could be taken quickly. The primary aim was to improve the quality of monitoring and to gain a clearer overview of the technical issues involved. The secondary aim was to improve the information being brought to the attention of the IEC. In addition as and when I attended the IEC meetings I would be able to see the response to such information and also be prepared to tender appropriate advice as and when asked.

After I had first arrived in South Africa I had a meeting with the IEC's Chief Director of Electoral Administration. The director was interested in my experience in Northern Ireland. He saw some similarities with South Africa. We discussed the steps taken to improve the transparency and perceived fairness of the electoral system in Northern Ireland and also how to operate in areas where there was active opposition to the electoral process. A few days after our meeting I prepared and forwarded to him a paper on the steps that could be taken to improve the transparency and perceived fairness as well as operational aspects of the actual poll including the selection, training of staff and guidance for political agents, their polling and counting agents. Shortly afterwards I received the invitation to advise the Election Administration.

During my visits I was kept fully occupied with both roles. The details are too wide-ranging to be included in this book because of the scale of its overall scope. I would attend the IEC meetings not only to advise, as and when so requested, but also to keep the European Election Unit aware of the progress of and difficulties being experienced by the IEC. That was to the advantage of both.

Of course there were some particularly notable difficulties. I attended the various meetings of the IEC and a particular one, on March 31st, highlighted the problems being faced. The training of officials was behind schedule not least because of ongoing delays in finalising the necessary Acts and Regulations. In addition to the total of 7,500 presiding officers that had to be trained there was a total 170,000 voting staff that required some face to face training.

Provincial Election Officers (PEOs) had been appointed for each province. Just four weeks prior to the poll the PEO for the Eastern Cape was hospitalised and was not immediately replaced. In addition ten magistrates employed as Senior Election Officials resigned. It was mentioned that in Natal 14 Deputy Electoral Officers had withdrawn because of fear or intimidation. In addition the recruitment, let alone the training of presiding officers, was well behind schedule. It could only be finalised when the exact number of, and the locations for, the officers had been determined and the staff recruited. This was at a time when the number, let alone the location of the stations in each magisterial area, had not been finalised and thus the number of presiding officers and other staff could not be determined. In addition there was concern about the target set of the number of electors to be allocated to each station. A total of 3,000 was the figure set. There was concern about that figure considering the large number of illiterate voters. Another area of concern was the provision of polling screens and ballot boxes. Consideration was given to the possible use of cardboard ballot boxes and also how temporary demountable shelves could be easily fitted onto the existing polling screens to enable a greater throughput of voters.

Difficulties were arising that made the task of running such an election – that would in any event be difficult – even more difficult again. They included changes in the voting and counting procedures, the late recruitment of staff affecting the training timetable, difficulties in accessing finance for basic training activities such as transport, the hire of venues, food and accommodation. In addition there was inadequate support at national and provincial levels resulting in, as an example, the payment of some staff being well behind schedule. In early March there were concerns among the international bodies in the country that unless the preparations were speeded up, the election would take place in some chaos, with confusion and long queues at voting station.

A meeting of the TEC took place on March 31st to review the preparations for the election. I attended that meeting and it seemed that many of the concerns expressed had been clearly identified and were being effectively addressed with the exception of proposals to deal with the problems in KwaZulu/Natal. There was one aspect under discussion that was causing me concern – the selection of polling stations and the number of electors allocated to each. Not unexpectedly the security forces were concerned about their ability to adequately provide security at a very large number of stations as well as having to plan for coverage should rioting or inter-ethnic violence erupt. From their perspective a smaller number of stations which would each have a greater number of electors allotted to them would be a better option. There were a number of possible adverse consequences to that over a wide range of areas. The number of premises capable of handling a large number of electors might not be available in many areas. In addition, should opposing factions come together, especially in the highly sensitive atmosphere of an election, this could well result in civic disturbance that could then overflow to larger areas.

In general I concluded that the timetable for dealing with the various tasks was tight but practical, given continued drive and determination. The result, I reported, would probably not be up to standards that could have been achieved if the preparations had commenced earlier. Having said that I did at the same time recognise the lack of any experience within South Africa in the organising of such a large democratic election and the very complicated political and ethnic backgrounds involved.

To maintain the security of the election from fraudulent voting, electors would have to produce a form of official identification before a ballot paper would be issued. South Africa did have an official ID card. Such official ID cards were issued from a special office situated in the capital, Pretoria. It required the applicant to fill out a detailed application form which was then fully checked out before the ID could be issued. The standard application form required full family details and date and place of the applicant's birth. A full-face photograph, as well as both profiles and fingerprints of both hands were required. It normally took some six weeks to obtain such documentation. In the past a large number of South Africans were not inclined to apply for such passes as they saw the information supplied being used for security purposes. That left a very considerable number without such a document. There was now the need to provide anything up to four million people with identity documents. The office involved could not deal with such a demand and certainly not in the available timeframe before the elections. The IEC decided that the use of Temporary Voting Cards (TVCs) would be the only way to address the need for such a large number of cards in time for the elections. The standard ID application form would still be completed and forwarded to the ID office for the standard identity document to be issued after the election. However the TVC would be issued on the spot.

I travelled to Pretoria to visit the office involved in the issue of ID cards. Whilst driving back to Johannesburg I experienced, a short distance out of Pretoria, a very intense thunder storm just ahead of me which proceeded ahead of my car all the way until near Johannesburg. I had experienced heavy thunder storms elsewhere in Africa but nothing like this one. It certainly illustrated the raw power of nature.

The Department of Home Affairs was responsible for issuing TVCs. In February two members of the Monitoring Division of the IEC and I formed a working party tasked to examine the potential for abuse in the issue, processing and use of identification documents at the election. We were assisted by two officials from the administrative division. We decided to closely examine the issue of TVCs and so paid a visit to the Department of Home Affairs in Market Street, Johannesburg where the issue of TVCs was under way. The office was very crowded with applicants and I estimated that it took in excess of an hour for an applicant to be processed. TVC issuing offices were to be set up in various parts of the country. During discussions I learnt that some mobile offices would also be utilised but I was concerned to hear that some such offices would be provided in political party offices where the particular party was willing to provide the space. To my mind that was not a sound proposal not least because not all the political parties would have offices of sufficient size in the various towns and districts. The issue of such documents is best done from a neutral venue. The TEC monitoring officials were in agreement with me and decided to raise the matter with the TEC. In addition we, as a working party, would draw up an audit system to ensure that the blank cards were properly accounted for. We also decided to consider arrangements for the random checking of applications. Having said that we left with the impression that attention and good care was being taken to minimise fraud.

Each TVC would bear a photograph of the holder, the date of birth and a unique serial number. They were printed on special card, covered with a special adhesive plastic film bearing a logo that was only visible under ultra-violet light. Polling stations were supplied with UV lamps to check each TVC. There was concern in some areas of the possibility of electors being subject to threat or worse if they were found to have voted. The possession of an ID card or TVC marked at the polling station when a vote had been cast, to avoid voting more than once, could identify those who had voted. It was decided that the ID card would be marked with invisible ink that would be seen under the UV lamp if an attempt was made to vote more than once. The use of a plastic coated card for the TVCs precluded the marking with invisible ink or the use of perforating or embossing to indicate that the holder had voted, as that would be obvious on examination. Accordingly it was decided that all TVCs used would be retained at the polling stations.

In the next month or so there were a number of technical and staffing problems that had to be addressed. The stock of special paper used in the production of TVCs was running low and it was necessary to arrange the procurement of new stock. One of the limiting factors was still the time required to fill out such applications. The answer was the use of a simplified form requiring less information resulting in a shorter time required for completion. Legal advice was obtained on this suggestion, leading to it being accepted. The TVCs so issued, would only be valid for the election and not for standard ID purposes. In Lebowa the staff issuing the TVCs went on strike and other personnel would have to be used. No units were yet in operation in Bop but staff had been sent to activate the sixty units to be located there. The system was not working well in Transkei and Ciskei and extra manpower was to be supplied as well as a better layout of the units.

Section 25 of the Electoral Act required the Transitional Executive Council to set up foreign voting stations to facilitate the casting of votes by electors outside the Republic at election times. The IEC was given some discretion as to where it was appropriate to do so and set the line at where it was estimated to be 50 or more eligible electors. Within 78 countries foreign voting stations were identified in 187 locations at which a total number of 92,268 votes were cast. People abroad could be identified by their passports.

I learned of an interesting development arising from the use of TVCs in the context of out-of-country voting. Some enterprising travel agents were offering holidays to favourite holiday resorts over the election period in islands of the Indian Ocean and so such holiday makers could vote in the Seychelles, Comoros, Mauritius or Madagascar away from any fears of violence. Many South African Muslims voted in Mecca during their pilgrimage there.

I was unable to pay even a very brief visit to South Africa when the country went to the polls. On April 26th, I had to make arrangements for the scheduled European Parliamentary Election under the Single Transferable Voting system, having Northern Ireland as the one constituency. Alongside these responsibilities, I kept a close eye on reports emanating from South Africa. Whilst the international observers were able to report on what they had witnessed both prior to and at the poll, one important sector of the overall process was not open to their inspection. The announcement of the election results was halted on May 3rd. How the final results were determined after that date was not open to public or international inspection. There have been strong suspicions that the results in some areas, including the highly volatile KwaZulu/Natal, were simply fixed among the various parties in order to produce the generally expected result and especially, in the case of Buthelezi's IFP, to ensure enough votes for office in the Government of National Unity. Nevertheless the general view was that the elections had been free overall. But in view of the allegations on the reported results in a few areas, the election might not have been fair to all. In any event the elections did give expression to the political will of the South African people.

On May 10th, 1994 Nelson Mandela was inaugurated as the first black President of South Africa.

NIGERIA

The Nigerian Government requested the Commonwealth Secretariat, headquartered in London, to assist in the organisation of training for senior election staff in preparation for forthcoming elections. I was contacted by the Secretariat in the autumn of 1998 to see if I could participate in that work. The terms of reference for the training included the following:

- The delivery of and safeguards for free and fair elections
- Transparency of election preparations
- Integrity of the key election processes
- The management of polling stations

- The role of election officers
- Voters lists
- Security of ballot papers
- Counting the votes

The Independent National Electoral Commission of Nigeria (INEC) was responsible for the running of the elections. The size of the overall operation facing the IEC was immense as the list of the geographical units involved clearly illustrates:

States within Nigeria	37
Local government areas	774
Wards	8,692
Polling centres	111,430
State constituencies	990
Federal constituencies	360
Senatorial Districts	109

A newspaper report in The Guardian (Nigerian) on October 29th, indicated the concerns of the chairman of the INEC. He referred to, presumably at recent elections, the forceful removal of ballot boxes by party thugs or agents. In addition he pointed out that a hitch-free distribution of election materials was the essential determinant of the success of any election. He went on to state: "Except there is maximum vigilance, election materials and ballot boxes could be tampered with or diverted by political hirelings." He did admit that there had been malpractices in the recent voter registration but promised that the Commission and the police would strive to plug all loopholes during elections. He implored the police to effectively utilise its intelligence services to forestall and apprehend all political mercenaries planning to thwart the efforts towards conducting free and fair elections.

As part of the nationwide orientation and state training workshops for senior electoral officials, I was asked to carry out the training workshops in Abuja, the capital, and the north-east part of the country, the latter being an area where there were ongoing security concerns. Two separate visits to the country were involved, the first in November and the other in January, 1999. In addition I operated a training session in London for Nigerian election staff that had been visiting there for other purposes.

I and fellow trainers covering other parts of the country met up in Lagos in November 1998 before visiting Abuja, for briefing by the INEC. Afterwards I travelled to the location of my workshop in Jos, covering eight states, which operated from November 2nd to 5th. In addition I travelled around parts of the region to get a feel for the topography involved. It was evident that in some locations motorised canoes would be required to service the elections.

During my travels I stayed for a couple of days in what had been a former colonial administration centre. It had a central administration building with a number of small circular, individual residential units, modelled on African huts close at hand. Meals were provided in the central building. Talking to the staff there I learnt that in colonial times district officers who worked out in the field were periodically brought back to the central administrative site for some rest and recuperation and contact with fellow Europeans. One evening after dinner, whilst I was walking along the pathway to my accommodation, I felt from time to time some things brushing against the top of my head. It was getting dark and so I could not see what they were. The path was lined with trees and so I assumed that I was brushing against low hanging branches. The next morning, whilst going for breakfast, I noted that there were no branches at head height. That evening I took a torch with me on the way to dinner and on the way back I shone the light at the trees and saw large spiders dangling from the branches. They fed off small bats that came out at night and flew along the tree line.

On another occasion when I visited a village the local chief welcomed me, gave me some refreshments, and as we chatted he explained that he believed that everyone had an animus in an animal, tree or other physical object. Should anything happen to it the individual would also be harmed in some way or other. In his case his animus was a large snake. He was keen to show it off and took me to a long and very deep pit where a very, very large snake lay. He then fed it by throwing down live chickens.

My training workshop was for a total of twenty-one senior officials from eight states – Adamawa, Bauchi, Borno, Gombe, Nasarawa, Plateau, Taraba and Yobe. The first morning session, scheduled for Monday, November 2nd, did not take place as only some of the election officials had arrived. The workshop did commence at 2pm that day. The late arrival of some of the trainees had been due to the combination of two factors – the short notice given to the staff, only a few days earlier, and the absence of some of the resident state commissioners who had to approve in advance any such travel arrangements.

From the very start it was evident that the election officers welcomed the opportunity to attend. They were both experienced and interested in their work. The initial feedback confirmed my fears that the new electoral commission was facing a daunting task both in the registration of electors and the running of elections scheduled over the next five months. The staff involved felt that they lacked the necessary tools to do the job and especially so in the field of logistics. I pointed out that the new commission was facing an immense workload and needed time to settle in. In addition I stressed that the window of opportunity provided by the transition to democracy had to be grasped even though, ideally, much more time would have enabled better preparations. I also pointed out that the forthcoming elections offered a good vehicle for them to fully demonstrate their commitment and ability and, hence, enhance their standing in the longer term.

The discussions during the training sessions identified a number of areas for concern. They included the following:

Logistics
Even at INEC state office level there were poor telephonic facilities and in practice none at all between the electoral officers, their supervisory presiding officers and polling station staff. Even if staff did attempt to use facilities at local government offices and police stations, the facilities were either not fully effective or not available when required, or in some instances access was refused. The use of mobile radio sets seemed at first glance a possible way forward. However a number of factors could negate their use. The first was the cost as the number of polling stations would be over 110,000. In addition I was informed that most polling stations would be sited in the open air and, hence, would lack electricity. Any radios provided would thus require additional batteries. An alternative approach would be to restrict the provision of radios to supervising presiding officers who each would be assigned between ten to twenty polling stations. That would result in the reduced requirement of between 5,000 and 10,000 radios.

Even at INEC state office level the telephone network appeared at times to be ineffective. To a large extent communications depended on the use of a Ceptron High Frequency Radio located at each such site. Those radios were an electronic version of a telex machine. Even so radio communication would at times have to be passed via a third office whenever atmospheric conditions or distance made direct contact impossible. All levels of the INEC suffered from communication problems. That would become a very serious handicap at election time and especially at electoral officer, senior presiding officers' and presiding officers' levels. Accordingly communications would be more dependent on physical contact between locations. From discussions at the workshop I calculated that only some 40% to 50% of the election officers had motor vehicles. The absence of transport would seriously restrict their ability to effectively perform their duties on polling day.

The option of using hired vehicle was one alternative but reports suggested that, even if available, the reliability of such vehicles was not of a high level. I saw the use of motor cycles or scooters as a good alternative and especially in rural areas where such two-wheeled vehicles could access pathways and tracks not suitable for an ordinary car or van.

Security
A review of the security arrangements at polling stations, the transportation of the election results and documentation identified problem areas. In some rural

areas the polling station staff had been intimidated by political party activists and thugs. It was reported that at previous elections polling station staff had been open to bribery and corruption. In a few instances ballot boxes had been stolen from polling stations. There were few police available to secure polling stations and in some instances the civilian population resented any police presence.

Registration of electors
The registration of electors had concluded before the training workshop had commenced. An enhanced system had been employed to assist in the prevention of multiple registrations by individuals. An elector would first have to attend the polling station during an accreditation period before he/she could vote. That would make it more difficult for a person registered at more than one place to vote twice unless the two polling stations involved were relatively close at hand. At the workshop I sought clarification from the attendees as to the precise procedure to be followed but there was some variation as to how the verification and voting sequence would be operated in practice. It was accepted that there was the need for some recognition of custom and usage such as, in some areas, the segregation of the sexes and in many areas the respect to be given to the elderly. Whilst there was the need to accommodate local custom and usage, it was also important to have a commonality of approach and decision making during the poll. There was the clear need for comprehensive instructions to be issued by INEC Headquarters.

Media reports indicated that *all* the printed registration cards had been taken up. A newspaper circulating in Abuja on Friday, November 6th, had the headline "Voting cards for sale". Such reports would raise doubts in the public perception of the integrity of the electoral process. The INEC chairman had already publically acknowledged that there were malpractices in the recent registration process. To my mind the absence of a comprehensive and accurate census of recent origin made it difficult to estimate the overall number of eligible electors and hence to evaluate the success or otherwise of the electoral registration process.

The new INEC had little time to settle into its role before the advent of the elections. Just prior to my departure from Nigeria I learned that all the state administrative secretaries were being moved. The reason for such a move was not stated but I surmised that it might well relate to the decision by the new INEC to restructure its organisation so as to address the problems identified. Such action may well have helped to address the concerns, but on the other hand could have had adverse consequences, in that the relocated officers would have to familiarise themselves both with the state topography and the electoral and political party personnel involved in the newly assigned area.

The training workshop went well and the attendees found the process very helpful. It also helped them to establish a group bonding that they would find useful during the trials and tribulations at elections. I left Nigeria content with the result.

After enjoying Christmas at home I received an invitation on January 4th, 1999 to return to Nigeria within a couple of weeks to carry out an orientation and state level training workshop for senior election officials namely the assigned National Commissioner for the region involved, the Resident Electoral Commissioners, Administrative Secretaries and other INEC electoral staff. As before, I was assigned to Abuja and Jos to cover eight states. The primary aim was to provide practical inputs on the management and conduct of free and fair elections and topics to be raised in the workshop sessions. In addition I was to pay particular attention to identified weaknesses at the previous local government and state elections. This time the attendees were much more senior officials than before. Having said that, the content of the workshop followed the same outline as before and this time lasted a little longer.

I arrived in Lagos on January 13th, stayed overnight in Lagos and then flew to Abuja to meet up with the INEC for a briefing before setting off to the assigned area. As at the previous visit I arrived at the international airport in Lagos – whilst the flight to Abuja on January 14th was from the regional airport. Interconnections between and from the two airports was by taxis so I experienced the very severe traffic congestion in Lagos that appeared to be the norm. It was good to reach the regional airport and better still to experience the hospitality of Bellview Airlines staff and the comfort of the very modern planes they used.

These two visits were my first time in Nigeria but I had been regaled with tales from the country as my late brother-in-law had served there for two assignments in the Diplomatic Service. My late sister would always describe her experience of that country whenever she visited me at home. One tale that always raised a smile with me referred to her husband's insistence on only using a particular brand of petrol in his car even if that meant that the petrol level got very low before the required brand was available from a petrol station. On his first assignment to Nigeria they both travelled out by boat, it was a long time ago, and he brought a new car with him. I understood that there was some financial advantage in getting a car that way and also the vehicle could later be returned to the UK without incurring taxation.

At the relevant time Lagos did not yet have deep water berths. Instead the ships would lie off shore and people and goods would then be transported to the shore by barges. Passengers would be transported first and then the cargo including any cars. Whilst my sister and her husband were waiting patiently for the car to be unloaded my sister noticed that in a nearby fuel storage tank area men were filling 40 gallon drums with petrol, presumably for onward transportation up-country. There appeared to be five separate lines of barrels being filled and as each one was filled it was capped and then a stencil was used to mark it. My sister went closer to see what was on the stencils and found that each line had a different brand name applied even though all the barrels were being filled from the one storage tank. That was the end of my brother-in-law's predilection for a particular brand!

My second workshop followed more or less along the lines of the first but with some aspects being discussed in greater detail. It was evident that the concerns expressed at the previous workshop had reached the more senior staff.

KOSOVO

The Security Council of the United Nations adopted Resolution 1244 on June 10th, 1999 concerning the grave humanitarian situation that then existed in Kosovo and the need for the safe and free return of all refugees and displaced persons to their homes. The Resolution included a reaffirmation of the call in previous resolutions for substantial autonomy and self-administration for Kosovo as well as a demand that the Federal Republic of Yugoslavia (FRY) put an immediate and verifiable end to violence and repression in Kosovo along with the phased withdrawal from Kosovo of all military, police and paramilitary forces according to a rapid timetable.

It was evident that the break-up of the former Republic of Yugoslavia had given rise to serious ethnic and political problems in the overall general area, of which Kosovo was only part, with a great loss of life and property. As a result there had been considerable changes in Kosovo in the ethnic composition in many areas and indeed for the country as a whole. On my first visit there I obtained the following data showing the estimated figures as at 1999 in comparison to the estimated 1998 figures.

Albanians	76% of the estimated 1998 figure
Serbians	51%
Croats, Romas and others	43%

On July 12th, the UN Secretary-General reported back to the Security Council on the then current security, political and humanitarian situation. It began as follows:

Following the deployment in Kosovo on 12 June 1999 of the international security presence known as KFOR, the Yugoslav army and the Serbian security forces began their withdrawal from the province …This withdrawal was completed by 20 June 1999. On 21 June 1999 the Kosovo Liberation Army (KLA) signed an undertaking on demilitarization.

The Secretary-General then went on to report that whilst the general situation had been tense, it was stabilising. The KLA had moved back into all parts of Kosovo and that a large number of Kosovo Serbs had left their homes for Serbia. This had been prompted by an increasing number of incidents committed by Kosovo Albanians against Kosovo Serbs including high profile killings, abductions, looting, arson and forced appropriation of apartments. The absence of law and order was being exploited by criminal gangs. Whilst the Kosovo International Force (KFOR) was responsible for the maintenance of both public safety and civil law and order, its ability to do so was limited due to the fact that it was still in the process of building up its forces.

In relation to the humanitarian situation it was estimated that out of a population of some 1.7 million almost half (800,000) had sought refuge in neighbouring Albania, Macedonia and Montenegro during the past year. An assessment indicated that up to 500,000 persons may have been internally displaced, many of whom were in worse health than refugees, having spent weeks hiding without food or shelter. By July of 1999 more than 650,000 refugees had returned to Kosovo leaving an estimated 150,000 persons in neighbouring regions and countries.

Among the various tasks assigned to the United Nations Interim Administration Mission in Kosovo (UNMIK) was the development of provisional institutions for democratic and autonomous self-government, pending a political settlement. That included the holding of elections. I was asked to carry out a preparatory evaluation mission for elections in Kosovo. Under the terms of reference I was first to discuss and assess the surrounding conditions for the organisation of elections with the Special Representative of the UN Secretary-General, his senior staff, relevant local authorities and other actors. Then I was to review the existing legal framework for elections in Kosovo within the overall context of the UNMIK mandate and assess the potential needs to revise the law. The scope of the voter population and the status of the constituent boundaries were then to be considered along with the need for, and the design and composition of, an electoral component for UNMIK. Finally a report was to be prepared on the findings of the mission along with concrete recommendations. This was the first of four missions that I was asked to do in Kosovo running into the latter part of the year 2000.

The first mission involved numerous meetings with a very wide range of people including UNMIK staff at various levels, the International Civilian Police Commissioner (CIVPOL) and the general in charge of Kosovo Force, the international peacekeeping force in country (KFOR). Confidential discussions were also held with Kosovars representing the various communities. A meeting also took place in Vienna with representatives of various missions to the Organisation for Security and Cooperation in Europe (OSCE) including those of France, Germany, Italy, Norway, United Kingdom and United States.

I ascertained that the residual law was that of the Federal Republic of Yugoslavia. Hence there was the question as to whether or not any election held should be conducted under the existing legislative framework. Security Council

Resolution 1244 did recognise the principles of sovereignty and territorial integrity of FRY. On the other hand it did call for substantial autonomy and overseeing of *provisional* institutions for democratic and autonomous self-government pending a political settlement and indicated that as being among the main responsibilities of the international presence. Accordingly I took the view that the initial elections should be regarded as part of the provisional arrangements and so should only as such provide for a two-year term of office. The new provisions and regulations should be drafted after due consultation with representatives of the Kosovar population and the Central Electoral Commission that my report recommended should be set up. Taking into account the prevailing tensions between the various communities I suggested that municipal boards should consist of both elected Kosovars and appointed UNMIK international staff.

Next I considered the electoral units, boundaries, to be used. A new boundary review would take an appreciable period of time and would be difficult to do in the existing circumstances. My recommendation was that the existing municipality boundaries should be used as the elected offices were to be only short term and the arrangements were transitional. A post election review of the existing boundaries could be carried out before the following election when there would be fully elected municipal boards having, where necessary, international staff in advisory roles.

The report I submitted was wide ranging covering many aspects of the arrangements needed to hold such an early election including its timing. A civic registration was the first stage. Many public records had been destroyed during the fighting and many individuals had lost their ID cards and other documents when they had to flee and/or their houses were burnt down. Detailed discussions with those involved in the programme, involving the issuing of ID cards and the preparation of an electoral role, indicated that a minimum of 35 weeks would be required if every thing worked well. That required the provision of the necessary hardware and software and that the finance for the overall project would be made available as and when required. My experience elsewhere indicated that that was not always the case and so many projects did not attain their projected timeframe. In addition any such timetable could be seriously affected should security in the territory become more difficult.

There were various other important aspects that I had to consider. It was an exceptionally busy time not least in meeting up with Kosovars, members of international bodies and diplomats. The various international bodies had different emphasis from each other on the way ahead and so I had to be careful in my approach to each. It was a very interesting time.

Kosovo was only one of the countries over a period of time where international bodies, including the United Nations, were involved in the introduction of democratic government to former states of the Soviet Union. In many cases various international bodies participated in that work as partners. The various sectors of responsibilities would then be assigned, by agreement, between those involved. Any appraisal of the overall situation needed careful handling. Such international missions were generally headed by persons of status who often had held senior posts in government back in their native states. As such they were keen to have a success, the earlier the better, particularly if it could result in the offer of a new senior post back home after an election there. Of course there were those who were very dedicated to the task in hand and were prepared to stay, within reason, until the desired status had been obtained. Nevertheless there could be differences of opinion as to when would be the appropriate time for elections. The more pragmatic might take the view that an earlier election, even if not up to the desired standard, would be better than one which met the generally accepted democratic standards – but would take much longer.

Some international office holders in the missions in Kosovo were pushing for an election to be held in the early summer of 2000 even if it would be of a lesser but acceptable standard. That viewpoint was made on the basis of the perceived need to have elected Kosovars actively participating in their own governance at a very early date and hence to demonstrate and assist in the movement towards democratisation. I was not inclined to such an approach. The preparation of the civil registry would have had to have been completed many months before then and a severe winter could delay the necessary work in the higher regions. Security considerations and other factors such as the return of refugees and IDPs (internal displaced persons) could also impact on the possible election timetable, as could any delay in the provision of the various electoral components.

Having carried out the review, I remained convinced that the earliest date for the holding of any election to the minimum acceptable standard remained September 2000 and indicated that in my report. Even so it was possible that because of various problems that could arise, the earliest time frame for an election to the minimum standards might not occur until the summer or spring of 2001. Situations can deteriorate unexpectedly but still I was hopeful that the election could be held in September. Lessons learned elsewhere illustrated the dangers of running premature elections or ones of insufficient standards.

Following the submission of my initial report I was then asked to revisit Kosovo on three further occasions to report back to the UN electoral division as to the progress on the preparations for the planned elections. Three detailed reports resulted covering all the various aspects involved. The following are just some of the key aspects covered.

The registration process
No figures were available as to the number of persons eligible for inclusion in the list of voters. Various estimates had been made with the largest estimate

showing 1.2 million. The registration process involved a number of procedures. Applicants had to produce sufficient documentation to prove their eligibility for registration. A significant number of applicants failed to do so – up to 11% in the first instance. That was due, at least in some cases, to the loss of personal documentation during the civil war. It seemed that women and the younger family members were disproportionately represented in those who failed the test. Those who failed the test had the right of appeal. Records showed that by the middle of July 2000 the number of applications received was almost 1 million, 994,450, of which just under 900,000 had been successful. There was a poor turnout by the minorities and especially the Serbs of whom very few applied. It was suggested that the safe return of Serb refugees would encourage Serb registration overall. Of course intimidation could effectively prevent such registration and there were some indications of that. There were also indications that some local Serb leaders were prepared to advise their community to register.

I was concerned that if only a small number of Serbs were to register in municipalities where they were the predominant community and the other ethnic group(s) did both – register and vote – then the latter would win all the seats. It was entirely possible that many of the non-Serb registered voters were no longer resident there having fled their homes. Under the registration rules applying, an individual could pick his or her present address or their previous address for registration purposes. That provision was designed to assist in the longer term the resettlement of those who had to flee from their long established homes. An unintended consequence could have been that in an overwhelmingly Serb municipality, both then and in the past, all, or a majority of the seats – could be won by the minority – some or all of whom did not presently reside there. Some of the international personnel staff involved were also concerned and so I recommended the postponement until the following year of the elections for the municipalities involved.

After the production of the appropriate documentation each applicant was photographed and then fingerprinted. That data was digitised, stored on a computer disc and sent off for processing. In some of the registration centres problems were encountered in that process. In those areas there were problems associated with the voltage in the electricity supply necessitating the purchase of UPS (uninterruptible power supply) units. Unfortunately that in itself gave rise to difficulty as the UPS units were found to require special cables, not available at the time, to enable them to connect with the special socket on the digital camera.

An appeals procedure had been established to deal with appeals against non-registration. An Electoral Appeals Commission (EAC) had been set up to administer the process. It was to operate as a judicial process having two chambers, both based in Pristina. Its restriction to the one location meant that would-be electors from areas at some distance would have to travel there to present their appeal. On one of my visits it became clear to me that the volume of appeals would greatly exceed the capacity of the process. Contingency plans were put in place to introduce a pre-appeal screening process so as to reduce to a more manageable number, the number of appeals that would have to go to a formal hearing.

The pre-screening process consisted of a check by registration staff of municipal records to see whether or not the individual applicant's right to registration could be confirmed. Municipal records, except in some areas where they had been deliberately destroyed, consisted of various items of personal documentation as, for example, applications for driving licences and passports. When an individual's application could not be verified from those sources the application would have to be forwarded to the EAC for consideration.

It seemed to me that a quasi-judicial process that provided registration appeal hearings in different parts of the country would have been a much better operation but the die had been cast and it was too late to change.

There were arrangements for the out-of-country registration of refugees. In the case of Albania, Macedonia and Montenegro each applicant had to attend a voter registration centre there. My enquiries showed that by the middle of July a little over 2,000 persons had applied to be registered. There were a number of likely reasons that could account for that low response. The out-of-country registration was for voter registration only – no travel documents were being issued. Those not interested in returning were unlikely to be interested in voting or indeed may hope to have left their present country of abode before the elections. By not registering they may well have being sending a signal of their intention of not returning. Some had reported their concerns about the possibility of the Serbian Secret Police getting hold of personal details from the electoral register. The number of refugees in Albania appeared to be quickly reducing due to the poor economic situation in that country and so the refugees were leaving for western countries.

In countries other than the three mentioned above a mail-in application system was applied. By the middle of July a total of almost 150,000 such applications had been received. The operation was controlled from Vienna with information offices in Belgium, Germany, Italy, Switzerland and the USA. The majority of the mail-in applications were from Austria, Belgium, Finland, France, Germany, Italy, Slovenia, Sweden, United Kingdom and USA. A low number of such applications were approved on examination with many being referred to the adjudication process.

The office in Vienna had a database of customers of the pre-conflict electricity and telephone utilities that could be used to help establish whether or not the individuals were qualified to be registered. If not the review process consisted of that office writing out to the applicant seeking more documentation, photocopies of which would be acceptable. If none were provided then the individual cases were referred to the ECA in Pristina. To enable the Vienna office to deal with the increasing demand, the staff level there was increased and extra computers purchased. I came to the conclusion that the appeals procedures both in and out of the country could well become the Achilles heel of the whole electoral operation.

The legislation required that voters at the elections would have to produce identification at the polling station to obtain a ballot paper. Identification cards were to be issued to those who had registered. The identification data obtained on the registration application along with the photograph taken would then be used to print out the ID card. Such information was available from the computer data base compiled from the computer disks received from each registration/polling station. Unfortunately the overall system was not working according to plan and so much so that it was estimated that only some 50% would have been produced in time for an October election. Unfortunately that was only part of the problem. The original plan was for the issue of ID cards to take place at each registration location during the period of registration and also at that place for the six week period after registration had ended. The delay in the production of the cards necessitated a new plan. It also raised the question as to how the cards would be issued, by whom and where. The organising of the elections had already put an immense pressure on those involved. The system was already severely over-loaded.

Even if the production of the ID cards was to be substantially enhanced, at considerable cost, that would still leave the question of how the cards could be delivered to the individual electors. I met with those involved to review the best way forward. After much discussion an alternative was identified. The electoral register could be printed bearing a photograph of each elector. In that manner the integrity of the voting process, in respect of anti-fraud measures, would be maintained to the same degree as originally planned. The additional costs involved were believed to be marginal. Some hardware and software modifications would be required to enable the biometric data to be converted to a suitable format for processing along with the alphanumeric data containing the electors' details.

That, to my mind, gave rise to some aspects that needed to be taken into account. I had in mind the overall security of the printing works to be involved and especially if it was located in Kosovo. A detailed examination of the overall security of the premises, the process and the staff involved would be relevant. I recommended that the UNMIK police or other appropriate source check out the proposed printing contractor to ensure that there was no direct or indirect link with mafia, political or paramilitary factions as, if such a link were to be discovered after the elections, the probity of the process could be seriously questioned. I put those comments into my report.

The EAC was heavily involved in the registration process as indicated above. It was only one aspect of its role. An international Chief Commissioner headed it up, with the support of three independent Kosovar Commissioners, served by three internal legal counsel and three international investigators. All registered voters, political parties, and accredited observers could file complaints with the EAC when they believed that the electoral rules and associated regulations had been violated. The EAC was given extensive powers ranging from levying fines; to the removal of a candidate from participating in the elections; to excluding a party from running in the elections; or even barring a party from taking part in the elections for up to six years.

My final conclusion was that the holding of elections in early October, which some senior members in the international missions were regarding as appropriate, would most likely give rise to serious operational problems and indeed to my mind were not realistically attainable. It was clear from all perspectives that the elections had to take place in 2000. In those circumstances I concluded that the realistic window of opportunity lay between October 21st and November 11th and so reported with the comment that a later rather than an earlier date within that time frame would greatly enhance the standard and acceptability of the elections. With that my involvement in Kosovo ended.

BOSNIA AND HERZEGOVINA

A week before Christmas in 1995 I received a phone call concerning plans for elections in Bosnia. (The term Bosnia was more commonly used than the full name of Bosnia and Herzegovina.) That was followed up a few days later by a letter. The Swedish Government was planning a meeting in Stockholm in mid-January to consider such elections and I was invited to attend. The purpose of the meeting was to focus on substantial problems relating to the elections and the organisational relations between the international organisations on the ground, the signatories to the Dayton Agreement and contributing governments. The Swedish Government proposed that the meeting should consider how an environment could be ensured for free and fair elections involving the following aspects:

- Safety
- Free and equal access to information for all voters
- Absentee voters
- Free electoral campaigning by political parties
- Electoral regulations
- Cooperation on the ground

It was indicated that the Bosnians proposed the use of the D'Hondt system, as used in Germany. That system does produce results that reflect very accurately the opinion of the electorate. To do so it needs well organised political parties fielding candidates for constituencies and party lists. If that system would be too difficult for Bosnia at that time then the Provisional Electoral Commission (PEC) would need to determine a suitable alternative.

The Organisation for Security and Cooperation in Europe (OSCE) had a Bosnia Election Mission which had sent an experts group to Sarajevo early in December. Their report suggested that the timetable for elections laid down in the Dayton Agreement, six months after signature, was extremely ambitious and that it would require a period of at least nine months provided that a number of specified requirements were fully met.

I attended the meeting in Stockholm and also, at a later stage, meetings in Vienna as a member of the Advisory Group. In addition I was part of a small group that flew in to Sarajevo via Serbia to carry out a brief analysis of the situation on the ground. We travelled by small private plane and had to circle the airport for a period whilst the runway was being searched for bombs and booby traps that might have been planted overnight. We also had the experience of travelling up the avenue in Sarajevo that became infamous due to the number of citizens who had been seriously injured or killed by snipers firing from the over-looking hills.

The Bosnian Municipality Elections that had been planned for November of 1995 had been postponed because of the lack of commitment of the Bosnian political parties and especially on the electoral rules and regulations to be applied. Until there was all-party agreement on the basic electoral principles, then detailed operational planning could not proceed for the rescheduled municipal elections to be held at the end of 1996 – the time when the OSCE's budget was to run out. The OSCE desired to have those elections held in the latter part of the year – whilst the International Force (IFOR) would still be in strength – in contrast to the situation at the end of the year when a substantial reduction of those forces was planned. That, together with the onset of winter snows, indicated a time frame for the poll in late November or early December. A tentative date of November 24th, had then been set. The mandate of the outgoing Provisional Electoral Commission (PEC) was extended until the start of December.

Not only were there differences of emphasis between the main political parties but also between the international contributors to IFOR. To some extent that was a reflection of the geo-political influences involved. A good example of that was when IFOR military forces were converging on the Sarajevo airport to secure it for military operational reasons. IFOR included Russian army units. The Russian State appeared to be more sympathetic to the Serbs. Obviously whoever controlled the airport was in a strong position as regards the supply and control of the overall military forces. The US general in charge of IFOR desired the UK general leading the non-Russian forces involved to prevent the Russians from securing the airport. That UK general realised that the Russians were most likely to arrive there first. Accordingly his plan, on arrival there, was to surround the airport with his troops so that they would have complete control of movements into and out of the airport. That was done and as a result a *modus operandi* was arrived at.

The three constituent ethnic groups in Bosnia and Herzegovina were Serbs, Croatians and Bosniaks. The Bosniaks had been converted to the Muslim faith when the region had been under the control of the Ottoman Empire. The Serbs were closely related to the Russians both ethnically and religiously whilst the Croatians were mainly Roman Catholic.

At the end of June 1996 I received a telephone call in my office from the outgoing deputy head of the Mission in Sarajevo. In that role he also chaired the PEC. Technically, the head of the OSCE Mission, was the head of the PEC – but the actual work was carried out by the deputy head. He invited me to act in the role of Deputy Head of the Mission. A short time later I received the formal request from the OSCE section of the Foreign and Commonwealth Office. The OSCE was particularly keen to obtain my services in the light of my experience in similar conflict situations in various parts of the world. Obviously I could only act as a temporary replacement due to my responsibilities in Northern Ireland. When I accepted the role President Izetbegovic, President Krajisnik and President Zubak, the presidents of the three states involved, were formally notified of my appointment as a temporary successor to the outgoing holder.

I left Belfast on October 30th to fly to Vienna where I stayed over-night and then travelled on to the Mission. When I arrived in Sarajevo I found my office to be in a former bank building that was not far from the spot where Archduke Ferdinand had been assassinated – the event that led on to the First World War. When I travelled around the city with the head of mission he always arranged the use of a Snatch Land Rover vehicle that had formerly been used in Northern Ireland. I found it not only to be most uncomfortable to travel in, but it also brought back memories and particularly the thought that the armour with which it was clad was not resistant to high velocity bullets.

As regards accommodation I was fortunate to meet up with three Scandinavians who were working in Sarajevo with the International Mission on a relatively long term basis and so had rented a house on the hills above the city. They invited me to join them and we got on very well. Attending my office involved a twenty minute walk down the hill overlooking the city and I found the exercise and the view to be invigorating. At the same time when passing by a couple of cemeteries I was made very much aware, from the large number of very recent graves, of the vicious conflict that had taken place. That was reinforced when, at the bottom of the hill, I passed near to the outdoor market that had been mortared from the surrounding hills resulting in many deaths.

On arrival I found that, *de facto*, a number of roles had been assigned to me: Acting Head of Mission during any absence of the ambassador (he did travel away from time to time), Deputy-Chair of the Provisional Electoral Commission (PEC) and Director General of Elections. A brief, initial evaluation of the difficulties being experienced by the Mission convinced me that, despite my reservations, I would really have to accept the challenges being virtually forced upon me. Not to have done so would have placed the preparations for the municipal elections in serious jeopardy. The succeeding weeks were somewhat hectic and challenging. Crisis management was the only appropriate approach in the circumstances.

<u>Duties as Acting Head of Mission</u>, as and when I acted in that role, included:-

- Holding daily meetings with senior staff
- Receiving visitors – senior military personnel, ambassadors etc
- Attending the Principals' meetings – the meetings when the principal international key players discussed strategy and key issues. Attendees included the High Representative, the Heads of Missions of UNHCR, UN, IPTF (The International Police Task Force) and Generals Commanding IFOR and ARRC (Allied Rapid Reaction Corp). I also attended those meetings when the Ambassador was in Sarajevo as it was the practise for the number two in the Mission to accompany the HOM to such meetings.
- Resolving operational and personnel problems.
- Submission of a detailed weekly report of the mission's work to OSCE Vienna Headquarters.

DUTIES AS DEPUTY CHAIRMAN OF THE PROVISIONAL ELECTORAL COMMISSION

Technically the Ambassador was the chairman of the PEC but the Deputy Chairman routinely chaired the meetings. During my period in the Chair the main business involved included:-

- The determination of the rules and regulations appertaining to the rescheduled municipal elections.
- The resolution of problems to, and challenges of, the calculation of the seats allocation at the September elections and the filling of seats becoming vacant through the resignation or non-acceptance of posts by those elected.
- Election Appeal Sub-Commission cases including those in which the PEC or the Mission were themselves the subject of complaints lodged.

The PEC had been meeting for an ongoing period of time as I noted from the first such meeting that I chaired. The minutes indicated that it was the 87th Session! When the PEC was equally divided on an issue I had to make a Chairman's decision.

AS DIRECTOR GENERAL OF ELECTIONS

A considerable workload was involved in the run up to the scheduled municipal elections to be run on November 23rd/24th. The available timeframe was really inadequate to enable a high quality election to be organised. In addition it was becoming clear to me that the political will did not exist within the body politic for those elections be held. That was especially the case with Republic Srpska (RS). It was evident to me that there was a difference of opinion within the Mission as regards contact with the President Plavsic of RS. The Russians were eager to have such contact made, whilst the other internationals were not of the same mind. It seemed to me to be appropriate to have a meeting, not to negotiate, but simply to hear their concerns. Within the majority of the international community there was widespread agreement that negotiation with the RS leadership would be inappropriate as it would meet with hard-line positions having nothing to do with the OSCE or elections *per se*, because, in part, the RS leadership was absorbed with other issues including the internal military unrest within their military forces.

The overall situation was very complex. There were reports of housing destruction being carried out in certain areas by RS and also of Bosniaks wishing to go home to property they owned in Kopaci and Trnovo. Refugees and Displaced Persons were threatened with eviction in Mostar by special West Mostar police who failed to disband despite an order from IPTF and IFOR. I did pay a visit to Mostar that made me very aware of the terrible things that had occurred there. The international community became aware of the partial destruction of the famous, ancient bridge that spanned the river. When I arrived there the missing central section had been replaced by temporary scaffolding but the divide between the two communities on either side of the river remained as strong as ever. That was not surprising considering the number of persons killed, so grimly evident from the need to use public parks as graveyards. The sight of the rows of many grave stones bearing the names of the deceased and the date of their demise over a relatively short time frame is something I will never forget. A short time later on I visited Metrovica, another location where a river separated two communities and where many Muslim men and boys had been taken prisoner, whilst supposedly under the protection of UN troops, by RS forces and then murdered and buried in mass graves.

Within the RS structures there were two competing forces. President Plavsic had ordered General Mladic to resign his command of the RS army following violence near the town of Gajevi. General Mladic refused from his power base centred in Banja Luka. President Plavsic operated out of Pele. My interest in having a meeting with President Plavsic was to pick up any comments she might make in relation to changes to the Electoral Rules and Regulations that had been formulated in the previous October and that the RS had found unpalatable, but were now up for modification. The Bosniaks had made proposals that were unacceptable to the Serbs and there was the need to arrive at rules and regulations that were acceptable to all concerned. That was of much interest to me as Chairman of the Electoral Commission. I had to be mindful that any concerns held by the RS could only be properly addressed if, by doing so, they would not adversely affect the proper operation of the Dayton Agreement and the due interests of the other parties in the Federation.

When I arrived for my meeting with President Plavsic I found a number of TV cameras awaiting me as I shook hands with the President. At the start of our meeting I politely indicated that I was not there to negotiate in any shape or form but simply to listen to any comments she would like to make. It was apparent that she was not too pleased with my approach and the meeting was relatively short. When we came out of the meeting the TV cameras started to focus in on us but the President waved them away and they duly left. Some years later she was brought before the International War Crimes Court's Tribunal for the Former Yugoslavia that had been ongoing from 1997. It dealt with a number of high officials on charges of war crimes including Slobodan Milosevic, ex-President of Yugoslavia, Dario Kordic one of the top Bosnian Croat politicians. Mrs Biljana Plavsic, who pleaded guilty, was sentenced to eleven years imprisonment.

Meetings with representatives of the Federation parties gave little hope for optimism. Nevertheless detailed planning continued for the municipal elections. At the same time the Chairman-in-Office of the Permanent Council of OSCE called for a postponement of the elections and indicated that, if they were to go ahead, higher standards than those achieved at the September elections would be required.

The new standards being demanded included a 100% level of supervision of the polling and counting stations. At the same time there were clear indications that the promised number of observers from international bodies would not materialise. Overall the Mission staff was becoming increasingly pessimistic about the possibility of the municipal elections being held even at a reduced quality level. The political problems continued and necessitated more of my time dealing with this aspect. RS was now signalling its opposition to the running of the elections especially after the decision by the Head of Mission to effectively remove the right of a voter to vote where he or she wished to live. In addition the RS instructed its representative on the PEC not to participate in the deliberations of the PEC but merely to attend as an observer – not helpful to me as Chair of the PEC.

The Ambassador remained hopeful that a compromise could be obtained. Accordingly planning for the elections continued but was severely constrained not only by the shortage of time but also by the failure to resolve the "wish to live" controversy. It was seen by some that such a provision would, in effect, enable land to be designated for ownership by one of the factions involved.

A review took place of the National Elections that had been held earlier. It identified weaknesses in the registration of eligible voters and the supervision of the elector process. The Steering Board of the Peace Implementation Council had indicated that the Mission needed to take steps to ensure maximum enfranchisement of eligible voters, especially of refugees, and to reduce the potential for electoral malpractice through better supervision of the registration, polling and counting processes.

Attempts to resolve the differences continued, including those by John Kornblum, the US President's Special Envoy, but failed. It was then decided to postpone the elections because of the lack of political consent – very much in line with my own view. I instructed the election supply store that, for security purposes had been set up in Vienna, to dispose of any stock that could not be used for the new projected election date. Then the emphasis switched to preplanning for those elections on the assumption that they would be held in 1997. Part of that planning involved discussions with IFOR and ARCC commanders to identify the probable level of logistical and other support that SFOR (the successor of IFOR) could be expected to provide.

During this period I had visits from all the senior commanders and attended informal discussions at the various command locations and addressed meetings of senior officers, some of which were on a question and answer basis. As and when new commanders took over from their predecessors, they would visit me to update themselves on the likely way ahead as regards the municipal elections and the associated security requirement. Individual meetings also took place with ambassadors and senior diplomats from various embassies. Those revolved around the likely timings of the municipal elections and the possible quality levels and financial commitments.

A three-day review conference of election staff took place involving not only headquarters staff but also field office staff. A detailed outline plan for the municipal elections was prepared on the basis of the requirement for higher standards. I arranged that the conference be held in Dubrovnik. I had the pleasure of being guided around that ancient port by three high ranking military officers who gave a wide ranging history of the site and explained that the eventual fall of the fortress was due to the invention of mortars. That enabled the invaders to site their mortars on the hills overlooking the town and then to lob mortars over the defensive walls until the garrison surrendered.

The current budget for the Mission was to expire on December 31. The contacts with the embassy staff, as well as other sources, indicated that there could well be difficulty in obtaining the necessary funding as well as the number of personnel to act as supervisors at voter registration and the poll. Accordingly I prepared a paper, based on the outline plan from the election review conference. The paper was designed to emphasise the correlation between the standard of quality that could be obtained and the level of funding and staffing supplied. The paper stressed the need to have the commitment made by the OSCE member states prior to the commencement of the detailed preparations for the elections.

In the conclusion to the paper I stressed that municipal elections differ from other elections in that they involve smaller units of electors. Accordingly the results can be more easily influenced by electoral abuse and so it would be particularly important to have a high quality of control and supervision. In addition I stressed that finance alone could not guarantee the attainment of the necessary standards. Adequate time must be provided both in the initial planning period and the subsequent operational phase. I concluded by saying that it is the correct combination of resources and time along with an appropriately geared organisational structure that would lead to the attainment of the desired standards. In so indicating I had in mind my view – that the dates set for the other elections had more to do with perceived political need, rather than the practicalities of running elections.

Just before Christmas I left Sarajevo to return home. However it was not to be my last word on on Bosnian municipal elections. I did pay a couple of very short visits to keep in touch with developments and also received, by fax and email at home, copies of relevant documents and minutes of meetings. At the end of January, I was asked for detailed comments on the ongoing planning for the municipal elections. My comments included reference to the fact that the Mission had yet to obtain the services of a Director General of Elections and that other senior posts had yet to be filled. To my mind there was some doubt in terms of experience and relevant expertise of the few remaining election staff in Mission. All that, I reported, resulted in grave doubts in my mind as to the feasibility of having a properly supervised election, of the right quality, in mid-July.

There were other areas of concern not least as regards the planned process for the registration of refugees which I regarded as a derogation of the OSCE's electoral duties. It was an easier and cheaper option but I viewed it as not providing the standard of election to a level that would overcome the justified criticism made after the September elections. I had made a number of suggestions as to the planning for the elections and it was clear, in the rather short time frame since then, that a different approach was being taken. In conclusion I pointed out that the municipal elections had to be postponed on two occasions and so OSCE should be concerned to ensure that adequate planning be provided. SFOR commanders had made it quite clear to me that the same logistical support that had been given last year could not be provided this time. In conclusion I did accept that the various factors involved may make it necessary to override the desire to have a higher quality than before and, if so, it should be clearly identified as such.

A BRIEF INTERMISSION

During several visits to Stockholm I had met with staff of the International Institute for Democracy and Electoral Assistance (IDEA). This is an organisation, supported by the Swedish Government, with the objective of promoting and advancing sustainable democracy and electoral processes throughout the world. At the end of December 1998 I was invited to a meeting at its headquarters in Stockholm to discuss the possibility of my employment with International IDEA. They arranged my flight and accommodation. The office was located on a small island just a few metres from the road and accessed by a very short bridge.

During my visit several senior staff members interviewed me in turn and afterwards the Secretary-General invited me to join the organisation to oversee and report on the development of democracy in the Southern Hemisphere. I would not have to be based in Stockholm but could travel to and from home and only attend Stockholm for a brief period once a month.

At the time I had being giving some thought as to when I wished to retire from the post of Chief Electoral Officer and also what I would like to do on retirement. On the other hand, the Northern Ireland Office had indicated that they would be very content for me to remain in post for some years ahead. Even so, the offer made by International IDEA both intrigued and attracted me. Accordingly I accepted the offer and decided to give consideration over the start of the New Year as to when I should resign from my office. Then the peace process in Northern Ireland began to run into difficulties and if there was to be no resolution, there was the possibility of a return to violence. Even if that was not to be the case there was the strong likelihood of a referendum being held in early or mid-1999. In the circumstances I reluctantly decided to stay in my post as Chief Electoral Officer and notified International IDEA of my decision and apologised for any inconvenience caused. I wrote a personal note to the Secretary–General and he fully understood the reasons for my change of mind.

In March of the following year, 1999, I was invited to the Electoral Assistance Division of the UN in the UN Plaza Building in New York for a brief visit. There had been some ongoing discussion as to my possible appointment there for a period of six months to assist in the updating and re-designing of their processes. There were also other matters for discussion. Certain bureaucratic rules precluded that appointment.

My visit did give rise to some interest from a Northern Ireland source. When The UN personnel who I was visiting were called away for a staff meeting, I took advantage to have an early lunch in the UN staff restaurant. A BBC Northern Ireland-based political correspondent, who for some reason or other was attending the building, suddenly appeared at my table. Apparently he had seen me arrive in the canteen whilst he was having a snack and decided to investigate the reasons for my attendance in the UN building. He wondered if there were some unpublished negotiations regarding Northern Ireland taking place that involved my attendance. I convinced him otherwise.

EAST TIMOR

East Timor had been a long established colony of Portugal. The other part of Timor had been under Dutch control as one of its colonies, as indeed had also been Indonesia. When the Dutch left their colonies that part of Timor was absorbed into the newly independent state of Indonesia. East Timor remained under Portuguese control until 1975. As a result of an armed forces coup in Lisbon in 1974, a new Government emerged which decided on a policy of decolonisation. In the case of East Timor that came into effect in August 1975 when the Portuguese governor and administration left. A brief civil war followed resulting in the left-wing Fretilin party declaring East Timor independent. Immediately the Indonesian Government made a declaration integrating the territory into Indonesia. On December 7th Indonesian troops invaded and during the military crackdown and occupation that followed an estimated quarter of the population, some 200,000 persons, died as the combined outcome of that action and the famine that followed. At the time Malaysia was in the midst of a communist rebellion against British rule there and there was in some adjoining countries concern of possible communist expansion into the general region. There were reports of the Indonesians being encouraged in their action with armaments being supplied to them to facilitate their takeover.

In July 1976 President Soeharto (Indonesian spelling, often Suharto in foreign press) signed a Bill formally declaring East Timor as Indonesia's 27th province. The United Nations did not recognise this and indeed went on to state that Portugal was still the administering power. In 1983 the UN Commission on Human Rights affirmed East Timor's right to independence. The East Timorese continued to resist the occupation including military action from the Falintil, a paramilitary force operating from the hills, who had taken up arms after the Indonesian invasion. Their ranks had been bolstered by those whose villages had been destroyed by militias backed by the Indonesian army. On November 12th, 1991 Indonesian troops fired on a procession in the capital, Dili, following on from the funeral of an anti-Indonesian activist, resulting in a number of deaths. The Indonesians reported fifty deaths but human rights groups stated that at least 180 had died. In August of the following year the UN formally condemned the Indonesian violation of human rights in East Timor. In November the guerrilla leader Xanana Gusmao was captured and sentenced to 20 years imprisonment.

In 1998 there was a change of approach by the Indonesians. On May 1st, the Indonesian President Soeharto was forced from power, after 32 years in office, following mass protests and riots. His successor indicated, whilst insisting that East Timor would remain part of Indonesia, that he would consider offering wider autonomy and special status to it. Portugal rejected that. The pressure on Indonesia increased in the following year. Australia stated in January that it would back independence for the territory if the East Timorese decided to reject autonomy. The Indonesians then announced that they may discuss independence for the territory if East Timor were to reject autonomy.

On May 5th, 1999 several agreements were concluded between the Governments of Indonesia, Portugal and the Secretary-General of the United Nations. One, 'The New York Agreement' (NYA), provided that the Secretary-General would consult the East Timorese people on the proposed autonomy by means of a direct, secret and universal ballot and to put in place an appropriate UN mission in East Timor to carry out the Consultation. The Indonesian Government was to be responsible for maintaining peace and security so as to ensure that the popular Consultation could be carried out in a fair and peaceful way in an atmosphere free of intimidation, violence or interference from any side. Another agreement, 'The Modalities Agreement' (MA), ranged over a number of aspects including the obligation of the Indonesian authorities to ensure a secure environment for the process and to be responsible for the security of United Nations personnel. It also indicated the appointment of an Electoral Commission the members of which would include:

…an elections administrator with world-wide experience in problematic elections; a political scientist with extensive human rights and political/electoral reform experience; and a senior judge with expertise in constitutional and electoral theory and practice.

I was invited by the Secretary-General along with Johann Kriegler, a South African human rights lawyer and constitutional court justice, and Bong-Scuk Sohn, a political scientist, academic and member of Korea's National Election Commission, involved in her country's movement for political and electoral reform, to be a member of the Commission. In a subsequent press release the Secretary-General identified the three members appointed as "having a proven commitment to electoral reform and political transition and a reputation for uncompromising independence". He then went on to stress the independence of the Electoral Commission:

In the performance of its function and powers, the Commission is not subject to the direction or control of any person or authority. The commissioners were appointed by and report to the Secretary-General; and their mandate obliges them to maintain manifest independence in relation to the consultation exercise.

He also emphasised that our concern was to be that the consultation be both transparent and fair, giving the electorate a genuine opportunity to make an informed and free choice. We were not to be concerned with the outcome of the Consultation, but with the legitimacy of the process and its reliability as a true reflection of the will of the people.

Our mandate specified a number of tasks including:

- To determine in our opinion whether the register of voters was of sufficient quality to form the basis for the conduct of the Consultation.
- To determine whether in our opinion the Consultation had been able to provide an accurate reflection of the will of the people of East Timor.
- To ensure that the process was conducted in accordance with the NYA.

July of 1999 saw my arrival in Dili, the capital of East Timor, which overlooks the Strait of Wetar. I met up with my two colleagues at the building in which we were to be based. It appeared to have been previously used for educational purposes, possibly I thought as a teacher training college. It was the headquarters of the UN Mission (UNAMET) and was enclosed by a high wall topped with razor wire. (That wall, at a later stage of my stay, was to be the scene of events that I would not forget.) Various arrangements had to be set up including a vehicle and an interpreter as well as our office. We held a press conference at which the international media attended – a large number of such media personnel present in the territory did attend. Afterwards there was much to absorb including discussions with the Chief Electoral Officer, his staff and then to read and analyse the various rules and regulations applying to the Consultation.

After a short period staying in a hotel we managed to get a house to rent in the pleasant suburb of Villa Verdi, one of 46 villages that comprised Dili. The tension in the overall area was palpable and so I managed to get a radio-telephone that could be used as and when necessary in case of an emergency. In addition to the Indonesian forces, there were shadowy figures moving around wearing a type of informal uniform – an armed militia called the Aitarak. As I later found out they were East Timorese who were paid by and worked for the Indonesian forces and were dreaded by the citizenry. They demanded that all houses fly an Indonesian flag.

Voter registration began on July 16th, both within East Timor and at registration sites around the world. There were thirteen registration centres external to East Timor with eight located in Indonesia, four in Australia and others in Portugal, Macau, United States and Mozambique. The registration centre in the village of Zumalai in Ainaro District did not open for security reasons following a clash on 15 July between pro-integration militia members and villagers. One centre in Alas in the Manufahi District was reported as inaccessible: both of those centres opened by July 18th. Other centres closed temporarily in the following days due to security concerns. The first few days of registration proceeded relatively peacefully with substantial numbers attending. Initially registration had been scheduled to commence on July 13th, but had to be postponed for a couple of days due to the serious security situation then applying.

The Secretary-General had written to the Indonesian authorities informing them of the slight delay in the commencement of the registration process due to the security situation, that the security situation in the territory as a whole remained serious and that it was not possible for him to conclude that the security conditions existed for the peaceful implementation of the popular consultation. He recounted earlier meetings that his senior staff in Timor had with the Minister of Defence, the Chief of the Armed Forces and several others. At those meetings the Government of Indonesia reaffirmed its assurances that affirmative steps would be taken to improve the security situation. The relatively calm situation over the following days seemed to have resulted from that.

The registration process was extended by two days to cope with the problem posed by about 50,000 internal refugees. After August 6th, the last day, it was reported that at the 200 centres located throughout East Timor – 433,576 individuals had registered. The stations outside the territory registered – 12,680 – making a total of 446,256 registrants. The number of rejected applications was 913, of which 900 were within East Timor, and 13 at external sites. The registration process and the poll were overseen by a large number of observers. Overall 1,700 individuals were involved including official observers, fifty each from Indonesia and Portugal and smaller numbers from seven other countries – Australia, Brazil, Canada, Chile, Ireland, New Zealand and Spain.

To be registered as a voter an individual must have been born in East Timor or have one parent born there or be married to an East Timorese. In addition an identity card or, in lieu, an affidavit signed by a priest or local official had to be presented. There were various problems that arose in relation to the required documentation. For example in the case of proof of marriage it was possible to get a certificate in the case of church and civil marriages but not for traditional marriages. Those who had been refused registration had the right of appeal to UNAMET Appeal Commission. My two colleagues and I met with the Chief Electoral Officer and his staff to keep ourselves informed on the progress of such cases. There was one particular aspect of the appeal procedure that I noted. Those appealing had to attend a hearing at which their individual case would be examined for adjudication during which they would be asked to identify themselves and their place for registration. Many were concerned and indeed afraid to identify themselves at an open hearing. Should the referendum result be very close and the number of such cases be large, we would have to consider whether or not the overall result could have been affected. Accordingly we kept a close watch on the position.

The fear indicated above drew my attention to the procedure set out for the counting of the ballots at the close of the poll. The procedure specified that the counting would be carried out at the individual polling stations. That raised a number of concerns in my mind. The counting of votes at a consultation or referendum is not universally carried out at individual polling stations. It is often done at a number of regional counting centres with the overall result collated centrally. An alternative, especially in the case of a relatively small geographical area, is for the counting to take place at one central location. Operationally there are advantages in having a centralised count including a much more consistent and controlled determination of doubtful votes. In addition a centralised count provides a better degree of confidentiality for the individual voter who may be, or perceived to be, open to intimidation. The secrecy of the ballot is most important not just for the individual but for all those voting in a polling station covering a village or small area where politically inspired violence and intimidation has been widespread. If the ballots cast there were to be counted at the local polling station and the result announced indicating, say, that the overall vote was in favour of independence whilst the overall Timor vote was not, then that would leave the voters involved in a potentially exposed position.

I believed that the count should be carried out centrally. Such a count would enable the three of us in the Electoral Commission to be present during the count not only to observe but to advise as we saw appropriate. After discussing this with my colleagues, we decided to write to the Special Representative of the Secretary-General to recommend that approach and indicated several steps that could be taken to enable appropriate representatives to observe steps for the receipt and overnight storage of the boxes. It was then agreed to have a central count.

I travelled around registration centres. On one occasion together with Ambassador Jamsheed Marker, the Personal Representative of the UN Secretary-General, I went by helicopter to visit one area where it was very difficult and unsafe to go by road due to the presence of active Aitarak militia. When we tried to land at the relevant site we were prevented from doing so by a lorry being driven in circles around the narrow site. We had to terminate the attempt and return to base as it would not have been safe in the circumstances to land any where nearby.

On two other occasions I made use of an available helicopter. The intention on both occasions was to meet with the Falintil guerrillas at their base in a high and secluded mountain location. I wished to find out if they proposed to take part in the Consultation and also if they were planning to take any action against the Indonesian forces or the Aitarak, as that would inevitably ramp up the already existing security problems. I had made contact with an individual in Dili who professed to know the exact position of the base camp. He did not have any co-ordinates or other geographical indicators but assured me that he could identify the site from the air. Unfortunately, once we were airborne over where he thought the site was, it was evident that he was wrong. We flew back to the helicopter's base. I was determined to try again. When we had dismounted at the base I asked the officer in charge if he could assist me in any way in the identification of the Falintil camp. He recalled that a month or so before one of his pilots had taken a person from UNMIK who wished to visit that camp and was able to find it after some searching. He immediately contacted the pilot concerned who indicated that he could find the site again. Arrangements were then made for the flight on the following day.

This time I decided that I should be accompanied by one of my two colleagues. The flight took place in the helicopter that was, as before, very clearly identified by its UN markings. When we landed we were met by the commander. He had drawn up his fighters, men and women, in a military style parade and asked me to inspect them. I managed to evade that request in a diplomatic way that caused no offence and we then had a discussion with him and a number of others during which I learned that they had been expecting the flight. I enquired as to their intentions over the election period and if they would cease military activities during that time. He advised us that some of his fighters had already gone down from the hills to register and more would do so. He said that they were determined to vote. After two weeks of difficult negotiations by the UN with the Indonesian authorities it was agreed that it would be safe for them to come down from their hiding place to do so.

The method of voting to be used by all electors was the placing of an 'X', or a tick, or by punching a hole in one of the two spaces – indicating the choice of either independence or autonomy. Each of the polling screens had a nail with which the elector could punch the hole if that was the chosen method for marking the ballot. That method was designed to cater for illiterate voters. Subsequently a slogan appeared, no doubt from some of those advocating autonomy and targeted at the illiterate voters, telling them to punch a hole in the choice they hated!

As well as paying visits to various registration locations my colleagues and I had sight of the routine progress reports sent from each site, not only giving the progress of the registration to date but also any security or other concerns. In that manner we were able to appraise the progress and any problems experienced.

In the run up to the poll there was a determined campaign by the pro-integrationists involving parades and convoys throughout East Timor with vehicles and public spaces festooned with posters and banners. There were reports of some of their supporters distributing rice and building materials to villages as part of the campaign to win support from the rural Timorese poor. In contrast there were some areas in which both the pro-integration and pro-independence organisations were working with UNAMET to address potential obstacles to the campaign process. For example in the city of Ermera the leaders of both sides signed a memorandum of reconciliation in which they promised to conduct a safe and orderly campaign. In contrast, in other areas militia attacks and intimidation kept many citizens from participating in rallies. Indeed an international observation team reported that pro-integration militias had assaulted those who had participated in pro-independence rallies.

The political arm of the pro-independence movement, the CNRT, did open offices in Lospalos, Baucau and Colima but attempts to open offices in other districts were resisted by the pro-integration militia. In Maliana some of the CNRT leadership had to seek refuge in the district police headquarters. Their office in Manatuto was attacked as were those in a number of other areas. During the week preceding the poll, not only did militia attacks continue – they escalated. For example in Suai, armed militia attacked a group of 2,400 internally displaced persons (IDPs) who had gathered in the grounds of a Catholic church.

UNAMET officials reported that the plight of IDPs had worsened. Some 1200-1500 persons remained in Ossu or the surrounding mountains. In Suai the numbers of those sheltering at the local Catholic church increased substantially. The reported local leader of a militia, who was a Government official, had the water supply serving the IDPs switched off leaving them in an even more critical position. After a delegation of American observers from the Carter Centre visited and talked with local officials the water supply was resumed.

In view of the ongoing political violence my two colleagues and I wrote formally to the Special Representative of the Secretary-General pointing out the failure of the Government of Indonesia to properly comply with the fundamental obligations it had undertaken under the New York Agreement (NYA) of May 5th, 1999. We stressed the requirement for us, as the Electoral Commission, to determine whether in our opinion the Consultation has been able to provide an accurate reflection of the will of the people of East Timor. We indicated that in carrying out that task we had continuously evaluated the progress of the Consultation process and that, separately and jointly, we had formed certain preliminary yet firm views that we asked to be drawn to the urgent attention of the Secretary-General. Unless there was to be a significant and immediate remedial action by the Indonesian Government, we would have to hold that it had failed to meet its obligations under the Agreements. In addition we might be obliged to conclude that that failure resulted in a perversion of the poll in favour of the pro-autonomy camp. Four days later, after the Special Representative returned from his subsequent visit to Jakarta, we wrote to him again. On this occasion we informed him that we had just received urgent representations from the Portuguese Official Observer Mission stressing their deep concern at the deteriorating climate and voicing their fears that the process may be spoiled irreparably.

Falintil maintained its non-confrontational posture. It celebrated its 24th anniversary by holding simultaneous ceremonies in its three cantonments that were attended by thousands of its supporters. They claimed that the intention was to draw thousands of pro-independence supporters from the towns and so reduce the likelihood of confrontation with their opponents during the campaign period.

There were reports on polling day of people having camped out overnight at the polling stations on the eve of their opening in areas where the militias were active. Those who had fled to the mountains and forests came down in large groups to vote and then went back to their hideouts. The large turnout at the polls was probably seen by those in the pro-autonomy camp as indicating a failure to obtain their desired result. There was an increase in violence. Armed pro-Indonesian militias acted to seize control of towns and main roads. The spokesman for UNAMET stated that security throughout the territory was deteriorating and that two East Timorese drivers, employed by UNAMET, had been shot dead in the town of Maliana by militias. That brought the number of UN workers killed in the past few days to four, with five other local UN workers missing in the same town. The spokesman added that the militia had gone on a rampage all night in Maliana and by morning at least twenty houses were burning. He also said that all the UN staff there had to flee into the police station for protection. Later on the forty international staff, in ten UN vehicles with an escort of 100 Indonesian police, left the town on the way to Dili which they reached that afternoon.

Other areas suffered at the hands of the militias including the mountain village of Hatakesi, a strongly pro-independence area, where thousands of displaced people had voted. Twenty to thirty houses were burnt there. The militia also burned houses and fought local youths in the Dili suburb of Bacora. The security situation worsened in Dili. In the Bacora area, where six people had died in militia attacks the previous week, young men gathered to watch over their district as they awaited the result of the Consultation. As in other areas the old people had gone to the hills sometime before, but came back first thing in the morning to vote and went back immediately. In the hills outside Dili pro-independence youths gathered and armed themselves with knives, the only weapons they had. The militiamen set up several road blocks around Dili. The result of the Consultation was awaited with mixed emotions – hope that the result would be in favour of independence, coupled with fear of the likely response to that.

At the conclusion of the poll the ballot boxes were taken to the count centre at the museum building in Dili. UN helicopters landed in a nearby field bringing the boxes in from the regions. An ongoing week-long rampage by the militiamen continued forcing UNAMET monitors to withdraw from towns outside of Dili. Mobs of anti-independence activists seized control of the town of Maliana causing a group of fifty-four international police officers to flee to Dili.

Following the closure of the overall poll a formal complaint was lodged by a pro-autonomy representative claiming malpractice at the casting of votes. The only specific case they did supply concerned an illiterate voter. The Electoral

Commission was the final court of appeal and we decided to hear the complaint at a public hearing. The hearing was attended by a large number of internationals who had been involved in different roles in and about the election.

The person in whose name the complaint had been lodged attended accompanied by an individual from the pro-autonomy movement. The complaint reportedly had alleged that the polling station staff, under the guise of helping her to complete the ballot paper, had deliberately marked it as a vote for pro-independence instead of her wish to have it marked for pro-autonomy. I questioned the complainant. Whilst doing so I realised that the individual was probably overawed by the number of those attending and especially so as she lived in a small rural community. Accordingly I explained the questions I would like her to answer and assured her that if she did not fully understand any question to let me know so that I could explain it further to her. I gave her time to relax as I asked her to tell the hearing what had happened at each and every stage from when she had entered the polling station until her vote had been placed in the ballot box. I took time to do so and ensured that she fully understood each and every question and if any answer was not clear, I gently explored her replies to clarify the position as and when necessary. She only spoke Tetun, a local language, so there was the need to have a translation of my questions and her replies. Her companion did interpret her replies but one individual present, who had a good knowledge of the language, stated that her companion was not giving a true translation. The fact that there was someone in the hearing who understood the language seemed to then stop him from any further such action. After I had finished it was clearly apparent that her evidence had completely contradicted the basis of the complaint and so we rejected it.

As the counting of the votes commenced so did the escalation of violence that swept through parts of Dili and further afield. We could hear gunshots. Four UN staff members had been killed and six others remained missing in the previous few days. They were not the only victims among the 4,000 East Timorese employed by UNAMET in the running of the Consultation. The large numbers of refugees roaming around Dili were being terrorised by Aitarak militia and Indonesian soldiers. Shortly afterwards the militia attacked Bishop Belo's residence burning a building and forcing the large group of refugees to leave and take to the streets. We heard other reports of the seriously deteriorating situation and Johann and I decided to drive the short distance to the house in Villa Verdi to bring back some clean clothes and property to store in the UNAMET headquarters. As we drove there we caught sight of two males one of whom was holding an object in his clasped hands. He came running towards us and we heard the sound of shots. We did a hasty three-point turn in the car and raced back to the compound. It was clear that it would be unsafe to return to the house that night so we looked around the building to see where we could sleep. There were 150 others within the building with the same thought in mind. We got some large cardboard boxes to place on the concrete floor but we then changed our mind and decided instead to sleep in our car. There was little sleep that night as the car windows could not be kept opened, despite the heat, because of the many mosquitoes. The next day brought even more problems.

In the morning the sound of gunfire could then be heard in the immediate area. I went out from the building to see what was happening – the others decided to remain in the building. The sound of firing appeared to increase and I was able, through a very small gap in a heavily blocked steel door at the surrounding wall that had once led to the outside area, to see a mass of terrified women and children milling about. They obviously were looking for sanctuary in the UNAMET building. They could not get access through the only entrance as it was being guarded by Indonesian soldiers and also there were shadowy figures hanging about a short distance away. Then I heard the sound of people climbing the high wall surrounding the building. They were women with children and young babies fleeing from the militia. Suddenly I saw women appearing over the top of the wall to get into the safety of the compound. Not only had the women to climb the wall, but also to pull up the children as well. Then they had to get over the razor wire that was on the top. Some of the children got nasty cuts in the process. Worse still was the way they had to get a baby across the width of the wire – at times the woman on the outside edge of the top of the wall would toss a child over the width of the wire between her and a woman standing precariously on the inside edge of the wall top.

After all of them had gained access, they gathered together in the grounds of the compound. I could see the extreme fear in their eyes and especially so the children. One woman had a few words of English and I was able to learn that they had had no food or water for some time. I led them into the large, empty assembly hall where they could at least lie down and get some respite. Then I was able to locate a very large plastic container of drinking water and decided to first give some to the children and then to the adults who had together started to pray and sing hymns. I was happy that they had found some safety at last.

During that period the militia also fired shots right outside the Turismo Hotel in the centre of Dili that had become the base for many of the international media who were covering the Consultation, causing them to seek shelter in the more secure parts of the hotel. An Irish press reporter, who had spoken with me on a number of occasions, telephoned me to say that he and some of his colleagues had decided that they should leave Timor because of their fear of what was likely to happen when the result of the poll was announced. He said that they and a number of other media personnel had managed to hire an aircraft to fly them out within a few hours and that he could arrange a seat on the plane for me. I was grateful for his concern for my safety but I felt strongly that I would have to complete my assignment and also support those staff who were still in-country.

We were able to get to the count centre the next day. My two colleagues and I observed the overall process in detail. There were observers from both the pro-independence and pro-autonomy camps. The Chief Electoral Officer informed us that four ballot boxes had accidentally fallen to the ground whilst the helicopter carrying them was taking off. They had been damaged and the seals on them had been broken. We examined the boxes and their contents and checked that the number of ballot papers found was in line with the number of votes recorded as having been cast. To ensure that there would be no grounds for suggesting that the original ballots had been replaced, I examined the ballots in fine detail. We then took particular care to observe the overall determination of invalid votes. The count proceeded over three days, with first; the initial sequence of verification of the number of votes cast; then the determination of the number of valid votes; followed by the allocation of each to the choice indicated.

The voter turnout was 98.6% of those registered. Even before the count proceeded to the determination of the referendum result the violence escalated further. My colleagues and I went back to the house each night keeping a low profile and I used my radio phone to keep in touch with the UNAMET security centre. From time to time we could hear the rumble of vehicles passing on the nearby road and a careful look showed militias as the passengers in the back of each vehicle.

When the result was announced, showing that 78.5% of the voters had endorsed independence and by so doing had rejected the Indonesian proposal for special autonomy under Indonesian sovereignty, the militias went on a determined rampage. Members of the UNAMET mission concluded that they could no longer protect themselves let alone the refugees that had flocked to the headquarters in Dili. Staff were staying inside the building and I could hear the occasional shot being fired at the building from the hills overlooking. I decided to see what the position was as regards security at the entrance to the site and went there to find a brigadier of the Bangladesh Army, who had been seconded to UNAMET, standing by himself facing a couple of Indonesian soldiers who were just outside, presumably guarding the gate, and beyond which there were a number of armed militias. I stayed with the brigadier for a period to lend him some moral support. After some time I went back into the building and later on, after the militias had gone, the three of us went back to our house where we kept a very low profile.

International pressure on the Indonesian Government resulted in the announcement of the despatch of 1,400 more soldiers and 400 specially trained police officers. With armed militias controlling the streets and the death toll reportedly rising into the hundreds, Australia announced that it was putting its troops on emergency alert. There was a worldwide demand for a peacekeeping force to be sent into the territory. Earlier the Indonesian foreign minister said that the Consultation had been conducted fairly but that there had been some irregularities which he was confident would be investigated.

There was concern that the allegations might be used somehow or other to tarnish the result. It was decided, with the agreement of the Indonesian Government that the three of us would fly to Jakarta to hold a press conference in the Government Palace to present our findings on the alleged infringements. After we had packed up we were taken under Indonesian army escort to the airport and put on a military passenger airplane. The plane was full of senior uniformed personnel who were departing Timor and there were only a few individual vacant seats left. Accordingly the three of us were seated separately. The atmosphere in the plane was somewhat subdued and I came to the impression that the other passengers had been stationed in East Timor and were being repatriated to Indonesia. The three of us were served with a meal along with the other passengers. I was fortunate enough to have a window seat and so could keenly watch the ongoing vista of a range of volcanic peaks stretching for a very long distance below us. Some were intact whilst others had large sections of the peaks missing, presumably caused by eruptions. Watching the changing visage below not only passed the time but was also very interesting.

Having landed at the Jakarta airport we were taken into the city and a short time afterwards the three of us went to the palace to commence the press conference. There was a very large number of international press reporters present as well as Indonesian Government representatives. Ambassador Marker, the Chief Electoral Officer and others from UNAMET sat alongside us. Sections of the Western media present questioned the Ambassador in a somewhat aggressive manner about alleged UN inactivity to deal with the security problem. He replied that he had made it quite clear that Indonesia had failed in its responsibility to maintain adequate security. An Indonesian reporter asked the Chief Electoral Officer about the various allegations that had been made by the pro-autonomy supporters about infringements of the electoral rules. The Chief Electoral Officer replied initially and then we, The Electoral Commissioners, categorically stated that each and every complaint was investigated whether it came from the Government, from the pro-autonomy, or from the pro-independence side. We stressed that the irregularities identified were not of significance. Ambassador Marker then stressed that there could be no doubt that the overwhelming majority of the people in the territory wished to separate from Indonesia. On that note the conference ended.

Afterwards we were informed that travel arrangements had been made for our homeward journeys. I was concerned about those staff left behind in Timor but I was assured that increased security measures had been applied.

I arrived home in the late evening. Passing by a local shop I stopped to buy a newspaper little thinking that I would be on the main front page headline. "Derry man under siege in East Timor" it screamed out accompanied by a photograph of me. It was a copy left over from the previous day when the editor was obviously unaware of my departure from Timor. I had an early night in bed, not only because I was tired but also because I wanted to get back to my office in Belfast first thing the next morning. I got up at the usual time of 4.50 am to wash and breakfast before walking to the bus depot. That took the usual 30 minutes to arrive in time for the 6.30 express coach to Belfast. I had a doze on the bus during the two hour journey.

REPUBLIC OF MONTENEGRO

The Office for Democratic Institutions and Human Rights (ODIHR), part of the Organisation for Security and Co-operation in Europe (OSCE), contacted me in late January 2000. A number of meetings were being set up in Montenegro and they invited me to join their team on a visit to the Republic of Montenegro to ascertain the legal and other arrangements for two municipal elections to be held in February. The two elections only covered part (involving some one third of the overall electorate), not the whole, of the Republic. Within the Republic there was an ongoing debate regarding possible moves towards independence from the Federal Republic of Yugoslavia. The two elections were an opportunity to gauge the effectiveness of the electoral process and the legal framework involved in the context of a possible referendum being held. In addition it could afford the opportunity to meet with the Serbian opposition and to seek their views both on the situation in Montenegro and indeed in the greater Serbian area. The political climate within the Republic became less conducive to such a visit and so it was abandoned.

Early in March 2001 I was sent details of the arrangements being proposed for a possible referendum and asked to assist ODIHR in the development of associated matters by drafting comments and suggested amendments. A parliamentary general election was scheduled for April 22nd, and senior ODIHR staff who had visited the country a week or so earlier had reported on the extreme polarisation of political life there over the referendum issue. The referendum was expected to be run as early as June. In the circumstances the scheduled parliamentary elections could act as an operational test bed for the referendum.

The ODIHR senior staff had discussions with the President, the speaker of Parliament and the Prime Minister regarding the existing referendum law and particularly regarding the introduction of some level of qualified majority. There was some readiness to considering amending the existing law. I was asked if I could, as soon as possible, go on a short mission to Podgorica, the capital, to help in persuading the Montenegro authorities to seriously consider the suggested amendments. Unfortunately I had made other commitments that precluded such a visit at that immediate time. Arriving on July 24th, I did pay a visit to Montenegro – enabling me to meet up with various political groupings along the lines proposed for the failed meeting and I then made recommendations to ODIHR.

MACEDONIA

Macedonia seceded from the then Republic of Yugoslavia after a referendum in September 1991. Greece immediately demanded that the international community not recognise it by that name as they viewed the proper use of the name as referring to part of Greece. The country changed its name to North Macedonia in February 2019. This came with Greek approval, who subsequently dropped their veto of the Macedonian application to join the EU.

The previous time that I had been in Macedonia was when I flew in by helicopter from Bosnia on my way back home to get a flight from Skopje Airport. Normally I would have travelled by car but the weather forecast was for a very heavy snowfall and the pass on the way had already become snow-bound and was blocked by stranded vehicles. I had to get back to Belfast the next day or so, and hence the helicopter flight was arranged for me. Flying over the pass the pilot had to virtually skim over the trees as, with the thick snowfall, visibility was somewhat difficult. The loadmaster was virtually hanging out of the door advising the pilot on the clearance from the trees. It was not a pleasant experience. However on arrival I was able to relax in the Aleksandar Palace Hotel for an overnight stay before flying out the next morning.

In the Spring of 2002, I was approached to carry out an initial assessment in advance of a detailed Conflict Impact Assessment. I was in-country from May 13th to 17th. Whist I had studied conflict resolution – that aspect had, up to then, been ancillary to electoral matters but now it was the reverse. Before the visit I had time to read up, briefly, on the history of the country and especially on the persons who, to my mind, were so closely associated with the country – Alexander the Great and his father, Philip of Macedonia. I also carried out a desk-based appraisal to select specific areas for detailed examination on the ground.

During my visit I picked up some similarities to Northern Ireland. There were ethnic tensions but in this case there were three ethnic groups; Macedonian, Albanian and Roma with corresponding languages. An armed conflict commenced in February of 2001 resulting in ongoing security and political manifestations. That led to further disruption of inter-ethnic relations, the effects of which would take time to reduce and then restore confidence. Conflict prevention was obviously a sector for incorporation into any programme.

As regards the ethnic minorities there was the need to include measures to address the information and advice needs of two of them – the Albanian and Roma communities – as it was evident that their access to social justice and support services was often restricted by state structures. Both communities had the need for information, advice and practical support in exercising their statutory rights.

A Framework Agreement had been signed on August 13th, 2001. It provided for new laws in relation to, *inter alia*, non-discrimination and equable representation especially in relation to employment in public administration and public enterprises. It included provisions for the use and official recognition of specified languages. Elections were scheduled for September 2002. There were plans for the reduction in the number of municipalities and the decentralisation of power. Those aspects could well lead to an increase in inter- and intra-ethnic tensions.

It was highly desirable to develop full inter-community relationships. There was the danger that each community could still be content to go their separate ways. The media reflected that and my investigation into the ownership and control of the newspapers published revealed a far from desirable position. The following shows the language, control and ownership of the individual papers:

Macedonian Language
- *Dnevnik* — independent
- *Utrinski Vesnik* — private but related to a particular party
- *Vecer* — Government
- *Nova Makedonija* — Government
- *Vest* — private company along with some of the small political parties

Albanian Language
- *Fljaka* — Government
- *Fakti* — private but associated with a party

Turkish Language
- *Birlik* — Government and a body Turkey-Founos

It appeared that, in essence, the *Dnevnik* was the only truly independent paper. At the same time it was in a somewhat exposed position, operationally, in that its press and offices were in a building owned by the supporter of a political party. The editor informed me that they did not have any tenure and so could be given a very short time to leave, say a few weeks. There were no suitable premises to which they could then move.

Dnevnik had a ratio of 60:40 advertisements: news and many of the advertisements are placed by the Government. The Government did provide a subsidy to it and also to virtually all the papers. Those factors meant that the Government had an easy means of applying an economic sanction should it wish to do so. The Macedonian language paper, Nova Makedonija, and the Albanian language paper, Fljaka, both Government owned, were published on the same printing press. The Faculty of Journalism had recently expanded its output but there was still a shortage of sufficiently experienced journalists.

The various factors mentioned above, highlighted the need for an in-depth

Conflict Impact Assessment to follow my initial appraisal. It would be important to ensure that any developmental intervention did not impact negatively on existing tensions but rather build on social cohesion, tension reduction and poverty alleviation. With the decentralisation of decision making and the restructuring of municipalities, the provision of the necessary funding could be problematic without external funding. A number of external donor agencies, including USAID and the United Nations, did indicate an interest in being associated with the project.

CAMBODIA

In 2002 Cambodia held Commune Council Elections. The UN unit in country reported that credible elections had been held under difficult circumstances but that there were significant problems in the overall electoral process. The Head of the European Commission in Cambodia remarked that whilst the elections had shown that the lessons learned in the two previous elections had been taken on board, there were still areas of concern. The European Union Observation Mission commented that the provision of media coverage, with equal access by political parties, could usefully be handed over to another national institution to avoid conflict of interest at National Electoral Commission (NEC) level. Also a standing list of voters, compiled at commune level, would in future save both time and money. A voters list was currently made up for each election.

In April the Cambodian Institute for Cooperation and Peace organised a National Conference (NEC) to review the electoral experience including the work of the NEC since its inception in 1998. A special session was held for that purpose to discuss key priorities for the NEC and possible models. The NEC's Secretary–General gave the closing address in which he indicated that the election organising process faced many difficulties leading to dissatisfaction and criticism from some national and international actors. The NEC, he said, would like to accept constructive criticism with a view to using lessons learned for organising the next elections.

The Commune elections were an advance on the previous National Assembly elections on which an international resident representative had commented that impunity from election law and human rights violators, unequal access to and unconstructive limitations on media and a poor legal framework, should not again be the starting point. Another international resident representative referred to aspects of the 2002 Commune Elections that had been identified as detracting from the overall achievement. He particularly identified the aspects that needed attention including the composition and mandate of the NEC, the electoral environment with reference to intimidation and violence, enforcement of the law, the electoral campaign and the registration of voters and candidates.

I was asked to assist in the design and formation of a reformed NEC and attended in Phnom Penh in late June and early July 2002 to carry out my evaluation and the resulting recommendations which I then included in a written report. During my visit I met with the members of the outgoing NEC, the Secretary-General, the various heads of departments and other staff as well as senior representatives of the political parties and also the staff, including legal advisers, of the several international organisations having a presence in Cambodia. It was clear from the onset that the ongoing debate on the composition of the new NEC was somewhat centred on the political dimension and somewhat abstract in nature. The following were the proposals from the three main political parties having seats in the National Assembly:

Party A
5 -7 members, selected from eminent Khmer personalities.
The Ministry of Interior would make the selection for presentation to the Royal Government in order for it to be approved by the National Assembly eleven months prior to election day.

Party B
6 members to be chosen from the three political parties currently holding seats in the National Assembly.
Each of the parties to propose two candidates at least eleven months prior to election day. Then the National Assembly would consider a vote of confidence, by a two-thirds majority of its members, on the joint list of nominees. Candidates should be at least 35 years of age, eligible to vote and not hold any position in the state institution, Civil Service, political party or social organisation.

Party C
5 members to be appointed.
The president and vice-president to be chosen from civil society and the other three members from the main political parties – one from each. In addition the structures of the Provincial Electoral Commissions and the Community Electoral Commissions should include representatives of political parties. As an after thought, Party C then decided to support Party's B proposals.

The total membership being proposed was relatively small in comparison to some other countries where there are up to twenty members. There is much to be said for having a compact and effective NEC, not least from the cost perspective. On the other hand consideration has to be given as to the precise role of the Commission and the duration of appointment. In the case of Cambodia it was the practice to appoint a new NEC twelve months prior to an election and then for it to only operate for that election period. A new NEC would then be appointed in the run up to the next election. The reform of the Committee would need to extend beyond the role of the members and their selection process and into the structure, duties and responsibilities of the NEC staff.

There was concern on my part on the emphasis being placed on the selection and appointment of members without due consideration on the precise duties that the NEC would, in the new context, have to perform. Of course there is the understandable interest by politicians in the selection of the members but, at the same time, there is a clear relevance between the collective functions and responsibilities assigned to the NEC members and the appropriate number of members for appointment. In addition the membership of the subordinate regional and commune commissions are of much importance as they are the electoral cutting edge.

One other important aspect is a major player in the effectiveness of any election – the accuracy of the list of voters. The past practise had been to use a periodic list. The somewhat infrequent top up of the register was rightly described as *inefficient, costly and confusing to the electors* (and) *that some type of continuous register should replace the periodic list.* The responsibility for the lists could be given to the Commune Clerks. There were 1,621 such clerks and they could regularly transfer updates to the National Election computer centre.

There was the option of the NEC operating in an oversight role rather than in a operational role. If so it could properly operate as a quasi-judicial tribunal for, say, complaints and appeals. As it would not have been part of the decision-making process, there would be no conflict of interest, and it could deal expeditiously and effectively with such complaints and appeals. The actual operation of the election could be carried out by a separate organisation manned by a coterie of experienced and capable staff under a chief executive.

There were other possible options that I considered after consultations with the various players and those options were also included in my report, which also stressed the need for stability after change. Experience elsewhere indicates that frequent or ongoing changes to electoral arrangements or electoral law can have an unsettling effect on the overall political climate. It can also lead to the general public itself becoming somewhat cynical of the political process itself: hence the need for stability. That was of particular reference to Cambodia bearing in mind the trauma that had been inflicted on the country over centuries down to modern times.

Many younger people in the West savour the beauty of Angkor Wat, built in the 1100s, as the iconic symbol of Cambodia. The abiding images for my generation are of horror and tragedy during the reign of the Khmer Rouge under Pol Pot from 1975 to 1978 – when up to two million people died through overwork, starvation, disease and execution. Even when the Khmer Rouge was overthrown in 1979, civil war continued for decades. The country had been down the centuries the target for exploitation by neighbouring countries such as Thailand

and Vietnam. In the latter part of the nineteenth century the French were invited by the Cambodian King to protect his state from those two countries. The result was that it became a French Protectorate. The French did carry out structural development but heavy taxes were levied and as a consequence Cambodian nationalism grew. The Japanese invaded in 1941 but after the Second World War the French returned and subsequently granted independence in November 1953.

In 1968 the Communists began a civil war and America bombed Cambodia to prevent, unsuccessfully, a takeover by the Communists who nevertheless captured Phnom Penn in April 1975. A war with Vietnam followed until 1989. Then a provisional government ruled until 1993 when elections were held and a Constitution framed. The Khmer Rouge refused to take part in those elections and tried to continue their guerrilla war, but peace returned to the country. The people remain poor but the economy is growing.

I departed Cambodia in the hope that at long last the people would find both long lasting peace and some prosperity and that the international community would actively assist in that process. It also, in my mind, placed Northern Ireland's problems in perspective.

INDONESIA

On June 7th, 1999 Indonesia held its first free and fair election in 44 years. The contest was for 462 of the 500 seats in the National Parliament with the remaining 38 seats being reserved for the military. It also included contest for seats in the provincial and regency/municipal legislatures. The 1999 elections were widely regarded, both domestically and internationally, to have been acceptable overall.

In 1998 the UN had been requested by the Indonesian Government for assistance from international donors for help in the electoral process. That assistance was considered to have contributed to the success of the 1999 elections which included a high voter turnout combined with the active involvement of civil society. Voter turnout was close to 86% of the total electorate of more than 104 million people across the largest archipelagic state in the world consisting of around 17,000 islands.

That achievement resulted from a number of changes to the electoral management combined with a strong official commitment and determination to have free and fair elections. Additional safeguards were introduced to prevent electoral abuse as, for example, the use of indelible ink to ensure that each voter could only vote once. Both national and international observers were utilised so that the result could be seen as free and fair. Foreign financial and technical assistance, totalling 90 million US dollars, played an important role. It was then the largest ever support programme to a nationally run election that had ever been seen in any country.

The transformation of Indonesia's systems of governance began after the resignation of the former President Soeharto (Indonesian spelling used here, foreign press generally use Suharto) in May 1998 after he had ruled for 32 years. His resignation was partly due to the ongoing financial crisis of the late 1990s to which the people responded with demands for a radical overhaul of the institutions of governance to make them more accountable and focused on serving the broad public interest rather than narrow private interests.

Following the 1999 elections a full review of the 1945 Constitution was initiated and resulted in fundamental changes in the political institutions of Indonesia. Those included the separation of powers and the principle of checks and balances. The police and military were separated and the representation of the armed forces in parliament was to be terminated by 2004.

Indonesia's State Guidelines on Policy had as its main goal "the realisation of an Indonesian society that is peaceful, democratic, just, competitive, advanced and prosperous". As part of that process the National 2000-2004 five-year plan had, as two of its main priorities, the development of a democratic political system and maintaining national unity, along with the realisation of the supremacy of law and good governance. In August 2002 the People's Consultative Assembly approved an amendment providing for the popular election of the President and Vice-President of the Republic beginning in 2004 by means of a two round direct election along with the establishment of a second regionally based elected chamber.

In September attention turned to the new political and electoral legislation required to fulfil the significant changes made the previous month. The election law itself, the law on political parties, the new law on presidential elections and that applying to the structure and composition of state representative institutions were for consideration. In addition the law relating to the new Constitutional Court had to be enacted.

The international community was asked to assist in the overall process up to, during and after the planned 2004 elections. I was asked to assist in the role of the Elections Evaluation Adviser. That required a good and constructive relationship with the members of the Electoral Commission and its senior staff so as to obtain their recognition of the problems that may arise and the necessary corrective action and organisational development required. It was a wide ranging remit including the provision of technical assistance to the various sectors involved in the electoral processes.

I had been involved in the oversight of the referendum in East Timor that led to its independence from Indonesia in somewhat strained circumstances, and I wondered if I would be persona non grata in Indonesia. Before accepting the post I had asked that enquiries be made with the Indonesian authorities to see if they had any objections to my involvement. There were none and so I arrived in Jakarta at the start of April 2003.

There were some tensions apparent in the city as instanced by the massive parades of men and, separately, women on the following day. Rightly or wrongly I had the impression that they were a protest by those opposed to some aspects of the Government policies, perhaps in religious matters. On the other hand I enjoyed on rest days the beauty of the island of Java and especially the multi-coloured fishing boats at the various bays. Accompanied by a couple of other internationals I dined at a beach restaurant at the very tip of the island overlooking the 'Son of Krakatoa' volcano that had arisen from the remains of Krakatoa, which had erupted in the nineteenth century causing a tsunami that had taken many thousands of lives in and about the very spot on which we were sitting. The geography of the immediate area, being a very flat landscape at a very low level above the sea, left it exposed to the massive tsunami.

My visit centred on contact with the General Elections Commission (KPU). After detailed discussions and analysis of past events I saw the main emphasis of my report as being in relation to the staffing of the KPU although the question of funding was of relevance. Funding was likely from outside sources if the KPU was viewed as being capable of running the elections fairly and effectively. That, to my mind, indicated a dual approach. The first was to identify expertise from outside the country that could assist the KPU in establishing itself as and be seen to be, effective and equable to all involved in the contests. Then there was the need to identify the permanent posts required to run the Commission at the required level of efficiency at future events. In my report I made recommendations as the following indicates in summary. (A Programme Advisor and Election Adviser were already in place.)

International staff for a limited period
An experienced Operation and Logistics Adviser, with experience specifically in planning and organising elections at least part of which has been in a transitional period towards full democratic development and consolidation. There was the need for the officer to have sensitivity and awareness of cultural sensitivities, empathy and the ability to gain and maintain the trust and confidence of electoral commissioners. There were other detailed duties specified against which any applicant should also be measured.

Election Monitor Specialist whose duties were specified including experience in dealing with both national and international observers and in the accreditation of electoral monitoring organisations.

Election Evaluation Advisor whose duties were listed in the report. It stressed the need for the appointee to have the experience and gravitas to be able to relate to the members of the Elections Commission and its senior staff and obtain their recognition of the problems that may have arisen and their acceptance of the necessary corrective action and organisational development required. That would be necessary to enable an appropriately phased programme to be prepared.

Nationals to be recruited as staff for the KPU:
A detailed list was provided governing not only operational matters but also important aspects such as, for example, public information and media liaison. The task for those would be quite challenging bearing in mind the geographic spread of the country having the largest archipelagic state in the world comprising, as indicated above, over 17,000 islands.

It was both an interesting and challenging task and I left hoping that the required action would take place.

LEBANON
The National Commission for Electoral Law Reform was created on August 8th, 2005 and was mandated by the Council of Ministers to propose a new draft electoral law, ensuring in the process the widest possible participation of the electorate from across the political spectrum and all segments of society. That was very relevant to Lebanon bearing in mind its very recent history. The Lebanese Civil War had lasted from 1975 to 1990 resulting in 120,000 fatalities and an exodus of almost one million people. Before the war Lebanon had been multi-sectarian but under the former French colonial system from 1920 to 1943, the Maronite Christians had been at an advantage, with the parliamentary system favouring a leading position for them even though the Muslims were in a majority. In more modern times, in June 1982 the Israeli army attacked PLO bases in Lebanon after the PLO had attempted to assassinate the Israeli ambassador in London. There had been retaliation and counter-retaliation by both sides until the Israelis, with the tacit support of the Maronite leaders and militia, drove into East Beirut giving rise to the Siege of Beirut that month. A multi-national force came into Lebanon in the following August in an attempt to resolve the situation. Despite that, during the period of September 16-18th, Lebanon's Phalangists allied with the Israeli army killed up to 3,500 Lebanese in what became known as the Sabra and Shatila Massacre. The same year saw the Islamic Republic of Iran setting up a base in the Beqaa Valley, an area that had come under the control of Syria. In 1983 there was a resurgence of violence. This rather brief potted history illustrates some of the problem that had to be faced in the process of establishing a new start for the country.

The Commission requested the United Nations Development Programme (UNDP) to provide technical assistance in the fulfilment of its mandate. The Commission was particularly interested in the holding of briefings by international electoral experts on specific electoral themes identified by the Commission. In turn the relevant UNDP section contacted me to enquire if I would attend the briefings in early December 2005. The Commission was aware of my experience in other conflict zones and especially in the Balkans and in their meeting with me they concentrated on how refugees from conflict, émigrés and economic migrants could be embraced in the Lebanese electoral process. The position in relation to Lebanon was common to some other conflict related areas. The Commission was particularly interested in my views on the registration of, and voting procedures for, refugees, émigrés and other migrants. One of their major concerns was the right of and the method of voting by those who had gone abroad or had sought refuge in refugee camps in neighbouring countries but who were desirous of returning home at the first opportunity when it was safe to do so. In many such cases their homes had been destroyed or occupied and hence they could not return unless and until housing was made available. It is possible even then that they might not be able to return out of fear or ethnic tensions.

Electoral registration of such persons usually takes place at the various refugee camps and not infrequently the registration is carried out by an international NGO which could also organise/supervise any poll. Would-be registrants are usually required to produce some evidence of entitlement although in many such cases the relevant documents may well have been left behind or destroyed in the conflict. In such circumstances the registration officers seek confirmation of entitlement through a search of available official documents in the home country by whatever means, direct or indirect. That type of issue has to be addressed and I had experience of that in various countries and especially in the former Yugoslavia. The overall approach should be one of enablement as opposed to a reactive one.

One aspect for consideration is the address/constituency for registration. In the case of émigrés/economic migrants – there are several approaches that can be adopted. They included:

- At the in-country address at which the applicant had been registered before.

- At the in-country address at which the applicant would have been residing except for his/her absence.

- On a special list of out-of-country voters for a particular constituency with which the applicant has had some association.

- On a special list of all out-of-country voters for whom a number of specific, special parliamentary seats are assigned.

The period for the duration of registration has then to be considered. It can be restricted to yearly on the basis of a new annual application. There can be a maximum fixed term for such yearly registrations, for example limited to a maximum overall period of up to seven years depending on the situation in the country. An alternative would be to restrict the registration to a particular election. A decision has then to be made as to which type of election the individual can vote in.

As regards émigrés and economic migrants it is not common for them to have the franchise at local elections but the practice varies as regards parliamentary, presidential and constitutional referenda. In the case of refugees from conflict, the decision can vary depending on the particular circumstances.

As regards refugees from conflict the various options above could also be applied depending on the probability of the return of the refugees to the places from which they have fled.

In Lebanon there was particular interest in the approach to émigrés/economic migrants. There is no widely accepted standard applying to the right or otherwise of émigrés/economic migrants to be registered, or remain to be registered as the case may be, as voters in their country of citizenship. Some countries permit such registration provided that certain procedures are followed. In some cases registration requires attendance at an embassy or consulate. Many countries do not provide any such entitlement except in the case of state servants who are required by their duties to be resident abroad. Examples of such include diplomats, civil servants and military personnel.

The visit to Lebanon was very short, only the matter of a few days but I did get a chance to visit some of the historic sites and to learn first hand personal experiences of the conflict from some of those living in the country. Of course Lebanon, like many countries in various parts of the world, had an Irish pub – owned by a local man I must stress, where I did enjoy a fish supper – not a usual choice for me but very enjoyable nevertheless and a change from the local, very pleasant cuisine.

GUYANA

Before describing my experience in Guyana I would like to indicate a change in the approach by international organisations to countries entering into a more democratic mode of governance whether following on from civil war or the removal of dictatorships. At first the approach had been to provide financial and other assistance in the expectation of a desired outcome. Unfortunately that was not to be the result in many cases over a number of years – with such assistance being provided without any perceived change from previous failures. Guyana is a clear example of that. The change in approach resulted in the desire to have the use of an election evaluation advisor whose task was identified in one document that I received as having:

> *At least ten years experience at senior level in the management and the full operational aspects of elections and especially so in countries undergoing democratic consolidation. Experience in similar post electoral evaluations is highly desirable as is the ability not only to carry out the evaluation in a constructive manner but also to be perceived to do so. The advisor needs to have the experience and gravitas to be able to relate to members of the*

Electoral Commission and its senior staff and obtain their recognition of the problems that may have arisen and their acceptance of the necessary corrective action and organisational development required so that an appropriately phased programme can be prepared.

I had been carrying out that type of role for a number of years. Guyana was just another example how the input of financial and technical assistance can be of little effect if not applied in an appropriate and effective manner.

Guyana, covering an area of some 83,044 square miles, has 90% of its population in the narrow coastal plain comprising only 5% of the total land mass. The population at the time of my visit was estimated to be some 800,000. It had a spread of ethnic groups and religions as the following figures show:

Ethnic groups – East Indian 50%, Black 36%, mixed 7%, Amerindian 6%

Religions – Christian 50%, Hindu 35%, Muslim 10%, others 5%.

In a letter of February 2005 to the United Nations Department for Political Affairs the Chairman of Guyana Elections Commission requested support for the Guyana electoral process leading to the National Elections scheduled for June 2006. He had in mind two critical areas namely technical assistance and coordination of donor assistance. The United Nations had been involved at previous elections there. For example the UN had provided technical assistance at the National Elections held in March 2001 and also played the role of coordinator of international assistance. The United Nations Electoral Assistance Division decided to have a Needs Assessment carried out to evaluate the conditions for holding elections in 2006 and to make recommendations as to the most appropriate form of assistance. I was asked to carry out the assessment and arrived in Guyana at the start of May, 2005.

The political climate within Guyana appeared confrontational. The two main parties, the People's Progressive Party (PPP), then in power, and the People's National Congress (PNC), in opposition, were perceived to operate mainly on an ethic basis with the PNC regarded as mainly Afro-Guyanese and the PPP as mainly Indo-Guyanese. Both appeared to be unable or unwilling to come to a workable accommodation that would facilitate a reduction in ethnic tensions. Instead there was a tense and polarised society with the potential for civil unrest, especially ethnic violence, following any election.

The PPP had initially emerged in January 1950 as the first nationalist movement. Then it had as its main leaders, the Afro-Guyanese, Forbes Burnham, and the Indo-Guyanese, Cheddi Jagan. In 1955 the PPP split with its former chairman setting up what became the PNC. Guyana gained its independence in May 1966 and became a republic in February 1970. Burnham had ruled Guyana from December 1964 until his death in August 1985, first as Prime Minister and later, after the adoption of a new Constitution in 1980, as Executive President. The elections held during that period were viewed both in Guyana and abroad as fraudulent. Burnham's position was one of state socialism and one-party control. The new Prime Minister, Desmond Hoyte, ascended to the presidency and he moved the country to a market economy. The elections held during that period were generally regarded to have been held according to international standards but still there were initially violent protests in the capital, Georgetown, which then led on to a serious deterioration over a six-week period.

The general electorate appeared to be somewhat estranged from the political process other than as an expression of ethnicity. The failure to hold local government elections since 1994 (1994 was the first time in twenty-four years that Guyanese had the opportunity to vote for local officials) did not help to inculcate much ownership of the electoral process. The reported removal of some local government representatives and their replacement by unelected nominees added, as it were, insult to injury.

The political climate remained confrontational and appears to have been operated on an ethnic basis. The parties were either unable or unwilling to come to a workable accommodation that would not only reduce ethnic tension but would also have greatly assisted the socio-economic development of the country.

Some commentators were of the view that the PNC did not want elections in 2006 or indeed in the immediate future but instead preferred some form of power sharing. If the scheduled elections were to be delayed, the PNC was then thought likely to argue for an interim power sharing government. The party and its supporters, despite international observation and the conclusions reached by the observation missions, did not accept the results of the 1992, 1997 and 2001 elections. Street demonstrations ensued. After the 1997 elections there was a deteriorating situation lasting for almost two months until the Caribbean Community sent in a mission. It had an audit team to review the count that the PNC alleged had been manipulated. The audit reported that whilst there had been "procedural omissions" and "irregularities" the overall conclusion was that "no significant difference in the result of the count was found". When the PNC petitioned the High Court it pronounced in its adjudication, not announced until January 2001, "… the elections were not conducted in accordance with the law."

I found it interesting to note that when I visited the Election Commission's premises, I could see the sealed ballot boxes from both the 1997 and 2001 elections stored in 40-foot containers stacked in the grounds of the premises.

Before I met with the members of the Guyana Elections Commission (GECOM), I had heard reports of the poor relations within and between the Commission members. My visit did not dispel such reports. It appeared that the six part-time members constituting the Commission regarded their primary function as defending the interests of their individual political parties. During a later meeting with an opposition party it was openly stated that ongoing discussions took place with "their" Electoral Commissioners. In my meeting with the GECOM Secretariat there were clear indications that the Commissioners were getting involved in at least some aspects of the detailed operations of the Secretariat. That undermines the authority and status of senior staff and especially the Chief Electoral Officer who should have been fully entrusted with and held accountable for such matters. My overall impression was that GECOM was not up to the task in hand. That view was supported by comments I received from some donor representatives who perceived that GECOM was not as effective or as efficient a body as could reasonably have been expected, and not as proactive as the situation required. There was the view among so many donors that the overall assistance required, both financial and technical, would differ little from that afforded over the previous fourteen or more years since the international community had first became involved in the electoral process in Guyana.

The cost of elections was very high considering the comparatively small number of electors involved, some 44,000 at the last election, 90% of whom lived in the narrow coastal plain. Enquiries ascertained that the number of staff in GECOM had grown steadily. There were 104 permanent staff with 1,705 temporary staff employed in electoral registration and 8,908 temporary staff on polling day. As regards the number of polling stations, my enquiries revealed that the number of polling stations had grown from under 1,000 at the 1992 elections to almost 1,800 resulting in the number of electors allocated to any ballot box not being in excess of 450. I was told that the allocation was to ensure that there would not be long queues at the poll. (If, for example, the turn out was 70% then the actual maximum number of electors to be serviced at any ballot box would be 315 voters.) As a result of that decision there was an increase of over 4,000 in the total number of polling station staff. In some of the remote hinterland regions the number of voters being served by individual ballot boxes was in single figures. An audit carried out by an international organisation after the 1997 elections showed that 145 of the polling stations then in use, had fifty or less voters. Indeed 12 of them had only one voter and 25 had two – in such cases this was, in effect, a *de facto* breach of the secrecy of the ballot.

GECOM's approach to the recruitment and training of election staff was somewhat unusual. Invitations were published to notify the general public how to apply for polling station jobs without reference to any criteria such as age or previous experience. All applicants were invited to attend training sessions. At the 2001 elections 12,941 individuals applied and completed the required test. Those who attended were supplied with lunch boxes and in some cases transportation. A considerable amount of logistical support and expenditure was involved. A GECOM nominee and two scrutineers, one each from the two major political parties, then screened the lists and intensive training programmes were offered to new persons proposed by the stakeholders. Not surprisingly some senior staff formally protested at the involvement of political parties in the final selection of polling staff.

The role of the Election Commission was spelt out in the Constitution – Article 161 of which states:

> *It is hereby declared that the role of political parties and their nominees in the conduct of elections by the Electoral Commission shall be limited to their participation in determining policy, monitoring the electoral process and the conduct of the election but it does not include active management of the electoral process.*

The legislation applying was the 1964 Representation of the People's Act. It stipulated that each one of the country's registration divisions established under the National Registration Act constitutes a polling division – and hence must have at least one ballot box. Despite population shifts the boundaries of the registration divisions had not been changed and that resulted in the somewhat incongruous position referred to above. The overall increase in the number of polling stations added considerably to the organisational requirements, as well as to the overall cost of the election, especially to the recruitment and training costs. I gained the impression of a somewhat ungainly organisation with either the inability or the unwillingness to remove ineffectual performers. I wondered if there was a level of political influence in relation to such employment and that the significant level of international assistance provided in the past was regarded as a means of providing jobs, even if in a very short term, and hence money into the local economies.

GECOM comprised a full-time chairman and six other part-time, members. The chairman is chosen by the President from a list of six candidates – "*not unacceptable to the President*" – presented to him by the Leader of the Opposition after meaningful consultation with political parties represented in the National Assembly. Three of the other Commissioners were in effect representing the PPP and the other three, the opposition. There was no specified term of appointment and no commitment to serve for a minimum term. With previous GECOMs that had been appointed only for the period of a particular election, some of its members did resign so that they could stand for that election leaving an understaffed Commission at a critical stage in the preparations for the election.

The registration of electors is such an important part of any electoral process. Voter registration had been a contentious issue over the previous number of elections with allegations of 'padding' and deliberate omissions. The National Register of Registrants (NNR) included those who at the time of compilation were of fourteen years-of-age or over, although voting was restricted to those of eighteen or over. The process of the compilation of the register involved several stages. The NNR, which was compiled at somewhat infrequent intervals, was used to prepare a Provisional Voters List (PVL). Then a period was allowed for the submission of claims and objections. After they had been dealt with, a Revised Voters List (RVL) was produced and after further scrutiny, a Final Voters List (FVL) emerged. National ID, cards based on the FVL, were then produced and distributed. Commentators reported that the whole procedure was too complicated, resulting in persons on the FVL not receiving ID cards, whilst some persons who did receive ID cards found on polling day that they were not on the copy of the FVL supplied to the relevant polling station, possibly due to computer error or being assigned to the wrong polling station. The practice was that those without ID cards were allowed to vote if registered.

International observers at previous elections did suggest that the responsibility for the registration process be removed from GECOM. The opposition parties demanded that for the 2006 election a household canvass be carried out. In contrast a report by an assessment mission carried out by the Commonwealth Secretariat in September 2004 recommended that a house-to-house voter registration should not be undertaken before the next General and Regional Elections. It went on to recommend that house-to-house registration should take place every seven years and that GECOM should ensure that the funding and other arrangements be in place for such an exercise to be held by 2011.

The two main parties remained deeply divided over the way forward as regards electoral registration. The PPP supported the view that continuous registration was the way forward. In contrast the PNC regarded the NNR as terminally flawed and hence not an appropriate foundation on which to move forward with continuous registration. The political divide was reflected in the approach by GECOM in its voting on this matter. The chairman was unwilling to exercise a casting vote. Parliament was of the view that this was entirely a matter within the competence of GECOM. Such an ongoing dichotomy, if allowed to continue, would have had serious implications both for the timing of the elections and the political process as a whole.

The assessment covered a wide range of electoral aspects and I was content that I had got a full appreciation of the situation necessary for me to write my report after I had got home and had time to review and reflect on my experience.

KYRGYZ REPUBLIC

After the collapse of the USSR, the Kyrgyz Republic (widely known internationally as Kyrgyzstan) obtained its independence in 1991. The country gained a reputation for being the most free and most democratic in Central Asia. Kyrgyzstan became very open to the rest of the world and actively cooperated with international development and financial organisations. As such it was regarded as a model for the rest of the region. It initiated a transition to a democratic system of governance with the election of members of parliament and the first elected President of the Kyrgyz Republic. Subsequent parliamentary and presidential elections were held in 1997 and 2000. However the process was also accompanied by several amendments to the Constitution resulting in a shift of power from parliament to the President and a diminution in the role of political parties. There was a shift towards authoritarianism, through the use of executive presidential powers. Human rights were violated, as were the principles of free elections, the freedom of political parties and of the mass media as well as the independence of the judiciary. Corruption and professional incompetence became more apparent within the public sector.

The President, Askar Akaev (foreign press spelling Akayev) had written to the UN Secretary-General requesting assistance in the electoral field. A Needs Assessment Mission (NAM) was planned for February 2003. However as the date for the NAM approached it became clear that the process leading to a referendum on constitutional amendments, scheduled for February 2004, was giving rise to mounting controversy and tensions. Previously the period from 2001 to 2003 saw elections for some vacant posts and also for the heads of local self-governing bodies for newly established territorial units. Observation reports on those elections identified major problems such as:

- The buying of votes
- Officials handing out multiple ballots to voters
- Ballot papers being issued without the required identification documents
- The number of ballot papers cast in some instances exceeded the number of registered voters
- In some areas the process whereby names could be added to the Register of Electors, just prior to the poll, attracted many more additions than would normally be expected
- 'Family' voting
- Administration officials present at the polling stations
- Violations during the poll and on the calculation of votes
- Candidates' agents, authorised representatives and observers were not fully prepared and had no clear understanding of their rights

Many of the problems were serious and rooted in the past, especially the tradition of 'family' voting. The range and level of the problems varied from election to election.

It was decided to postpone the mission pending a reassessment of the situation in the country. On October 3rd, 2003 the President met with the Secretary-General and he reiterated his request for assistance. Tensions had subsided somewhat.

The Constitution specified that a presidency could only last for a maximum period of two consecutive terms. The President announced his intention to step down in 2005, at the end of his second term of office. The attainment of a smooth transfer of power, after the holding of legitimate and fair elections would be seen as good proof of the country's progress in democratisation and the rule of law. In addition it would set a positive precedent for other Central Asian countries. It was then decided to proceed with the mission.

I was asked to carry out the assessment and arrived in the country in November 2003. Just prior to my departure I was informed of a rumour that the President, despite his public announcement, was not going to resign but would continue in office.

On arrival in the country an early meeting was arranged with the President during which I was hoping to establish what exactly he had in mind. During this meeting I expressed the view that he would be relieved to be able to put aside the onerous duties of the office and enquired what plans he had in mind for the period after his resignation. He was quite straightforward in his reply. He said that he was not leaving the office but would stay on as President. I replied that I was under the impression that the Constitution did not permit that, to which he replied that the Constitution would be changed to accommodate his intention. At the end of our meeting he indicated that he had full confidence in the Chair of the Central Electoral Commission (CEC) and that the Chair was the person to whom all international bodies should relate.

I met with a wide range of national and international actors working within the country and also with the Kazakhstan, German, Russian and US ambassadors, the Speaker of Parliament, the President of the Supreme Court, the Chairperson of the Constitutional Court and the leaders of some of the political parties. In addition I also met with the leaders of various civil society organisations during which the clear message coming across was that there was considerable doubt on the perceived impartiality of the CEC itself and not only the CEC but also the Government as regards the effective and fair operation of the electoral process. There were also serious questions about the impartiality of the subordinate commissions that organised the poll and the counting of votes at individual polling stations.

Indications from international observer missions at recent elections also suggested that the accuracy of the voters lists continued to be a major problem. The register of voters is one of the foundation blocks of any electoral system. The registration of electors was not a function of the CEC or its components: rather it was the responsibility of local executive bodies except in the case of military voters, their family members and other voters who live on the territory of a military unit – where it was the responsibility of the military unit commander. Electoral registers were updated twice yearly – on July 1st and January 1st. The Head of Local Self-Government or military commander as the case may be, signs the updated register and each such register has to be delivered to the relevant Precinct Election Commission (PEC) not later than twenty days before an election. There was the provision for updating by the PEC by the use of additional lists. I learnt of reports that at some polling stations the number of additional voters had run into the hundreds.

My investigations identified the counting of the ballots cast as an area of concern. Both political party representatives and reports from international observers identified an insufficient oversight of the counting process. In some instances the level of lighting was inadequate, in others the sorting process was carried out in a very rough and ready fashion and there was insufficient room to accommodate observers. The completion and despatch of the protocols and the formal declaration of the counting result at each polling station was by far the sector that gave rise to most concern. An international organisation's report on the 2000 Presidential Election contained the following findings:

- Various locations where protocols were filled out using pencil and some were later changed. At other locations blank, signed protocols were forwarded to the Regional Election Commissions where some observers saw such blank protocols being filled out.

- Observers were denied access to the tabulation process of protocols but managed to obtain a copy of an official protocol for a polling station in Osh which differed substantially from the data entered into the computer:

Candidate	Protocol	Computer entry
Akaev	487 votes	887 votes
Tekebaev	450 votes	50 votes

On a challenge being made, the result on the computer was changed to agree with the protocol.

In addition I received reports from reliable sources of alleged planting of ballot papers in both Osh and Bishkek. In Osh bundles of folded ballot papers were found when the box was opened for the count. The ballot paper account was amended to agree with the number found in the box. In Bishkek at one polling station 701 ballot papers were found in the ballot box before the poll had opened.

Reports that I examined from more recent elections indicated similar problems and that there was, at the very least, the perception that the various levels of electoral commissions were open to pressure from the Government. There were clear indicators that such influence had impacted on election results. One way of having such influence was by the appointment of persons in controlled employment to membership of commissions who then, either willingly or under pressure, acted in a partisan manner. A report on the local Kenesh Elections held on September 21st, 2003 indicated that some PEC members had relationships with candidates that called their impartiality into question. In one instance the PEC chairman was a direct employee of a candidate on the ballot paper in his polling station.

I then revisited the CEC and raised the overall issue of commissions' membership with the chairman. He responded that the reason the same personnel were always used was that they were the only ones available and suitable. That may well have been the case in, for example, rural areas but not in cities and larger towns. On my first visit to the CEC I had been surprised to see that the office of the CEC was co-located in Government House in the capital, Bishkek, alongside the offices of the President and Prime Minister. In general, electoral commissions see the need to be located in a separate building so as to avoid any perception of lack of independence and impartiality. My unease was compounded when I ascertained that the CEC had the shared use of the Government computer and e-mail system to send out instructions at election times and the receipt of the election protocols from the polling stations. In addition visitors to the CEC had to go through the strict security system used for the overall site. The names and details of their visits were recorded.

The State automated computer system, *Shailoo,* was installed in 1998 as a joint project with international assistance to provide an informational, telecommunication and computer network, including e-mail. Its use by the CEC in the processing and transmission of information was regarded in an International Observation Mission Report at the 2000 Presidential Elections as providing ... *a remarkable level of transparency for the tabulation of results, allowing observers and candidates the possibility to audit the aggregation of results from the polling station to the CEC level.* Of course the system in itself cannot guarantee the accuracy of the information displayed and hence there was the need to ensure, and to be seen to ensure, that there were adequate safeguards installed.

Amongst the key areas of concern that had been identified during my meetings with both national and international actors were those in relation to the production, distribution and usage of ballot papers. International observers had identified occasions when marked ballot papers had been introduced into ballot boxes prior to the opening of the poll and also that official ballot papers had been in circulation other than within the polling stations. The lack of a proper system of audit and control of ballot papers facilitated attempts to thwart the democratic process.

The various political parties emphasised that there was a lack of interest by the general public in the electoral process. According to one estimate the majority of the people, 56%, lived in rural areas and their level of participation at the polls ranged from 15% to 55%. Some party activists inferred that at least some of the fraudulent practices identified were done to ensure the minimum required overall turnout of at least over 50%. A passing reference was made to Serbia where the recent elections there had been invalidated by a low turnout.

The role of the media is crucial in any civic education campaign. Media representatives made reference to the very useful seminars they had held with the assistance of the United Nations Development Programme (UNDP). At the same time they identified a number of constraints that made their task very difficult. The main, nation-wide, TV station was owned by the President's family. In addition the distribution of independent newspapers outside the main cities was very difficult. After the 2000 Presidential Election some private newspapers which had provided a platform for opposition candidates were said to have been faced with vexatious lawsuits, tax inspections and also the State-owned distribution network at times refusing to distribute their prints.

International observation reports on the 2000 election characterised the media environment as having an overwhelming tendency to portray opposition candidates in negative terms leaving concern about the future of freedom of expression and the autonomy of the media in Kyrgyzstan.

During my evaluation I spent just under a week travelling out to several rural areas to assist my understanding of the overall situation. That included the beautiful area around Lake Issyk Kul relatively close to Bishkek, then on to Naryn and the south-west of the country near Tajikistan and which, in one particular part, was a well known route for drug trafficking. Part of the journey took me up to the high mountains near the Chinese border where there were empty lorries travelling on the road into Kyrgyzstan with the intention of getting scrap metal or other recyclable material to bring back into China to meet the insatiable need there for such material. I saw a group of lorry drivers disassemble an old metal building at the side of the road to load up on their lorry for the return trip to China. High up at a mountain pass I saw a lorry driver lying under his lorry carrying out some type of repair. On my way back the lorry was gone and so I assumed that the repairs had been successful.

Down in the lower levels there were very large herds of horses. When I enquired of my translator as to why there were so many, he informed me that horsemeat was the preferred meat. During my travels I met with the local electoral commissions, political parties, civil society organisations and any international organisations' local staff. The regions were keen to portray their historic relationship with the Silk Road and several hotels and guest houses where I stayed overnight bore that name or one related to it such as 'Green Yard'. There were banners bearing the legend of the Silk Road and obviously the locals were very proud of the past connection. They were also keen, understandably, to attract tourists.

Back in Bishkek I compiled my notes in preparation for my report to be compiled back home. Sitting in the business lounge at the airport waiting to board a flight to Moscow, for onward transfer to London, I noticed a small group of men coming into the business lounge. A member of the staff attempted to stop their entry upon which a heated argument broke out. One of the men, better dressed than the others, entered into a fierce interaction with the staff member. A local person sitting near me, who spoke English overheard the argument and told me that the group were not entitled to be there and that the apparent leader of the group was a very minor politician who, with his colleagues, was going to a meeting in Moscow. As a result of the argument, which I was told contained some threats, the staff member withdrew and the group of men then made full and free use of the refreshments available.

When we boarded the aircraft the group of men were shown into the rear section, the economy section, of the plane. After all the passengers had boarded the plane the group leader came into the business section and took a seat there. The air hostess approached him and asked to see his boarding pass which he showed her. According to the person next to me the boarding pass was for economy class and so the man was told to return to his original seat. He refused and, apparently, made threats to the air hostess. She told the airplane captain, a Russian, who came out and told the man to return to his original seat. He again refused and the captain went into the cockpit from where he contacted the police. The plane sat on the runway for some time awaiting the arrival of the police. Apparently the pilot then informed the control tower that the airplane would not take off until the police had arrived and dealt with the situation. After some further time several police men appeared at the top of the aircraft steps from which they observed the individual for a brief period and then went back down the steps. A few moments later they reappeared at the top of the steps and went into the cockpit where apparently they told the pilot that they would not take any action and they then left the plane. My neighbour told me that the man involved was known to cause such problems before but was never dealt with due to his contacts with those in power. The pilot, after some more delay, decided to take off for Moscow.

My next visit took place in December 2005. Much had changed in the interval. Parliamentary elections, a two-stage system had been held in February-March of that year. The build-up of public resentment on the poor democratic quality of those elections erupted into the storming of Kyrgyzstan's White House (presidential building) on March 24th. President Askar Akaev fled the country and later submitted his resignation. With the flight of the President and his key ministers and the poor democratic quality of the elections, it was surprising that the new parliament gained both legitimacy and political recognition. It decided to bring forward the scheduled Presidential Election of October 2005 to July 10th – which resulted in the overwhelming vote for a former opposition leader. The overall political climate remained fragile.

At a meeting of the national Security Council on November 21st, the new President expressed his concern about the effectiveness of the country's law enforcement agencies and especially in the context of economic crimes. (The blatant buying of votes was perhaps a reflection of that. In the ongoing bleak economic climate some citizens perceived elections as an opportunity to obtain badly needed money or food rather than the opportunity for the exercise of the franchise in its own right. Some local commentators observed, "they vote with their stomachs".) An amendment to the Constitution was indicated – the former president had initiated four rounds of constitutional change that concentrated power into his hands. This time, one of the proposed amendments was the prevention of changes to the Constitution being used to prolong a term of an incumbent president. The draft amendments, which were published on November 21st, gave rise to controversy as regards certain aspects. The drafts included the abolition of the post of State Secretary, the merging of the Supreme and Constitutional Courts and, from 2010, the reintroduction of party lists at parliamentary elections. Initially the media had reported that the President was also considering the abolition of the post of Prime Minister and the creation of the post of Deputy President. The President made public the intention to hold a referendum on some key issues as, for example, the system of governance (presidential or parliamentary republic) and the immunity automatically provided to certain office holders.

The elections for the Heads of Local Self-Governance took place on 18 December, involving some 1,600 candidates, and were conducted in a relatively calm environment with only isolated incidents. The support being provided by the United Nations Development Programme was not solely related to the successful completion of the scheduled elections but rather was an integral part of a holistic process of democratic transition and governance. The purpose of my evaluation was to provide the UNDP with a clear analysis of the process and lessons to be learnt and to make strategic recommendations for the consolidation of good governance and democratic practices in Kyrgyzstan.

The preparation of the evaluation involved an extensive desk review of documentation, including reports from observation missions, NGOs and international partners, key actors in the field of electoral administration and processes, electoral system reform, electoral assistance, civic and voter education and other key persons and institutions involved. The interviews took place in Bishkek and also in the Naryn and Issyk-Kul oblast [regions or administrative divisions]. Feedback, whether in person or through documentation, will vary in terms of range, accuracy and intent and that had to be borne in mind during the evaluation process. The calendar for elections for the next two years indicated there were to be local elections in October 2004 and in 2005 parliamentary, presidential and local government elections. Clearly there was much to plan for and the feedback from previous elections would assist in the identification of areas for particular attention. The overall evaluation was to provide a clear analysis of the progress and lessons learned and to make strategic recommendations for the consolidation of good governance and democratic practices in Kyrgyzstan.

A report was then submitted to the UNDP including recommendations for a new programme, and associated objectives, covering the period 2006 to 2010.

REPUBLIC OF TAJIKISTAN

The country is landlocked and consists almost entirely of folded mountains. Only some 10% of the land is suitable for cultivation although the available, significant water resources do permit intensive agriculture and especially the cultivation of cotton. The population in 2004 was estimated to be 6.3 million with an ever increasing youthful sector. Almost two thirds of the population were living in poverty and one third of the workforce, 630,000, migrated each year to other countries for economic reasons.

Tajiks formed almost 50% of the population with Uzbeks 25% and a small number of Russians and others. As regards the religious composition 85% are Sunni with Shiites (Ismaili) 5% and some Orthodox Christians and Jews.

Like its neighbour, Kyrgyzstan, Tajikistan declared independence from the Soviet Union in 1991. Prior to that there had been violence between groups aligning themselves for or against the pro-Soviet nomenklatura in anticipation of the split from the Soviet Union. By the end of 1992 civil war had broken out between the United Tajik Opposition (UTP) and the Government of President Rakhmonov (he shortened his name to Rakhmon) resulting in some 30,000 deaths and the displacement of around a million. In October 1994 a cease-fire took place after UN-mediated talks. In June 1997 a General Agreement on Peace and National Accord was signed in Moscow. The Peace Accord was threatened by warlords fighting to keep control of parts of the country. In 1998 a renegade commander (an ethnic Uzbek) led an armed incursion into northern Tajikistan and was only repelled after some fighting. Then in 1999 and 2000 Tajikistan got caught up with disputes in neighbouring Kyrgyzstan and Uzbekistan when armed Islamic rebels used its territory as a launching base for forays against those two countries. That well illustrated the overall tensions existing in the region.

There are both ethnic and clan-related divisions within the country, perhaps aggravated by its mountainous nature. Corruption was seen as one of the most sensitive development challenges in the country. Such corruption was cultivated through the shadow economy, much of which was linked to the transit of drugs. Abuses in law enforcement were a serious problem. Police operations did not reflect legal practices and there were concerns about the independence and capacity of the justice system.

In April 2006 the Government of Tajikistan requested that a UN Needs Assessment Mission be sent to evaluate conditions for electoral assistance prior to the November 2006 Presidential Election. I was asked to carry out the mission and was in country in May. There had been parliamentary elections in 2005 and whilst they had been run in a peaceful manner one of the international observer missions commented that there was the failure to meet many key commitments for democratic elections and large scale irregularities had been evident.

One particular area of concern was the actions of some members of the District Electoral Commissions who had been appointed from senior officials of regional and local government associated with the ruling party. The actions reported included some instances where precinct protocols were altered on their receipt at District Electoral Commissions or, in a few instants, influence was brought to bear to have blank protocols submitted. As elsewhere I got the feeling that aside from the desire to have a favourable result there may have also been the desire that the Government candidates be seen to win by a comfortable, as opposed to a narrow, margin. The manipulative actions may also have been designed to ensure that the prescribed minimum turnout of over 50% would have been reached and so avoid a rerun that would otherwise be required under the legislation.

The principal objective of my mission was to provide an assessment of the Tajikistan electoral institutions and legal framework and then to indicate areas where they might be strengthened by the provision of United Nations electoral assistance. In addition the existing activities and plans of international donors in their provision of assistance to the democratic process were to be considered with a view to overall coordination and the avoidance of duplication.

Under the 1997 Peace Accord the ruling People's Democratic Party (PDP) agreed to share 30% of all governmental positions with the opposition Islamic Revival Party (IRP). The IRP was the only officially recognised Islamic party in the region. It focused more on national issues and identity in contrast to the banned Islamic movement Hizb ut-Tahrir that pursued a more radical pan-Islamic agenda. There were six other registered political parties – the Agrarian Party (AP), the Communist Party (CP), the Democratic Party (DP), the Economic Reformist Party (ERP), the Socialist Party (SP) and the Social Democratic Party (SDP).

Reports from the 2005 parliamentary elections referred to difficulties being placed in the way of some non-government parties. The head of the DP was detained in Moscow on various charges including terrorism and embezzlement. Within Tajikistan charges were brought against the leader of the unregistered Tarraqqiyot Party and he was arrested and detained. That action presumed that persons held in legal custody, even pending trial or on remand, were not eligible to stand at parliamentary elections.

An examination of the law relating to the registration of candidates at parliamentary elections revealed the following requirements to be met by each candidate for inclusion in the poll:

- A deposit equivalent to 200 minimum monthly salaries
- The signature of 500 eligible voters in the case of independent candidates

- Proof of higher education
- A mental health certificate
- Not being in legal custody and that included on remand or arrested and awaiting trial
- The submission of property and income statements

The first two of the listed requirements appear to have negated a significant number, some 100, of would-be candidates at the 2005 elections. Given the state of the economy at the time it is not surprising that a requirement for such a deposit, then the equivalent of US$800, was a very severe constraint and especially for those in the more rural areas and for women in general. Whilst the collection of 500 signatures would have been an irksome task, the main problem reported was the inconsistent approach to the validation of the submitted signatures and the vague nature of the provisions applying. It was reported that if more than 3% of the first 500 signatures examined were found to be invalid then, irrespective of the number of additional signatures on the paper, registration as a candidate was refused. The requirement for a mental health certificate was not reported as a difficulty on the day.

Disqualification on the grounds of being in legal custody or on remand or under arrest was in conflict with the provisions of the Constitution. Article 27 of the Constitution stated *…no one shall be considered guilty of a crime except by sentence of a court in accordance with the law.* Article 27 stated that *… a citizen shall have the right to take part in political life* but qualified that by stating *that …persons who had been deprived of liberty in accordance with a court sentence shall not have the right to take part in the elections and Referendums…* There were reports of two well known opposition leaders being excluded from the 2005 elections by the misuse of that provision. It was claimed that other opposition party members had been detained in the run up to the elections and so debarred from standing at the poll.

One aspect relating to the parliamentary elections that clearly needed attention before the next such election was the wide variation in the size of the electorate in the various constituencies. The size of constituencies varied greatly from some 50,000 electors in Vanj, to over 103,000 in Isfara – despite each returning the same number of parliamentarians. The electoral law permitted a maximum variation of 15% except in remote areas where it can be 20%. Clearly a boundary review should be carried out before the next parliamentary elections in 2010 in line with the prescribed permitted variation between constituencies.

A separate legal framework applies to presidential elections. The nomination procedure is quite different. Nomination can be effected through political parties, parliament and other bodies such as Federation of Independent Trade Unions of Tajikistan. A candidate has to have the support of 5% of the citizens and has to lodge the requisite number of signatures. For the 2006 November Presidential Election, I calculated that a minimum of 120,000 signatures would be required. The collection of the signatures is limited to 21 prescribed days and that is a very onerous requirement and especially for the smaller parties or those with limited resources. Unlike at parliamentary elections there was no restriction on candidature on persons being in legal custody such as on remand or awaiting trial.

The registration of electors was the task of the individual Precinct Electoral Commission under the supervision of the District Electoral Commission. This was done in conjunction with the khukumat [local municipal body] supplying relevant data on residents within its area to enable an initial voters list to be compiled. This was then checked and amended by means of a house-to-house canvass although it was not clear whether the latter was obligatory or a matter for discretion by the individual PEC. Reports from various international observers in the previous year, 2005, indicated that the process appeared to have been carried out carefully but that the process was open to multiple registrations with electors being registered in two or more areas. Electors could be included in the voters' list up to and including polling day on the presentation of identification. There was no legal requirement that an applicant produce proof of residence and hence there was both the possibility and perception of scope for artificial inflation of the voters' list on polling day. The experience of the 2005 parliamentary elections indicated that the number of such additions was not significant.

The existing registration process was generally recognised as being somewhat outdated. That was particularly the case as regards the registration of migrant workers who formed a significant sector of the overall electorate. There were some 3.1 million eligible voters at the 2005 elections. A centralised voter database was the way forward.

Looking at the overall situation it was apparent that whilst political reform had commenced there was much more to be done including democratising the state, increasing the efficiency, transparency and accountability of key state institutions as well as providing effective protection of human rights and freedom. My travels within the country had identified both north-south and east-west divides coupled with regionalism and clan-orientated policy, corruption and the infiltration of criminal elements into public life. There was the clear need to strengthen the capacity of democratic parties as their enhanced role could contribute to political stability and the fostering of national unity. Such a role was important in the circumstances of the existing strong presidential, much centralised, control then existing.

During my travels around the country I had a driver with a fine sense of humour. On one occasion whilst we were driving in the south-east of the country near to Afghanistan I asked him to be very careful to avoid accidentally crossing the un-demarcated border – he simply smiled and told me that we had just been across the border for a short time. I was very much aware of the long salient of a valley that formerly had been in British-governed India at the time of the long ongoing British-Russian Great Game over both sides' interest in the Indian subcontinent. Apparently both sides had come to some form of an understanding and Britain, wishing to preclude easy physical access for Russian influence, had that salient transferred to Afghanistan thus ensuring no direct physical contact with Russian controlled territory to and from India. It can be clearly seen on a map as the long thin, isolated finger of land on the top, eastern portion of Afghanistan.

Over some years Afghanistan featured in a number of approaches made to me concerning governance and related matters. I was very aware of the long list of those who had tried to conquer that country from Genghis Khan, Alexander the Great, Britain itself and more recently the Russians. The history of Afghanistan did not, to my mind, suggest that the combination of geographical features, the ethnic and tribal divisions along with geopolitical factors would be easily overcome so as to facilitate an infusion of democracy and central control. Accordingly I declined the various invitations.

SIERRA LEONE
The name Sierra Leone was applied by Portuguese explorers when they first caught site of the land from their ships. From the sea the hills behind the coastal plain appeared as the shape of resting lions and hence the name. Portuguese slave traders used a small island, Bunce Island, as a base to hold captives and then to transfer them to ocean-going ships. Later on British slave traders took on the role with 10,000 slaves being shipped to North America, mainly to the states of South Carolina and Georgia. Britain banned the slave trade in 1807 and used the Royal Navy to enforce it.

In 1787 British abolitionists established Freetown, the present capital, as a settlement for repatriated and rescued slaves. The early arrivals were American slaves from Nova Scotia. Sierra Leone became a British colony in 1808 as part of the British Territory of West Africa. Those two factors played a role in the two of the languages used to this day – English and Krio. The latter is derived from a combination of English and Creole. The repatriated and released slaves remained there with their descendants forming the bulk of the present day population on the coastal plain. Sierra Leone became independent in 1961.

My first visit to the country took place in 1994. During that time I became aware of the long history of Freetown and also of the differences between Freetown and the interior of the country. The inhabitants of the interior were native to the area and had their own customs and social relationships with chiefs and paramount chiefs. There was a clear divide between them and those in the coastal strip.

1991 saw the start of a civil war. The Revolutionary United Front (RUF) started its campaign by capturing towns on the border with Liberia. In 1992 the President was ousted in a military coup led by a relatively junior army officer, Captain Strasser, who then under international pressure announced plans for party elections. I was asked to form part of a three person team to review the position in country in relation to elections. It was to be a general, outline review.

On arrival in Lungi International Airport there was the usual emigration and customs checks and whilst going through customs the official asked me if I wished to contribute towards the kitty used for the purchase of their coffee refreshments. I put a small donation into the indicated box whereupon my suitcase was immediately marked with a chalked X and I was waved through. I stopped a short distance further on and observed how the next person was treated. He declined the requested contribution whereupon his luggage was immediately opened and all the contents were strewn across the table and examined in great detail one by one. I did not stop to see the outcome as I had to catch the ferry to cross the estuary to Freetown. There was a road to the capital but it was not safe to travel.

I stayed in the Mammy Yoko Hotel situated overlooking the ocean and the numerous fishing boats that seemed to go out during the night and which attracted, on their return each morning, numerous housewives buying the fish.

On my first day I took advantage of some spare time to tour around Freetown and visited the Anglican Cathedral which was reminiscent of British rule. It was a rather small church but the plaques around the walls were clear evidence of the price paid by the English upper-class in their role of overseeing the Empire. Each plaque was dedicated to an individual who had joined the Foreign Service and had been posted to serve in one of the various roles such as District Officer and had died quite young as a result of the tropical diseases that were prevalent there. Next I went to the Official Stationary Office to get copies of the relevant electoral legislation and found it to be virtually a shed. That and a brief walk around the town clearly highlighted the general poverty of the area.

The following day my colleagues and I paid a visit to the National Election Commission to get an update on its role and work to date. Next we visited Captain Strasser and his fellow coup d'état members to establish their perspective as to the way forward. The area we visited was secured by UN troops who were from the Nigerian Army. I was mindful of the fact that they were from a country that was itself not under democratic rule. It was then time to pay a courtesy call to the British High Commission.

It was important to travel to various towns such as Bo, Makeni and Kabala in the interior of the country to get the perspective away from Freetown. There were areas where diamonds had been found and where the ground had been entrenched in the search for them. In some instances the floors of houses and outside latrines had been dug up in the search. The RUF was being supplied with weapons and money by Charles Taylor then President of neighbouring Liberia. In addition they had the use of Liberia as a safe area. Taylor did support the rebels for a decade and received what became known as 'blood diamonds' for his help to the RUF. Such diamonds were illicitly processed through the normal diamond marketing arrangements.

The RUF had a brutal approach to the recruitment of fighters. It had a dual purpose approach. One aim was to frighten away the population from areas where diamonds could be found. The other aim was to isolate their very young recruits from family and other connections so that they had nowhere else to go other than to remain with the RUF. After selecting a village for attention the RUF fighters would surround the area and immediately butcher some residents. In addition they would pick out some people for special attention. They would be asked if they wanted a short sleeve or a long sleeve. A short sleeve was the amputation of an arm just above the elbow whilst the long sleeve was amputation at the wrist. Young boys were then instructed to kill a member of the family or otherwise they themselves would be killed. Having seen the action of the RUF fighters the individual would be in no doubt as to the threat being made. The young boys so recruited would be fed with drugs to make them fearless during fighting.

Whilst driving in the north west of the country, part of the road I was travelling on had been washed away by torrential rain. I enquired at a nearby hut as to an alternative route. I was told of a short timber road nearby that connected to the road I wanted. It very briefly passed through the neighbouring country of Guinea but would enable me to get back on to the road that I desired to use. The timber road turned out to be a road consisting of a raised wooden platform supported on timber pillars to enable it to pass over small ravines. The road had two parallel sets of tree trunks, the width of a vehicle apart, so that the wheels would be guided to avoid them going over the edge. Unfortunately at some points the timber guides had been worn away and whilst I was driving the front nearside wheel went out of the guides leaving the front of the vehicle body resting on the timber platform. Despite all my efforts I could not retrieve the situation. Eventually a local man passed nearby and I was able to ask him to get some help. A short time later a group of men appeared from a nearby village and did manage to get the vehicle back on track. It did cost me some money but I was happy to be able to drive on.

I drove on a short distance until a normal road appeared. It led to the frontier and much to my surprise I saw a uniformed man standing outside a small sentinel box. He was immaculately dressed in a uniform, crisp and ironed with a kepi on his head. The former French connection was very evident. He stamped my passport and waved me on. By now it was beginning to get late and I had been told that if I ran into problems there was a former Rice Research Station, at one time the most prominent in all of West Africa, where I could spend the night in if necessary.

Driving back into Sierra Leone I was able to find the Rice Research Station. It had been abandoned and was somewhat derelict. Nevertheless it provided shelter for the night although the shrill cry of monkeys and other animals in the adjoining forest kept me awake for most of the time.

During my travels it was important to visit and pay respects to the 'Paramount Chiefs'(the highest-level political leader in an administrative area) and tribal chiefs. It was clear that they were not very content with the central government in Freetown. This dichotomy was to become much more evident on my next visits to Sierra Leone. On one occasion during my travels I met up with a local villager, a teacher, who indicated that food aid being supplied to the area was being partly purloined on its way for delivery to the villages. Apparently the lorries carrying the aid were stopped at a secluded site; the sacks of rice were then partly emptied and re-sewn after being cut down in size. The process, he said, was overseen by a Paramount Chief who, no doubt, got a share of the booty. The lorries then continued on to the designated area with, apparently, the correct number of sacks.

There was a United Nations helicopter based near the Mammy Yoko hotel and it would transport personnel to the airport across the bay as opposed to having to use the somewhat decrepit ferry. I used it to get to the airport to start my trip home. Two days later, whilst taking staff out to the airport, the helicopter crashed into the sea and all the crew and passengers were lost.

In March 2001 the Sierra Leone NEC requested assistance from the United Nations in the form of electoral observation, technical assistance, logistics and security. It was decided to field a preliminary Needs Assessment Mission to assist in the preparation of a draft operational plan. I was asked to carry out that assessment and report back so that the UN could prepare the required draft operational plan. There had been significant developments since my previous visit. The UN troops helping to end the war came under attack in the east of the country and a number had been abducted. The rebels were closing in on Freetown. Britain sent 800 troops to evacuate British citizens and to secure the airport for UN peacekeepers. This was all despite the signing of an Agreement in Abuja, Nigeria on December 10th, 2000 on a ceasefire and cessation of hostilities between the Sierra Leone Government and the Revolutionary United Front (RUF). That Agreement had been witnessed by the representatives of six African countries – Ghana, Guinea, Liberia, Mali, Nigeria and Togo.

Leaving my hotel, the Mammy Yoko, on the first few mornings I noticed that the fishing boats were lying empty on the beach and with no sign of having been used for some time. The few fishermen who were about appeared to be poorly dressed as opposed to what I had seen on my previous visits to the country. In contrast to the past there were no women seeking to buy fish. I decided to make enquiries. Two very large trawlers were being used to intercept the shoals of fish far out at sea. The fish were then transferred at sea to Russian and other

East European factory ships for freezing and packaging for onward transmission to the countries involved. Thus not only were the local fishermen deprived of their livelihood, but the local inhabitants of their source of healthy food. I was ashamed to learn that the two massive trawlers involved were Irish. There were certain allegations about how the permits for fishing in the territorial waters had been obtained.

The Needs Assessment Mission (NAM) followed the same lines as that of 1994 and I reported back to the UN.

In the next few months the situation on the ground in Sierra Leone became even more fluid and rapidly deteriorated. The UN decided to have a much more detailed analysis covering a wider range of sectors in the political, security, constitutional and legal aspects. The overall situation was causing great concern in the greater West African region. The NAM's composition was widened to a total of three members. In addition to me there was a constitutional lawyer who had been a former South African Chief Electoral Officer and a Malaysian UN political affairs officer. In addition we had, as advisers, a Pakistani colonel and a UN administration and logistics staff officer who was a Canadian. Under the terms of reference the mission was to determine the type and extent of the UN involvement in the electoral process, to ascertain whether the UN had a role to play in meeting the needs identified and whether the UN had the capacity to play the proposed role. We were in country from August, 18th to 29th.

The mission consulted widely including with the Sierra Leone Police, the National Commission for Disarmament, Demobilisation and Reintegration. We also visited the cities of Bo (Southern Province) and Makeni (Northern Province) and conducted meetings with civil society, traditional leaders and regional ministers. An extensive reading list was consulted including the Sierra Leone Constitution, NEC documents and reports from the 1996 elections.

A number of significant changes had taken place since my last visit. The Government's term of office was to expire on September 30th, and the normal situation would be the holding of elections before that date. For various reasons the Government's period of office was extended by six months, as provided by Article 85 of the Constitution. Even so, the date for elections was not determined. Within parliament there was no agreement between the two main parties as to the format of the election. The two parties did not have sufficient seats to control parliament, and even if they did, there was much debate as to the type of electoral system that should be used. In contrast the Constitution was quite specific on the matter – it prescribed a constituency based electoral system and we gained the impression that that was also what the general public desired. The situation had become even more complicated as a consequence of the RUF action in May of 2000 which resulted in their exclusion from the political scene. There was the need to bring the RUF party back into the political process. There was still a deep divide between the political elite in Freetown and the rest of the country. In particular the 154 Chiefs, if fully engaged in the process, could greatly assist in the development of the body politic.

The Government had neither proposed to Parliament an electoral system nor consulted widely. We had concerns regarding the legality of an electoral system being imposed. The NEC was working on the consolidation of the various laws and decrees of the pre-1996 regime that formed the basis of the legal electoral framework. At the same time it was working on preparations to meet an election date of December 2001 but it did admit that that date was not possible. If so, another six-month extension to the Government's term would be required. The NEC staff complement was not yet completely filled. In addition the Government had only contributed 31% of the projected budget. Donors had come forward but only with part of the remaining amount. In addition the NEC had yet to identify all of the required 5,400 polling stations because in some parts of the country disarmament had not yet been completed and also some of the buildings previously used had been destroyed during the war.

The police were keen to be the prime mover in securing the election process but there were doubts that they had the capacity, in terms of personnel, infrastructure and equipment. Futhermore, they did not enjoy creditability in all parts of the country. The police had not been in some areas for ten years. A security plan was needed. We had the impression that the sense of security prevailing in Sierra Leone was fragile and that it would remain a risk factor in the electoral process if any party was not committed to peace. It was important that all the parties involved would perceive the electoral process as operating on a level playing field.

Given all the current circumstances in Sierra Leone, it was particularly important that the timing of elections had to be co-ordinated with all other relevant factors such as the time frames for disarmament and demobilisation and assistance to returnees, just to mention a few.

The Needs Assessment Mission report was quite detailed and specific. One of its proposals was that the UN mission in Sierra Leone should get more involved in both the oversight of the electoral process by having a robust engagement in the preparatory phase and possibly leading on to assistance in the delivery stage.

SAUDI ARABIA

In June 2004 the Royal Saudi Government sent an urgent request to the UN Secretary–General for expert advice in the running of the municipal council elections scheduled for October. I was asked to head a three-person needs assessment mission that was in country from July 17th to July 25th. The other two members of the mission were Palestinians who spent time doing the Hajj pilgrimage.

The Country Background
Geographically Saudi Arabia is divided into four (and if the Rub' al-Khali is included, five) major regions: the central Region, Western Region lying along the Red Sea coast, the Southern Region in the southern Red Sea border area and the Eastern Region, the stormy and sandy part. Administratively the Kingdom was divided into thirteen provinces having in total 178 municipalities.

The Constitution is based on and governed according to Shari'a (Islamic law). The Basic Law, introduced in 1993, constituted the basis on which the Kingdom was governed and the rights and obligations of both the State and the citizen. The Law defined the division of the power of the state between judicial power, executive power and organisational power subject to the provision that the king is the ultimate source of all those authorities.

The Consultative Council (Majlis Al-Shoura), inaugurated in 1993, had as its primary function the provision of advice to the King. In practise the Council was able to initiate legislation and review the domestic and foreign policies of the Government. Any action not approved by the Council had to be referred back to the King and hence the King remained the final arbiter of state affairs. Members, then numbering a speaker and 120 members, were appointed by the King and represented a wide mix of clan and religious leaders, business and professional men, academics and ex-government officials.

The Electoral Background
Elections were not new to Saudi Arabia if we take into account the municipal elections during the late 1950s and early 1960s. However, in the intervening period, there had not been any elections. A new municipal law had been enacted in 1979 to reorganise municipal administration but it was never implemented. Then in October 2003 the Council of Ministers announced its intention to re-enact the 1979 municipal law, with modifications, to provide for the election of half of each municipal council's members with the remainder being appointed. The Government's intention, as announced by the King to the Shoura Council in May 2003, was to increase citizens' participation. That included the election of officials for each local and provincial assembly and a third of the members of the National Consultative Council, incrementally, over a period of four to five years. Appointees were to fill the other seats on the various bodies. I understood that the intention behind that process was to ensure during the interim period that there would be sufficient qualified and competent members so as to provide effective governance. In that respect the forthcoming municipal elections were regarded as a test and, if successful, all municipal council seats may well be filled by election.

I ascertained that the franchise at the forthcoming municipal elections would be confined to male Saudis, 21 years of age or over, provided that they had been resident within the country at one address for a period to be specified immediately prior to the registration period. It was anticipated that the required residential period would be twelve months or perhaps less. There was one important exception to the right to the franchise – those who were members of the security forces. When I enquired as to why that was the case I was informally advised of the reason. The security forces were comprised of members of various tribes/clans that have had, both in the past and perhaps also, ongoing conflicting interests. Accordingly there was the perceived danger of introducing or increasing tension should such security force personnel participate in the election.

The limitation of the franchise to males was another aspect that I explored. Newspapers and other sources suggested that women would likely be enfranchised at the next municipal and subsequent regional and national elections. I could not confirm that. Indeed I sensed that this was a most sensitive issue that required very careful handling even during private discussions. At the same time I was well aware from my work, of the situation in the neighbouring country of Yemen where women were entitled to the franchise. That suggested to me that there were no religious constraints applying. Indeed, after careful enquiries, I was informed that neither secular nor religious laws forbid female participation but rather societal norms. The impression I gained was that the concern was focussed on the more radical religious elements that could use any such female participation to foment opposition, possibly by acts of violence which could lead to a destabilisation of the Government and of the overall security. I observed the number of military vehicles driving around with their machine guns manned and ready for action if necessary. In addition, in the government guest house where I was staying there was always an armed soldier close by my accommodation.

A National Society for Human Rights (NSHR) had been set up some four months prior to our arrival. The Government selected its members who included women but when I met with the NSHR only males were in attendance. I enquired about the absence of any woman member. It was stated that when women members attended they sat in a different room connected to the main room by microphones and speakers. It was clear that the NSHR was only in the throes of determining its own agenda and role.

Another human rights issue was the constraint against candidates standing as members of political parties – the requirement being that candidates stood as independents. The authorities appeared to be of the view that political activities, at least in the present, constituted a potential for destabilisation of the Government and the overall security situation in the same way as the extension of the franchise to women might. The expressed concerns could be seen in the high level of security visible on the ground. On the other hand there was a precedent for limited reform, as could be seen from the action of King Faisal in the 1960s when schools were opened for girls and a national TV station was launched. Of course what had changed since then was the introduction of external influences relating to international terrorism in general, and the war in Iraq in particular.

From my conversations I became aware of two opposing views within the ruling elite in relation to reform. There was the more positive approach recognising the need for an accelerated reform process. The other regarded the introduction of democracy as having the potential to give rise to something similar to the Taliban. Even the more moderate wing saw the need for a cautious approach with each step being evaluated before the next step would be proceeded with. The municipal elections were viewed in that context with, on the one hand, a concrete signal of change being given whilst, on the other, only one half of the seats being up for election so that continuing control could be maintained in the interim.

In the previous year Crown Prince Abdullah met with reformers and sponsored three National Dialogue rounds in June, December and just prior to our visit. There was talk of holding elections for the Shoura and Regional Councils. Then women were permitted to get commercial licenses in their own name as opposed to the provision whereby the name had to be that of a male guardian. However in March, twelve pro-reform activists were arrested. That may well have reflected the unease in the ruling elite of any tendency for the pace of reform being forced and especially so in the context of the deteriorating security situation with attacks on ex-pats on whom the oil industry was so dependent.

There were geopolitical aspects involved. Its neighbour to the south, Yemen, had recently introduced democratic practices. That was the exception to the general rule. Neither its neighbours in the east – Oman, UAE, Qatar, Bahrain and Kuwait – nor its neighbours in the north, Jordan and Iraq, had, as yet, proceeded down that pathway.

During the visit I met with a wide range of senior Saudi Arabian officials and visited various parts of the country. In addition I was invited to a formal, Arab-style, reception by the Crown Prince in his residence. He led me down the row of welcoming guests. In contrast to the various tribal guests, I was offered a chair to sit on but declined it and instead joined them in like style. Afterwards the Crown Prince took me for a drive around his gardens in his golf-buggy-type vehicle bearing a Rolls Royce badge during which he, with much justification, lauded the work of his Lebanese head gardener.

The report to the UN gave an assessment of the preparedness towards holding the elections and included a review of key issues such as the franchise and electoral institutional assistance needs. The report did indicate areas of concern.

CHAPTER 7
Academic and other conferences attended

There were plenty of invitations to attend such conferences that almost invariably were held in Europe. It was only possible to accept some and the following are representative of those I found more interesting.

CONFERENCE ON INTERNATIONAL ELECTORAL
EXPERIENCE IN THE BALKANS
This conference, organised by International IDEA, was held in Stockholm in September 2000 over three days. Senior representatives attended from the various international bodies that had been involved in the Balkan region. I was invited to attend. The sessions held covered the experience gained by the various international organisations involved in specific countries followed, in each case, by a discussion on the lessons to be learned. The studies included:

- Democratic Development in Kosovo – the issues and challenges faced followed by a discussion with members of the Central Election Commission involved.

- Members of the Council of Europe reported on Kosovo Election Observation Reports followed by a general discussion.

- Next other case studies took place involving other countries in the region. The first was on Bosnia and Herzegovina in 1996 and was headed by the Ambassador who had been the head of the International Mission in charge of the country then.

- The focus was then on the events in Albania in 1997 and was headed by a member of ODIHR.

- A senior journalist then addressed the conference on relations between Election Management bodies and the Media. That led on to a spirited discussion.

- The case study on Croatia 1999-2000 was led by senior members from ODIHR.

The conference then switched to a more general perspective including Election Management and Civil-Military Relations, Election Management Bodies and Political Bodies. On the final day a summary of the lessons learnt during the conference was drawn up along with specific lessons for Kosovo itself.

The event was very successful and enabled the experience gained in the several countries involved to be documented and with relevant aspects that could have reference to other countries tabulated.

BONN CONFERENCE ON FACING ETHNIC CONFLICTS

This conference, over the period December 14th – 16th, 2000, was organised by the University of Bonn's Centre for Development. It was opened by the mayor of Bonn along with the rector of the university and the director of the Centre for Development and then followed by a traditional German dinner and reception. The attendees were from a wide range of countries ranging from Africa, America, Australia, China, Europe, and Indonesia. I had been invited to chair a panel on 'Electoral Systems and Power-Sharing Arrangements'.

In all there were a total of twelve panels some of which ran parallel. There was a wide range of the topics down for discussion at the various panels each of which consisted of a chair and three speakers.

The wide range of the topics included:

Nation-State, Nationalism, and Democracy

Politics of Mobilisation

Prevention

Accommodation of Minorities

Ethnic Violence

Negotiating Peace 1: Strategies and Tactics

Negotiating Peace 2: Success and Failure

Ethnic Accommodation and the Economics of Violence

Peace Building and Mediation

Reconciliation

Federalism

Electoral Systems and Power-Sharing Arrangements

It was a very interesting experience with the opportunity to discuss hands-on experience with other practitioners and academics.

WORKSHOP IN WARSAW ON CONFLICT MANAGEMENT FOR ELECTORAL OFFICIALS

The workshop was held on October 9th -10th, 2001. to discuss and finalise a draft Conflict Management Training Course for Electoral Officials. The author was from the Centre for Study of Violence and Reconciliation and had invited comments from me and two others prior to the finalisation of the draft being presented.

After the objectives and the format of the workshop had been explained the author introduced and gave an overview of the draft paper. This was followed by general comments and a *tour de table*. It was then my turn to chair a discussion on key issues covering such aspects as 'taking action', the timing of such action and the potential dangers involved. A number of speakers developed the theme.

The next session focussed on priority issues and was followed by a discussion led by an academic from a Department of International Politics. There then followed a discussion on adapting the course material into three modules:

- Negotiation Module
- Third Party Intervention Module
- Facilitation Module

The framework for implementation was debated next followed by the conclusion and summing up.

It was very well attended with a widespread range of personnel having relevant experience in various countries of the world.

ANOTHER WORKSHOP IN POLAND

In January 2006 a conference was held in Warsaw on the possible implementation of an anti-corruption strategy in Poland. It was to review the provisions relating to corruption in the Polish election law and the available countermeasures. The Chairman of the Dutch National Electoral Council, who was also a professor of Comparative Constitutional Law, and I, were invited to give a comparative analysis of the electoral law and associated anti-corruption measures in our own individual countries by means of two papers to be presented at the conference. In addition we were asked to deliver a short report summarizing our evaluation of Polish election law and the anti-corruption actions in that field.

The first session, an introduction and briefing, outlined the perceived main problems of the existing Polish legislation relating to electoral law and corruption. Next there was a meeting with a senior Polish academic who presented his arguments for the change of the electoral system to a proportional system which, he argued, offered less scope for corruption.

In the afternoon there was a detailed presentation by a technical expert of the existing Polish election law. He regarded it to be, from a legal point of view, modern, sophisticated and almost perfect. After his overall analysis he then went on identify three specific areas having a high potential for corruption:

a) Supervision of the electoral process

b) Campaign funding

c) Suspect signatures

There then followed a team analysis and discussion on the information and material presented to us that day. The next day started with a seminar on the general topic with invited representatives from:

- Ministry of Interior and Administration
- National Electoral Bureau
- State Electoral Commission
- Anti-Corruption Bureau
- Ministry of Justice
- Supreme Court
- Internal Security Agency
- Institute of Public Affairs
- Other experts and university professors

Then it was the turn of my colleague and I to present our papers outlining the relevant legislation in our two individual countries in relation to corruption in the field of elections. I presented copies of relevant extracts of the UK legislation and quoted specific examples of reported cases. A lengthy discussion ensued. Then it was the time to deliver a short report summarising our evaluation of the Polish election law and the relevant anti-corruption legislation. We felt able to offer some thoughts for consideration based not just the legislation in both our countries but our experience abroad. Some of the aspects are listed below.

During a formal dinner that evening we participated in informal discussions with Polish legal experts and afterwards my colleague and I did our own analysis of the various papers presented and the ensuing discussions. The third day was less formal. We had informal discussions with fellow attendees and were able to meet with political process insiders to identify their proposals and concerns.

Poland had adapted a number of Acts to enhance the legislation relating to the financial side of political party electioneering. The first, under the campaign against corruption, was the 1997 Act on Political Parties. Since then it had been amended no less than five times. The last and very significant amendment, of December 2001, introduced a large-scale State financing of political parties along with expanded procedures and regulations designed to prevent funding from illegal sources. In addition the Finance Ministry introduced several Ordinances that addressed party financing issues. Legislation, no matter how appropriate and encompassing will not by itself prevent corruption. The National Electoral Commission (NEC) has an important role in the oversight of the financing of political party electoral funding including the financing of specific electoral campaigns. Whilst the specified requirements includes independent audit reports, we felt, that not only was it somewhat reactive, as opposed to proactive, but also that the NEC had limited capacity.

Under the legislation the time limit set for the acceptance or otherwise by the NEC of individual accounts was up to four months from their receipt. Closely following elections would result in a very heavy workload over a relatively short timeframe. We could see various scenarios where the sheer pressure of work could negate the prescribed oversight. In any event it is often the case that political parties establish transitory bodies for the election period only and they are then disbanded making it difficult to discipline months later.

Party funding is not confined to the period in and about elections. Accordingly there is the need for a general oversight throughout the year and that, combined with the time to process cases post-election, identifies the need for appropriate staffing outside election periods and the immediate post-election periods.

Another aspect we covered was the need for a well-defined audit trail. We viewed the existing lack of any prescribed penalties for an incorrect or illegitimate manner of managing the finances of an election fund as a serious omission. A proactive approach prescribing an effective audit trail through Ordinances could play a crucial role in the prevention of the corrupt practices that so far have been difficult to deal with. Example of such practices include 'anonymous' donations, 'generous' bank loans and the payment by donors of amounts well in excess of the stipulated maximum by the device of 'purchasing' through grossly inflated prices party programmes, publications and such like.

We learnt that at the nomination of a candidate at presidential elections, the forging of signatures of those on the nomination paper was not uncommon among the various parties. That did not surprise us when we learnt that 100,000 signatures were required as part of the nomination process. Indeed we had experienced the same situation in other countries where a similar requirement was specified. Where such occurs not only is it sending out a wrong signal as regards the need to comply with other requirements but it can adversely affect the public perception of the whole process. Such a requirement may well have been designed to prevent "unrealistic" candidatures from obscuring the real contest. An equally effective and more reasonable approach would be to require a more reduced number of signatures encompassing electors from all of the various parts of the country and thus showing a countrywide support. Alternatively a substantial deposit, to be forfeited unless the individual candidate obtains a minimum number of votes cast, perhaps one twentieth, could be employed in lieu of any substantial number of signatures.

One important aspect we recommended was the requirement for each registered political party to have a person registered as the party treasurer. The treasurer should have the power to delegate specific duties to a limited number of named, designated persons whilst at the same time continue to bear overall responsibility under the law. The duties of the treasurer should be specified including the duty to keep accounting records that are sufficient both to show and explain the party's transactions. The records should be of sufficient accuracy so as to indicate, at any time, the financial position of the party including a record of all assets and liabilities with past records having to be maintained for a period of at least five years. The accounts for each financial year should be in a prescribed format and approved by the party management committee or party leader before submission by the prescribed date.

In relation to election campaigns a party can appoint a person as its campaign officer who, in turn, may appoint up to a prescribed maximum of deputy campaign officers for the party. No payments should be made or costs incurred, in respect of campaign expenditure on behalf of a registered party other than by the party treasurer, deputy party treasurer, campaign officer or deputy campaign officer. All payments above a prescribed amount should be supported by an invoice or receipt. A time limit should be set for the submission of bills and their subsequent payment. It could be set, say, for 21 days after the end of the campaign period. Any bills submitted after that date should not be paid and listed in the accounts as such. This timeframe is to enable the party treasurer to meet the deadline for the submission of his /her accounts.

Certain problems had been identified in 2005 when presidential and parliamentary elections coincided. Different regulations applied to the two campaigns. At the minimum the two Electoral Acts should be harmonised or better still a single Act covering all elections of political bodies could be utilised. We examined the legislation for a penalty applying in the event that an individual gains or holds a parliamentary seat obtained through bribery or any other form of corruption. It was not clear to us what the effect of a specific order could be in certain cases involving the hearing of a complaint against the validity of an election. We were not able to get an English translation of the Polish Constitution of which we were told that under Article 105 the lifting of parliamentary immunity has to be regulated by statue. No English translation of that statue was available.

In conclusion we referred to the important role played by the media in many countries as important guardians of democracy seeking to counteract corruption.

DRAFTING AND THE PUBLICATION OF A PAPER ON THE PROPOSED INTRODUCTION OF INDIVIDUAL ELECTORAL REGISTRATION IN THE UK

The principle of individual electoral registration, as opposed to the then existing registration of an address and its eligible occupants that was based on the information supplied by the householder, had been on the UK political agenda for some years and had all-party support. A White Paper and Draft Bill were introduced in 2011 with the intention to have legislation introduced in 2012 after public consultation.

During the consultation a number of substantial problems were raised and indeed the likelihood of it being achieved was questioned. I was asked to produce a paper as a contribution to the debate. The twenty-two page paper I produced was entitled 'Comments on the proposed system for Individual Electoral Registration in Great Britain.' Copies were circulated to Members of Parliament.

In the preface to the paper I made it clear that I agreed in principle with the proposed concept and quoted one of the reasons put forward in the White Paper for the change:

> *We think that the current system of electoral registration is unacceptably exposed to the risk of fraud.*

I wholeheartedly concurred with that perception. I stressed that there was the clear need, whilst enhancing or changing the existing registration system, to take into account the changes that have taken place in society. I emphasised that whichever process was to be introduced it was essential it be both accessible to and easily understood by the wide range of qualified individuals whatever their ability, socio-economic status, cultural background, gender or age. In addition I pointed out that good and effective legislation by itself is no guarantee of success without the required level of staffing, coupled with adequate resources and timely finance. As an aside, I also referred to a particular aspect of the overall electoral process that for some time had given cause for concern – the failure of those who are registered to go and vote at elections.

The paper went on to indicate the changes that had taken place in society including, for example:

- Increase in population mobility
- Increased number of elderly
- Increased and more diverse range of cultural identities
- Reduction in the status of the nuclear family
- Increased emphasis on the rights of the individual
- Data protection and the right to privacy

The paper indicated that the Fixed-term Parliaments Act 2011 did make it easier for electoral officials as regards detailed planning and the operational aspects of both electoral registration and all types of general elections. That included the Scottish Parliament and the National Assembly for Wales.

One of the aspects I argued against was the proposal to make registration voluntary as opposed to the existing legal obligation. An accurate and inclusive electoral register is a fundamental requirement for the demarcation of electoral boundaries. In addition I had concerns about the proposed methodology for the changeover from the existing registration process to the proposed individual registration. There was the need for a commonality of approach throughout Britain, involving 380 registration officers, in the preparation of the electoral register. I did indicate specific reasons for my comment. Contacts with and information from personnel involved in registration in Britain had made me aware of the considerable differences in approach that could only result in different levels of accuracy or indeed inaccuracy. I had been aware for a good number of years of, in my opinion, a very lax approach in some areas. The paper also made reference to electoral abuses as regards registration and associated matters and how the process could be tightened up under the changes being proposed.

There were concerns in some sectors of the public about the security and privacy of the data in the electoral register. Shortly after my appointment to the post of Chief Electoral Officer I decided to reduce the stock of printed registers held outside of periods when any elections were likely to be held. It was possible to have a stock required for an unexpected election to be printed at very short notice. In addition I saw no good reason why copies of the electoral registers had to be supplied to any one asking at a price that neither reflected the value of the information contained nor gave an appropriate contribution towards the cost of its preparation. In general the public supplying the information were not aware that the details of their names and addresses could be passed on to others for non-electoral purposes. I became aware that certain councils in England, responsible for the preparation of the register in their areas were of the same mind and had acted accordingly.

Electoral registers were seen by various businesses, particularly the credit industry, as a good means of checking the accuracy of the information being supplied by applicants for their services. The Prime Minister at the time was very supportive of the expanding credit industry. She saw its right to purchase copies as important and so, in effect, the law was changed accordingly. I could see some merit in that perspective but that did not mean that the legally prescribed purchase price reflected an appropriate portion of the cost involved. The credit industry would have had little trouble in paying an appropriate price and the monies so obtained could then have been used to enhance the process of preparing the registers and hence their accuracy.

My paper did point out that for a considerable period of time the use of the register had mainly been confined to the electoral process, the selection of jury panels and the work of boundary commissions. With the provision of access by others, especially the credit industry, a new type of response arose from some members of the general public. On one hand some members of the public, because of the perceived breach of their privacy, became antagonistic to the registration process. On the other hand some sought to have a fictitious name included to support a fraudulent application in the knowledge that checks would be made to see if that name appeared on the register at the stated address. The change did have one positive side. A genuine resident seeking to have, for example a mortgage, would sometimes learn that the application had been refused because the applicant's name was not on the electoral register at the residential address given on the application. It did give encouragement to be registered in future.

Debates in Parliament indicated widespread agreement that the goal of a complete and accurate electoral register was highly desirable but there were many questions raised regarding the likelihood of either being largely achieved and concerns about the proposed timing and arrangements. I saw it likely that the debate would continue for another year or more.

CHAPTER 8
Developing computerisation of STV counting

During my time as Chief Electoral Officer I had introduced increased computerisation into the various routine office operations and especially the compilation of the annual Draft and Final Registers of Electors. They had been previously processed and compiled by an outside computer system from manually prepared input documents that had to be physically transported from the various area offices located across Northern Ireland. There was one sector that was not open to computerisation, the counting of the votes cast. The legislation applying explicitly prescribed a manual system with visual oversight to be provided to representatives of the various candidates standing. However on one visit to an election in Russia, I was able to observe an experimental trial on the automatic scanning of each ballot paper as it was inserted into the sole ballot box involved in the experiment. That ballot box had a scanner mounted on the top in such a position that any ballot paper inserted into the scanner would, after being scanned, then be automatically inserted into the box. At the end of the poll the scanner would print out the allocation of the number of votes cast for each candidate and hence the formal result. I did notice the potential for a breach of secrecy as regards the choice of individual voters. Each such voter would place the completed ballot paper onto a feeder tray so that it could then be automatically fed into the machine. Voters were placing the ballot papers face up onto the tray and hence any other person close by would be able to determine the choice of that particular voter. The answer was simple – to get voters to insert the papers face down. The idea behind the scheme was to determine a methodology whereby the time taken to obtain an election result would be significantly reduced especially in the case of those areas having sparse population over a vast expanse of the country. For me it was an interesting side event but not of any immediate relevance.

After I had retired from my post of Chief Electoral Officer I was approached by a local firm who were endeavouring to develop computer programmes for use in Scotland in the counting of local elections employing STV. I understood that they had being utilising the services of a person to advise on their trial efforts but that he had decided to withdraw from the experiment. I was then contacted.

It was both interesting and challenging. I decided to adapt an incremental approach. That involved preparing batches of dummy ballot papers each filled out separately in accordance with a theoretical predetermined stage-by-stage result that I prepared. It took me considerable time and effort both to set it up and to prepare all the individual ballot papers involved. The early batches only involved relatively straight forward features but then I made them increasingly more complicated as and when any computer/scanning problems arising from each previous batch had been overcome. I then designed other test batches of papers so that all the permutations of possible variations would have been covered. Eventually the system was fully developed to enable the system to be tested at real elections. That involved the staff travelling over to Scotland with the scanners and associated items being packed into vans and the staff remaining there during the counting process. After a number of successful election counts, the firm was then purchased by a Scottish firm who moved the operation over to there.

CHAPTER 9
A Brief Epilogue

When I took up a totally unfamiliar post in my home town in 1974, I little dreamt that in a few years time I would take over the role of responsibility for all electoral operations in the whole of Northern Ireland and especially so at a time of very serious public discord. There were very active paramilitary activities involving not just many deaths and multiple bombings but also the further cleavage of society as a whole. What I could not have even imagined at the time was my progression onto the international scene. It was not something that I had even thought about, let alone planned for. It crept up on me.

A favourite saying of mine is, politics is all about obtaining access to power and some politicians will do whatever it takes to attain power. Of course there are very many politicians who, individually, have a very deep-seated desire to serve their constituents and work hard to do so. On the other hand effective politicians have, by necessity, to be in a political party – in other words in an organisation. A basic instinct of any organisation, whether political, religious, secular, or whatever, is self survival and so its natural instinct is to take whatever action is required to maintain its interests, appropriate or otherwise to the society in general.

In my work, both at home and abroad, I experienced *realpolitik,* the power of geopolitics, in the design and implementation of plans for the introduction or enhancement of democracy. Of course one has to live in the real world but that should not prevent us from trying to improve it. The contest between communism and democracy, the Cold War, led to the superpowers on both sides safeguarding or expanding their respective spheres of influence. If that meant supporting a vicious dictatorship then so be it. Democracy was not always *the* prime concern of the Western super-powers. Whilst the Soviet Union had imploded and democracy has seeped into its former vassal states, the competition between the super-powers continues.

Political scientists have long debated the various aspects of democracy and how elections play a role in the process. It was only in the latter part of the twentieth century that the important role played by the organisations responsible for the running of elections became fully appreciated. Then the main international bodies such as the United Nations set up dedicated units to assist in the establishment of appropriate bodies to organise and oversee elections in various countries.

After I had retired from my post in Northern Ireland I decided to get more involved in a proactive approach to political events abroad as opposed to the somewhat reactive aspects that I had mainly been involved in up to then. One of my concerns abroad had been the emphasis by *some* international organisations on a particular, almost standard, framework that should be introduced into the arrangements for democratisation regardless of the country and the society involved. Not infrequently it was a reflection, in the case of such organisations funded by their national government, of their home country standards. Of course there should be basic rules and entitlements but the implementation of those can be obtained within a relevant and appropriate variation. In addition it was not helpful if the organisation involved was from a country that did not have 'clean hands' as regards such events at home, otherwise it was somewhat hypocritical. In some instances it can be more to do, as referred to above, with geopolitics as opposed to true democracy.

I enjoyed my overall experience despite at times the stress and dangers involved. It was most satisfying both at home and abroad and especially so the operational success of the two closely following elections in Northern Ireland in 1998. The first was the referendum on the Good Friday Agreement in May and the second, a month later, for the new Northern Ireland Assembly involving a party list system. They were both crucial to the new peace process and any critical comments on the running of those two elections could have had adverse consequences on the likely overall acceptance of the results.

Whilst meeting with friends and interviewers I was frequently asked if I was writing a book on my experiences. There was no such thought in my mind until very recently. As I started on the task there were indications in my home town of the re-emergence of a very small number of individuals in paramilitary activities. Just as I was finalising the draft of this book a young female journalist was murdered whilst reporting on street rioting in Derry between the police and those supporting the 'New IRA'. She had been born in Belfast and had recently come to reside in Derry and became very attached to the city. There was widespread condemnation of the murder with public meetings being held both in Derry and elsewhere.

A very unique funeral service was held in St Anne's Cathedral, Belfast attended by a wide-spread cross-section of Northern Ireland society. Leading politicians from Ireland, North and South, also attended including the Irish President as did the UK Prime Minister and the Northern Ireland Secretary of State. The service was conducted by the Protestant Dean of the cathedral and a

Catholic priest and made an immense impression on those attending and also on those who watched the television coverage broadcast in Ireland, Britain and further afield.

I am hoping that this book will go someway towards indicating how conflicts in many other countries have been overcome despite them having much more substantive problems than those existing within Northern Ireland. It can illustrate that the problems here are very far from being insurmountable. The book describes the difficulties that we have already overcome. There is still some way to go and especially in the need to discard what I would term 'digging-a-trench politics'. That, in the eyes of those who do so, may be seen by them as patriotism. Bertrand Russell, the renowned British philosopher, took a very, very different perspective of patriotism when he commented that, in his view: "Patriotism is the willingness to kill and be killed for trivial reasons." On the other hand those who are very much inclined to hesitation on taking the required steps forward would be well advised to consider the quotation from the Talmud: "Three things are good in little measure and evil in large; yeast, salt and hesitation."

We surely must apply ourselves to the task in hand, not tomorrow but today.

APPENDICES

The following are designed to explain, or to highlight, some of the important aspects to be considered in the design and operation of an effective, reliable and democratic electoral system for the top tier of governance. They are outline in nature. There are various factors that may negatively impact on the ability to attain the desired standard and particularly so where there is, or has been, conflict, ethnic or religious divisions.

APPENDIX 1

COMMON TYPES OF DEMOCRATIC GOVERNANCE

In general there are two main types – presidential and parliamentary. In the former the president can be directly elected either by popular vote or by an electoral college, and is not responsible to the Legislature and not normally dismissible by the Legislature except in special circumstances such as impeachment. The office is held for a fixed term. A typical rule, under the Constitution applying, is that a President is limited to no more than two consecutive terms. I did come across on one particular occasion the incumbent president, towards the end of his second term in office, indicating that he would seek a further term. When I met with him he confirmed his intention. When I indicated that the Constitution appeared to forbid that he simply replied that he would have the Constitution changed! Within a Presidential system there can be a tendency towards authoritarianism and the lack of accountability. For example on one occasion I had experience in Central Asia of a country where an initially democratically elected President became tainted by authoritarianism and corruption. He was overthrown by a citizens' uprising.

Presidential cabinet members can be from outside the legislative branch, unlike parliamentary systems. When the President is from a different party from that of the legislature majority party gridlock can ensue. Presidential systems have a tendency towards fewer ideologically based political parties than parliamentary systems. Presidential systems are particularly dominant in the Southern Americas where at the last count 19 of 22 sovereign states employed that system.

Subordinate states within a country, such as the USA, can sometimes utilize a presidential system for the head of the individual states as such a president is less dependent on legislature support.

In a parliamentary system the Head of Government is elected through a directly elected legislature and can be subjected to a vote of confidence. If that is not obtained, when called for, a new election has normally to be called if a new government cannot be formed, usually within a prescribed period, even though the specified term of the parliament has not yet expired.

When no one party has a majority in a legislature a government can be formed through power sharing. That can leave the resultant government open to a threat by a coalition party to leave the coalition government unless a particular policy is followed. Minority parties having a more intense political philosophy are more likely to adapt such an approach. The need to form a coalition government is more likely to occur much more frequently where a proportional representational electoral system is in operation.

The Prime Minister in a parliamentary system is constrained by the need to maintain the confidence of the legislature, in contrast to the position in a presidential system. There is the counter argument that parliament has more control than that in a presidential system. David Lloyd George, British Prime Minister 1916 -1922, was not inclined to that perspective. He commented, in evidence to a select committee that *Parliament has really no control over the executive, it is pure fiction.*

Generally speaking both presidential and parliamentary systems have an Upper and Lower House. Whilst the Lower house is elected that is not always the case with the Upper House. In some of the latter the members can be nominated, as opposed to elected. In other instances there can be membership through privilege or descent – the British House of Lords is a well known example of that.

The above is a very brief outline of the differences between the two systems – there are many tomes that go into a full and detailed analysis and thus interested readers can get a full perspective that way.

There are various types of voting systems that can be utilised in the election of the individual members of legislatures. Those are identified in appendix 4. Other appendices indicate various factors that should be taken into account in the selection of an appropriate electoral system for individual countries. The selection of an inappropriate system, by itself, may give the appearance of democracy but not the actuality. If so the longer term stability of the country can be put at risk.

APPENDIX 2

LEGISLATION AND RESPONSIBILITY FOR ITS APPLICATION

In outline terms the legislation applying can be categorised as being at two levels – <u>primary</u>, where an individual statute (Act) sets out the general principles whilst also delegating specific authority to an executive branch for more specific laws to be made, under the auspices of the principal Act, by means of <u>secondary</u> legislation. The operational aspects of elections fall mainly under the latter.

Well designed and effective legislation precludes the need for frequent or ongoing amendments having to be made to it. Where such a scenario does occurs it may lead to a loss of confidence among the citizenry in the overall process and especially when the political atmosphere is somewhat strained.

There are various types of management styles that can be employed in the application and operation of the legislation at democratic elections. The following are some of more common.

CHIEF ELECTORAL OFFICER

I operated in that role in Northern Ireland for over twenty years in the very wide range of duties that can be applied to such a post. My post involved the full range of duties from the preparation and updating of the electoral register for all of Northern Ireland, the determination of claims and objections received in respect of entries in the Draft Register prepared each year concluding with the publication of the final register. The published register showed the allocation of separate groups of electors within each ward register to blocks indicating the range and number of ballot boxes to be assigned. That required the prior determination of the overall number and locations of the various polling stations. A periodic polling station scheme was prepared to show the overall allocation of the sub-groups of electors to the individual polling places within each electoral area. An electoral area varied according to the type of election involved ranging from a Westminster parliamentary election to a District Council election.

The duties also included the formal public notification of the date and timetable for each election including where and when candidates' nominations had to be submitted. Also involved was the determination of the validity of the nominations received, of applications at elections for postal or proxy voting, the counting of the votes cast as well as the formal determination and announcement of the successful candidates. I had a number of Deputy Electoral Officers under me each of whom was given, under my control, responsibility for certain duties over an assigned area. Whilst as Chief Electoral Officer I could delegate those duties I remained personally responsible, under the law, for any errors or deficiencies in the process.

In other countries there can be variations in the overall authority given to such Chief Electoral Officers. As was in my case, some such officers may hold an independent post and thus are only answerable to the courts and parliament. Others, whilst being responsible for the running of elections and associated functions, such as the registration of electors, may operate under the direct supervision and control of a higher authority such as an electoral commission. Sometimes the title *Chief Electoral Officer* has been applied to designate, in effect, a much more junior officer who is responsible only for limited aspects of the operational running of the election under the direction and control of higher management.

ELECTORAL COMMISSIONS

The role of an electoral commission can vary from country to country. Some commissions are more permanent organisations with the individual members holding office for a stated period, usually for a number of years, whereupon the membership is reviewed. The composition can range from members being independent and perceived to be so or, instead, having as its members representatives of various political parties. In the latter case it may well be the intention to have such members acting as a check and balance on each other. There can be and indeed has been the danger of the membership being restricted to only a few of the major parties or to parties that have been officially registered. Authoritarian inclined governments have been known to restrict such registration as a means of indirectly controlling the electoral process.

In some countries the custom has been to appoint a separate electoral commission for each and every election rather than having a standing electoral commission. Certain potential problems can arise from such an approach. There might be a political imperative to have an election timetable that does not provide sufficient notice to enable fully effective and adequate preparations. There is the need for adequate time for the recruitment, the appointment process for and training of the commission's membership. Problems have also arisen in some instances when a member, who has been appointed as a political party nominee, decides to resign at short notice so as to be able to stand as a candidate at the election. I have been aware of such occurrences that clearly were not conducive to the public perception of an independent and impartial system.

Electoral commissions may be responsible for the determination of both electoral boundaries and the number of representatives to be elected from each. Alternatively such determinations may be the role of a Boundary Commission, a separate body especially set up for that purpose and generally chaired by a senior, experienced and perhaps retired judicial officer.

STATUTORY OFFICE HOLDER

This can be illustrated by the role of the Chief Executives of Councils in Britain. The chief executive of one of the local government councils within a parliamentary constituency is usually responsible for the organisation of the parliamentary elections for that constituency. The formal declaration of the result falls to the mayor or other individual. Prior to the establishment of the Electoral Commission in the United Kingdom the system operated independently of any external direct control. With the establishment of the United Kingdom Electoral Commission there is now an overall control by that body. In many countries the appointment of an electoral commission has become commonplace.

APPENDIX 3

ELECTORAL BOUNDARIES

The establishment of fair boundaries is one of the foundation blocks of any democratic electoral system. It is equally important that the boundaries are periodically reviewed to take into account any population changes or other relevant factors. The number of constituencies and the representation to be afforded to each is dependant on a number of aspects. They include the size of the country, the varying density of the population, the electoral system to be applied and the number of representatives to be elected.

In general terms the following are two of the frequently employed models but may be slightly modified from country to country.

An ongoing Boundary Commission comprised of independent members under a senior, sometimes retired, and judicially qualified Chair. The Commission usually has the assistance of suitably experienced advisors. Generally the Commission is required to carry out specified periodic reviews although, if necessary, an interim review may be required in special circumstances. The membership is reviewed periodically.

In some countries the Boundary Commission may have the membership drawn from representatives of political parties. This, possibly, is on the assumption that the members so appointed will keep an eye on each other although there is the possibility of a trade-off occurring on a *quid-pro-quo* basis. In some countries concerns have been expressed that the membership has been constrained to just a few of the political parties.

With an ongoing Commission there is the ability to have a timed programme of work enabling a draft scheme to be prepared and then put out for public consultation. Following on from that the final Boundary scheme is prepared and then submitted to the legislature for consideration. That preliminary stage does not occur in some countries.

A short term Commission set up just prior to a particular election. There have been instances of the time frame involved being very close to the scheduled election period and indeed so close as to require the preparations for the election to be set in motion even before the details of the boundaries have been notified. That can result in a very limited time frame for the recruitment and any necessary training of staff. Commission members are often representative of their parties. I had the experience of meeting with members of various political parties to identify any problems they had with the electoral arrangements only to be informed that they would, in such circumstances, talk to *their* Commission member.

<u>Variations in the geographical size and electoral numbers of electoral units</u>
Urban areas are much easier to delineate than very rural areas. The latter can cover a very wide range of territory difficult to transverse due to the presence of mountains and lakes. Offshore islands present a different scenario – they can be relatively small, very isolated and so are not easy to be linked up other populated areas to make up an electoral unit having the requisite number of electors that would otherwise be required for representation. In such circumstances a much lower level of electorate may be acceptable for determination as a separate unit.

The type of the electorate voting system does affect the flexibility of boundary determinations. With a majoritarian system the object is to obtain, as far as is possible, units that are reasonable close to each other as regards to the number of electors contained in each. It is necessary to have some flexibility within a stated range above and below the target number – a plus or minus range of 10% is not uncommon. On the other hand proportional systems provides more flexibility as units having varying sizes of registered electors can each be allocated the relevant ratio of members to the size of the electorate involved. Various factors, such as the geography, racial or ethnicity, may indicate consideration of such an approach.

APPENDIX 4

VOTING SYSTEMS

The following are the more commonly utilized systems. Some of these, especially the first three, can be also be used for the election of a president.

FIRST-PAST-THE-POST

This is where <u>the electoral constituency returns one candidate</u> with the elector indicating his/her choice of candidate usually by marking the choice on the ballot paper with an X or a similar mark. The candidate who gets the most votes, not necessarily an overall majority of all the votes cast, is declared elected.

TWO-ROUND SYSTEM

This is a variation of the First-past-the-post system that requires the winning candidate to obtain a majority of all the votes cast to be eligible for election. If no candidate obtains such a majority then a second stage election has to be held, within a specified period, to determine the successful candidate from the top, usually the top two, candidates at the first round.

ALTERNATIVE VOTE

This is used for <u>single member constituencies</u> where the voters are asked to mark their order of preference of the various candidates. A candidate receiving over 50% of the votes is declared elected. Where no candidate obtains such a majority the votes are then re-allocated according to the preferences stated on each ballot paper until one candidate obtains a majority of the votes cast.

SINGLE TRANSFERABLE VOTE

This is used for <u>multi-member constituencies.</u> Candidates who obtain or exceed a specified quota of first-preference votes are declared elected. The quota is calculated on the number of seats and the total number of valid votes. Any surplus votes of a successful candidate, over and above the quota, are transferred to other continuing candidates according to the choice shown on the individual ballot papers. The count proceeds in separate stages by the election or elimination of candidates until the requisite number of members have been elected. Where at any one stage when there are still seat(s) to be determined but no further candidate has obtained or exceeded the quota, the candidate(s) having the least number of votes is eliminated and the ballot papers are then individually transferred to the next continuing candidate in accordance with the individual choices indicated. In the process any choice indicated for a candidate who has been already elected is passed over to leave the remaining choices for consideration. Not all successful candidates have to reach the quota. For example if there is one vacancy remaining and all but one of the candidates who have not attained the quota have been eliminated then the last remaining candidate is declared elected even though the quota has not been obtained.

SINGLE NON-TRANSFERABLE VOTE
This combines multi-member constituencies with a First Past the Vote counting system where the elector has only one vote. It is semi-proportional in operation.

THE BLOCK VOTE
The Block Vote is used in multi-member constituencies with the elector having as many votes as there are candidates to be elected. There are two variations:-

- The voters having the choice of individual candidates

    or

- The voter selects a party which has listed its choice of candidates.

The candidates with the highest vote totals win the seats.

LIST PROPORTIONAL REPRESENTATION
Each party participating presents a list of candidates and the electors then vote for the party. The parties each receive the number of seats in proportion to their overall share of the national vote with the winning candidates being selected from the rank order of their respective lists.

MIXED MEMBER PROPORTIONAL
This system provides for a proportion of the members being elected from plural-majority constituencies, generally 50%, with the remainder selected from proportional representational lists. The intention here is to enable the PR seats to compensate for any disproportionality resulting from the other seats.

APPENDIX 5

THE FRANCHISE

Age – The age for entitlement can vary from country to country. There has been the trend down the years of the age requirement being reduced. For example in the UK when women first got the vote, under the Representation of the People Act 1918, the specified qualifying age for a woman was 25. Much later on the qualifying age for both men and women became 18.

Nationality – In most cases an individual has to hold the nationality of the state but there are exceptions. In East Timor, for example, at the referendum on independence, a non-Timorese individual married to an East Timorese qualified for the vote.

Address for registration – Here also the rules can vary. The general approach is to have registration at the elector's place of residence. The legislation can require a minimum, set, period of residence to qualify. In the UK the legislation recognises that a person can have more than one residence and so can be registered more than once but, if so, it is an offence to vote more than once at the same general election.

There have been ongoing problems in countries involved in conflict and where there have been refugees and internally displaced persons (IDPs). Those involved had to flee their homes and so have no permanent residence. The general approach has been to register them under their former home addresses provided that there is proof of their past residence at the addresses concerned. The experience in Bosnia-Herzegovina indicated the problems arising in trying to address that problem following ethnic cleansing.

Where ethnic cleansing has taken place, even a generation or so before, those who have been dispersed elsewhere may wish to be registered at their former location in furtherance of their desire to return. The 'wish to reside' location for registration was one of the stumbling blocks at elections in Bosnia-Herzegovina. It was perceived by some as a means of claiming or re-claiming territory.

Voting entitlement – If there is an age requirement then the registered elector has to have attained the minimum age either by the publication of the electoral register or, if not, by the date of the poll. In the latter instances the electoral register usually indicates the date on which each such elector becomes entitled to vote. Where the electoral register has been produced specifically for the particular election, bearing in mind the prescribed criteria required, all those listed are entitled to vote.

In some cases a registered elector may not qualify for all types of elections. For example an individual may be eligible to vote at parliamentary elections but not at local government elections or vice-versa. The local government franchise may depend on the payment of rates or other contribution towards the running costs of the council. If the register has not been compiled for the specific election then it will indicate any restriction on the franchise. In some instances an elector can be debarred from voting for a specified period as, for example, if convicted of certain offences. Some countries permit prisoners to vote whilst others do not.

APPENDIX 6

VOTING METHODS AND PROCEDURES

The various individual methods generally employed by which a registered elector can exercise the franchise are as follows:-

Attending in person at the designated polling place during the hours set for the poll and completing a ballot paper there.

Voting by post subject to making the required application within a specified time frame and it being approved. In such circumstances the ballot paper is sent out by post and has to be received back at the designated return address by a specified date and time. Postal voting is more open to abuse in comparison to voting in person. Forged applications can be submitted and especially so in the names of those who, whilst registered, are known not to routinely vote. Where the legislation specifies a minimum turn-out of electors, otherwise a second round of the poll has to be held, the misuse of the postal voting facility may be exploited so as to obtain the minimum required voting turn-out and thus avoid a re-run. In the case of a country having a somewhat autocratic government, such abuse may well be employed to show a much higher electoral turn out than what actually exists so as to give more credence to the government. It is important that a close oversight and control be operated of the granting and issuing of postal and proxy voting to prevent abuse of the electoral system. At some elections a very small number of votes, even as low as single figures, can sometimes determine which candidate is elected.

Politicians may become concerned about an ongoing fall in the voter turn-out at elections and particularly so when it falls close to or even below 50% as that could reduce public confidence in the process. In such circumstances the easier provision of postal voting may be viewed as a means of obtaining an increased turn out. Recently in the UK research has indicated that in this regards the benefits of postal voting and also electronic voting have been exaggerated and especially so in relation to claims about increased turnout and social inclusion. It was also reported that greater use of postal voting has not only made UK elections far more vulnerable to fraud but indeed has resulted in a number of instances of large-scale fraud.

As an aside I would mention a system I observed at elections in Russia following on from the collapse of the Soviet Union .It was a somewhat unusual means of enhancing the turnout at elections. At some of the polling stations that I visited there was a one-way system operating at the polling station. Electors going to vote would enter by one door but exit by a different door after they had voted. I found that those who had voted would, on the way out, pass by stalls containing food, clothes and other products that were hard to find elsewhere and were at sale at a lower price.

Voting by proxy where the voter appoints a named person to cast the vote on his/her behalf. There are generally certain requirements relating to the qualifications of the proposed proxy and the attendance of the proxy at the polling station or voting by post.

Voting out of country In some countries, where there is an overseas Diaspora, arrangements are often made to establish polling places outside the country, including overseas, where there are a sufficient number of eligible electors living there.

Location of polling places The term 'polling place' generally relates to an individual building or location to be used by the electorate to cast their ballots. Some polling places can have, especially in built-up areas, two or more ballot boxes with each assigned to a separately designated group of electors. A common and indeed necessary usage is to label all ballot boxes with a unique individual identification sign.

There are two common approaches to the determination of those premises to be used as polling stations, referred here as a Polling Station Scheme. The first can be described as an as-and-when-required-approach for each election as it occurs. That has two disadvantages in that it increases the work load at an already busy time and there is less opportunity for the public and political parties to make representation as to the appropriateness of the selections made. In contrast the legislation can require the preparation of a polling station scheme at periodic intervals with the draft scheme being open for public inspection and with a period specified for the receipt of objections or proposals by any registered elector. Any such objections or proposals received are considered and the draft scheme amended to take into account any changes decided. The amended scheme is then published as the approved scheme.

The selection of polling places should first involve the visiting all of the likely locations so as to determine which are more suitable or better located for the electorate. A list of all the polling places for a particular constituency is best prepared well in advance of any election. Just prior to an election it should then be reviewed so as to ensure that there has been no change in availability or appropriateness since the initial selection. In deeply divided communities there can be the complication of particular locations being viewed by some as partisan or indeed, in very deeply divided communities, as problematic. In addition election administrators can be faced with a desire of the security forces for a restriction in the overall number of polling places to be utilised so as to more easily facilitate the employment of security arrangements. Such an approach, if accepted, can sometimes result in the aggregation of a very substantial number of electors in the one place and maybe in excess of what the location can comfortably handle. The allocation of a large number of ballot boxes assigned to the one polling station can result in excessive numbers of voters arriving to vote at busy times. Where there is a deeply divided society the close encounter of different factions during the hours of the poll can even lead to civil unrest with possible adverse consequences for the voting turnout and the general acceptance of the result.

In lesser developed countries there may be few or no suitable buildings in some areas and, if that is the case, the poling stations may have to be located in the open air utilising tents or other temporary facilities. That can make security and ballot secrecy more difficult and also arrangements will have to be made for the provision of lighting to cover the timeframe after dusk whilst the polling stations remains open and during the period after the poll when documentation has to be completed. Electric generators may be required to service any computer systems and other equipment.

In the run up to an election it is important that the individual electors are notified of the particular polling place that each should attend to vote. A copy of the overall polling station scheme should be provided to each candidate on nomination so as to assist in his or her organisation of the election campaign and the attendance of assigned polling agents.

It is important for an effective oversight to be maintained throughout the progress of the poll at the various polling stations so as to identify and correct any problems as and when they arise. That can be attained by the use of supervisors travelling around the various locations and ideally in radio or telephonic contact with a central control base where any special corrective action required can be quickly organised and implemented.

VOTING PROCESS AT THE POLLING STATION

It is important that the secrecy of the ballot is maintained. At the same time the various candidates should have the entitlement to see that the process is being both efficiently and fairly operated. That means that a candidate should be able to appoint, if so desired, a polling agent to <u>observe</u> the process at each individual ballot box. The person so appointed should be of legal age. It is important that the procedure for the appointment of such agents is clearly stated and also the time by which the returning officer has to be notified and by whom. Generally that is done by an individual candidate's main election agent and specifies which ballot box or ballot boxes a polling agent is to attend. The returning officer has, in turn, to notify the polling station staff of the details of any polling agents appointed and the ballot box or boxes to which they have been appointed. The election agent should ensure that each polling agent appointed is made aware of the prescribed role and what can and cannot be done by him or her.

There is a duty of secrecy placed on polling agents that forbids the communication to any person before the poll is closed of any information as to the name of any elector or proxy who has or has not applied for a ballot paper or voted at a polling station or the number on the register of any elector who, or whose proxy, has or has not applied for a ballot paper or voted at a polling station. An illegal action on the part of a polling agent can have adverse legal consequences for the candidate for whom he or she has been appointed. For my own elections in Northern Ireland I prepared a booklet outlining the precise role of an election agent and the range and scope as well as the limitations applying. Copies of the booklet were supplied to the various political parties prior to the poll and individual copies supplied for issue to the agents at each and every polling station.

Immediately prior to the opening of the poll the individual ballot boxes to be utilised should be shown to be empty and then officially sealed and remain so until the poll has been completed at the prescribed time. It is important for polling agents to be present then as well as observing the overall process. At the conclusion of the poll any unused ballot papers and the counterfoils of those issued should be sealed in the supplied envelopes for retention by the returning officer.

The number of ballot papers supplied to the individual boxes should relate to the number of electors assigned to that box and that the total number of ballots papers issued is recorded. Ballot papers should contain the name of the constituency involved and the date of the election. It is common practice for each such ballot paper to bear a unique serial number that identifies it. A general practice, as and when a ballot paper is issued to an elector, his or her electoral number is entered on the ballot paper counterfoil before the ballot paper is detached and issued. Some people have raised concerns over such marking of ballot papers. They see the provision of individual serial numbers on each of the ballot papers as a potential breach of electoral secrecy as to how an individual elector has voted. I am not inclined to that view provided that adequately security is applied.

Prior to my appointment as Northern Ireland Chief Electoral Officer the policy applying to the storage of the ballot papers cast at an election and the relevant counterfoils was to have all them collected, sealed and stored in a secure place. If a person was to seek to identify how a specific elector voted and was able to overcome the security arrangements involved then a very substantial amount of work and indeed space would be required. For example in the circumstances where the number of ballots cast was 40,000 it would require two separate stages after the investigator had found out, from the electoral register, the ward number and electoral number of the elector involved. It would then be necessary to access the records and go through the 40,000 ballot paper stubs until the one bearing the relevant elector's serial number has been found. Having acquired that serial number the 40,000 ballot papers cast would then have to be individually examined, sorted until the one bearing the corresponding identified serial number has been located.

The purpose of having a specific serial number on each ballot paper is both to identify it as an official ballot paper, as opposed to a fraudulent one, and also to enable an Election Court to make a determination if and when an election petition has been lodged – a somewhat rare event and one that would be held under strict confidence. However to address the perception held by some I set up an arrangement whereby the used ballot papers were sealed up and placed for the prescribed period before destruction in one secure location whilst the counterfoils were likewise sealed but stored for the prescribed period in a separate and secure location some distance away.

THE ISSUING OF BALLOT PAPERS
The number of staff allocated to each ballot box depends on the requirements prescribed. In any event one of the officials should be in overall charge. The title 'presiding officer' is often used to designate that official who is assisted by subordinate staff sometimes known as polling clerks.

There is a range of requirements to be met by a person applying for a ballot paper. A very basic approach is where the applicant has only to state his or her name and address which is then checked against the electoral register to establish that the name does appear on the register under that address. In many cases the applicant may also be required to produce an identity card or other such document – the range of acceptable documents has to have been identified prior to polling day in sufficient time for any elector who does not possess such identification to be able to apply and obtain the specified document in advance of polling day. Where the production of a specified document is a legal requirement the polling station staff have no discretion in this matter and thus none can be lawfully exercised.

It has been the practice in some countries to have a finger of one hand of an individual marked with indelible ink on being issued with a ballot paper to show that he or she has applied to vote and thus prevent that person for voting more than once. The ink used is especially formulated to ensure that it is not easily removed for a period of time. There is a downside to the use of such ink when there are factions who are actively opposed to any participation in the election and who threaten physical action against any individual who can be seen to have voted. The security forces may be able to secure the area immediately adjacent to the polling station but not necessary elsewhere.

As and when each voter is being issued with a ballot paper the entry in the electoral register against his or her name should be marked to indicate that a ballot paper has been issued. The usual practice is for the ballot paper to be stamped with the official mark to confirm its official issue – a different mark is used for each election. Occasionally an elector may accidentally spoil the ballot paper by accidently placing a choice against a candidate other than the preference intended. That is easy to understand when there two or more of the candidates have the same surname. The elector can be supplied with a new ballot paper provided that the spoilt paper is returned to and immediately cancelled by the presiding officers. The spoilt ballot paper should not be destroyed but rather at the close of the poll has to be enclosed with the unused ballot papers for despatch to the returning officer.

THE POLLING STATION AS A NEUTRAL ENVIRONMENT
Within the polling station it is important that no literature, emblems, posters or the such-like exhorting electors to vote for a particular candidate or party are displayed. The electorate should be able to cast the vote in a neutral environment. The polling station staff should be made aware of that need and told to remove any such items from any part of the polling station and in particular to frequently check each polling screen to ensure that no such publicity items have been deposited by electors who have already voted. . In addition the bearing of any type of weapons within the precincts of a polling place should be both banned and enforced. Where it is necessary to have security forces present they are best confined to areas outside the individual rooms used for voting. Where polling agents from the various parties involved are in attendance it is important that they are aware that they are only there in an observational role and not perceived otherwise by the voters. It is important that they do not wear any emblems or the suchlike exhorting electors to vote for a particular party or candidate. I saw no problem with such polling agents wearing a simple coloured rosette having only the name and symbol of the party. Indeed it was operationally useful as it was then easy to establish when there was more than one agent present at a time for any one of the candidates.

Should an elector need assistance to complete the ballot paper that should be supplied by a member of the polling station staff or a family member as opposed to one of the polling agents. It is best that the individuals appointed as polling agents by the candidates have some familiarity with the specific area. The duties involved demand tact, judgement and discretion and this should be borne in mind during the appointment of persons to the post. It is advisable that each such person so appointed should be provided with a written appointment for presentation to the presiding officers in charge of the particular ballot box.

It is important that the neutrality of the polling station is maintained at all time during the hours of polling and immediately afterwards when the accounting of the number of ballot papers cast is being determined and the overall result ascertained and declared. As the hours of polling are usually lengthy an election agent may appoint two or more polling agents to attend at the one ballot box. If so only one such duly appointed polling agent can attend at the particular ballot box at the one time on behalf of the candidate.

AT THE CLOSE OF THE POLL

Different approaches can be applied to the procedure applying at the precise time stipulated for the close of the poll. One approach is that the issue of ballot papers has to stop precisely at the stipulated time whether or not there are still persons present who by then have not been supplied with a ballot paper. A different approach is for the entry to the polling station to be closed but to permit each registered elector within the premises, who have not yet voted, to be supplied with a ballot paper and to cast their vote.

APPENDIX 7

COUNTING THE VOTES AND THE DETERMINATION OF THE RESULT

According to the type of election and the legislation applying the counting can be at each individual polling station with each ballot box being counted separately at the room or location used during the balloting process and with the relevant polling agents in attendance. Alternatively the various ballot boxes may be transferred to a central counting centre and that takes more time and organisation. It does however have the advantage of a more uniform determination on doubtful ballot papers but some would regard it as removing the oversight of the process from the various local areas. In the case of a large geographical area a number of such counting centres may be necessary.

<u>Where the counting of the votes is to take place at a central counting centre</u>.
At the close of the poll the slot for the insertion of completed ballot papers into the ballot box is to be immediately sealed shut. A form, generally known as the Ballot Paper Account, is then to be completed. That includes the total number of ballot papers that had been supplied to the individual ballot box and the number of papers remaining as unissued thus identifying the number of votes that should be contained within the ballot box. The unused ballot papers, along with any spoiled ballot paper for which a replacement has been issued, are then to be inserted and sealed in the special envelope supplied for that purpose and likewise the counterfoils of the issued ballot papers in a separate sealed envelope also supplied for that purpose. All the other stationary and miscellaneous items are to be placed in the separate bag provided.

All those items are then to be taken by the Presiding Officer to the designated counting centre for delivery to the counting staff there. At that centre all Ballot Paper Accounts for the entire number of polling stations for that constituency are opened, checked and verified against the number of papers then found in each ballot box. The overall total of votes cast is then identified and the ballot papers are then allocated to the individual candidates according to the choices shown and the successful candidate or candidates, according to the type of electoral process being used, determined and officially announced.

<u>Where the counting of the ballots is to take place there and then on the closure of the poll at the room used during the balloting process</u>
It is highly desirable that the relevant polling agents remain to observe the process. The Ballot Paper Account is completed and so the number of ballot papers issued is identified and compared with the number of papers found within the ballot box. Should there be a difference a recount of the ballot box contents should take place. It is possible that very occasionally an elector who has been

issued with a ballot paper does not complete the paper in the polling booth but instead pockets it and departs the polling station.

The number of the votes cast for each of the candidates is then determined during which any invalid papers are excluded from consideration. During this operation a polling agent may request a recount and the presiding officer can carry it out where there appears to be reasonable grounds to do so. When all that has been done a designated form, sometimes known as a protocol, is then completed and signed by the presiding officer indicating the result of the poll. That form, together with the sealed ballot box and associated documents, is then taken to a designated centre.

In some countries emerging into the democratic mode, as well as some that have been there for some time, allegations have been made of fraud being perpetrated by fraudulent misuse of protocols. In some instances there have been claims of the polling station staff being in sympathy to a particular party's candidates and whilst a correct protocol has been completed in front of opposition polling agents and countersigned by them a blank or inaccurate form has instead been substituted in its place. The false details are then used in the calculation of the final, overall, result There have been occasions when such action has been identified resulting in the recorded data being amended to the correct details. There have also been instances where the proper protocols have been forwarded without any covering envelope with the correct data having been entered by pencil enabling alterations to be made before the official receipt. Such actions have being addressed by having each of the polling agents being supplied with a verified copy of the protocol at the polling station and which they then can take to the central count location for comparison with the data recorded there.

That overall process of the counting of the votes is common to both the counting at the individual polling station and at a central counting station. It is described below. Where polling by qualified electors takes place in foreign countries special arrangements are made including the method by which the results are notified to the appropriate in-country officials and then to the home state.

IN THE CASE OF A REFERENDUM
In East Timor a referendum was held to determine whether the electorate wished to become independent from Indonesia or, instead, desired to remain under Indonesia on a pro-autonomy basis. I was one of the three Commissioners appointed by the UN Secretary General to oversee the process and to report on whether or not the result of the referendum accurately reflected the will of the East Timorese people. I discovered in advance that the initial intention, as regards the counting of the votes cast, was to have that carried out at each and every polling station immediately after the poll had closed. However I had doubts about the wisdom of that and especially so in the circumstances appertaining at the time in East Timor.

The referendum took place in an atmosphere of extreme violence with those in favour of pro-autonomy running rampage, resulting in death and destruction. If the referendum was to result in the overall choice for pro-autonomy then, to my mind, that could place those electors in fear in any area where the counting of the poll at individual polling stations showed the majority favoured independence. The possibility of revenge taking place against them could ensue. After discussing this with my fellow Commissioners we were able to have the counting of the votes arranged to take place at one central location.

Having just mentioned a referendum there is one relevant comment that I would like to make and especially in the context of deeply divided communities. It is on the question as to whether or not a referendum should be run in the context of a weighed majority being specified for the outcome to be officially recognised for implementation. In a deeply divided society there would be little likelihood of overall acceptance if, for example, a proposition was only carried by 50.01% versus a vote against of 49.99%. That, obviously, is an extreme example, but never-the-less highlights the need to establish what could be, or indeed would be, appropriate in the circumstances. In the case of the referendum in Northern Ireland on the Good Friday Agreement, described in the main body of the book, there was no requirement for a weighed majority. There were indications of an informal weighed majority being promulgated by at least some of those who were in opposition to its proposals. They argued that at least a 70% vote in its favour was required for it to be accepted. The question as to whether or not a weighed majority should be set for an individual referendum is a matter of much debate in itself and also at what level it should be set. There are a number of other requirements that can be introduced for the result to be effective. For example a requirement could be set that the turn-out has to be over 50%, if not higher, of the registered electorate.

Where it is evident that there are widely conflicting views held by the electorate, a simple yes or no option may be too broad an approach. An Alternative Voting system could be utilised. That would enable each voter to identify his/hers first choice and then to indicate any views on the other options. Those would be taken into account in the rank order expressed. In that manner it is more likely to result in a much broader representation of the collective opinion.

The counting of the votes at the Northern Ireland Referendum took place at a central count as the area concerned was relatively compact. Where that is not the case then there can be a number of regional counting centres and good planning and care is required to obtain an effective and timely flow of information so that the central control site is able to announce the overall result within a reasonable timeframe.

DETERMINATION OF VALID AND INVALID VOTES

A valid paper is one that clearly indicates the voter's intention. An invalid paper is one where it is not clear as to what precisely is the choice. There are differences in this regards according to the type of voting system applying.

It is relatively straight forward with a simple majoritarian system involving the filling of one vacancy. If the indicated choice is not clear then the paper is invalid. The polling agents have no role to play in that decision although they may lodge an objection at the time. The presiding officer would obviously listen to those comments but the decision remains with that official. At times and especially when the result is seen as being very close a polling agent may well endeavour to try and influence the decision on the validity of any ballot paper that <u>may possibly</u> indicate a choice for his or her candidate. The presiding officer would be well advised to be both consistent and firm on the decisions being made. It is not what could or could not be interpreted but what exactly is marked on the ballot paper and if it is <u>absolutely clear.</u>

Where a proportional voting system, such as STV, is involved a different approach is relevant. If, for example, the elector has marked first preference for more that one candidate then the paper is invalid. On the other hand if the voter has marked a first preference for only one candidate but has marked a second or other preference to more than one candidate the ballot is still valid. In such cases the vote can be allocated to the first preference candidate but it cannot take part in any subsequent stage involving the transfer of the first choice candidate's surplus votes where there is more than one preference stated at that stage.

Rules can be applied as regards writing on the ballot paper. One such rule can relate to writing on the ballot paper by which the voter can be identified. If so the vote is invalid. It would appear that that such a rule originated in times, some considerable time ago, when an elector could be promised to receive payment if the vote was cast for the particular candidate. The writing of the voters name on the ballot paper would be obvious to a polling agent and so would be seen as proof and hence the promised payment would be made.

Where the election rules specify that a ballot paper has to bear the official stamp then absence of the mark indicates an invalid paper.

APPENDIX 8

PERMITTED EXPENDITURE IN FURTHERANCE OF CANDIDATURES

The provisions applying vary from country to country can be variable as prescribed by the relevant legislation in force. Hence this appendix can only comment in general.

Money can have a powerful impact on the outcome of elections and particularly so at general elections with marginal constituencies being targeted over a lengthy period of time both prior to and during the election period. Separate provisions can apply as indicated below. The overall approach is to prevent the democratic system being, in effect, manipulated by those who have the finance and intent to do so. Such action in this respect is commonly referred to as 'corruption'. There has been, for example, much discussion in legal circles down the years as to what exactly that word means. The UK Court of Appeal, in the case of Harvey [(1999) Crim L R 70 CA], confirmed that dishonesty is not an element of the term 'corruptly'. It approved the following interpretation – *"corruptly" means purposely, deliberately doing an act….. which the law forbids as tending to corrupt.* It is most important for the legitimacy of any democratic system that no one may gain or hold a parliamentary seat through bribery or any other form of corruption.

1. <u>Limitation of Candidate's expenses.</u> It is common practice for the legislation to prescribe a maximum amount that can lawfully be spent on the furtherance of a candidate' election expenses – those incurred by the candidate personally and those incurred on his or her behalf by the candidate's election agent.

2. <u>Party funding.</u> There are varying opinions as to the need for restrictions on the amount of funding that a political party can spend during elections. It was not until 1997 that the UK began to consider the introduction of a limit. The then Home Secretary, in evidence to the Home Affairs Select Committee, acknowledged that the then current law on party funding was outdated. "We need to modernise our approach to election spending" he said and pointed out that whilst the current laws impose strict limits on the amounts individual candidates can spend in their constituencies there was no control on what is paid out at national level. The chairman of the Committee commented that there was the need to return to issue-driven rather than money-driven elections. The Conservative opposition party at the time had only recently ended its opposition to a ban on foreign donations. There were concerns being expressed that Britain was heading towards the American system which was viewed as lavishing vast sums of money on advertising leaving politics in a back stage to image.

The UK system has been amended together with the establishment of an Electoral Commission with powers to oversee election expenses in all aspects. That requires a general oversight throughout the year with detailed accounts being submitted for audit.

3. <u>Funding from other sources</u>. Such funding seems to have become a major issue in some countries in recent years including Britain. It would appear that the intention is to influence, directly or indirectly, which of the candidates will be elected or else, for example, to influence the overall successful legislators in their selection of future economic policy. It can be the desire of very wealthy companies or individuals to obtain, by the use of money, a government with a political philosophy that aligns with their views. More recently there have been allegations of certain foreign governments spending considerable amounts of money, to obtain an electoral result that they see as being more amenable to them for political, security or trade advantage or, at times, for strategic purposes.

Legislation by itself, no matter how appropriate and encompassing it may be, will not prevent corruption. There is the need to have an effective oversight of the financing of elections. That is best effected by an independent body with clear and effective oversight coupled with precise timeframes for the submission to it of specified accounts from candidates, their election agents, political parties and others who have contributed to the electoral process.. There is the need for the submitted accounts to be audited. In the case of party funding the system has to be able to have a general oversight throughout the year. An appropriate complement of available, qualified and experienced staff is required over and above the election period and the immediate post-election period.

It is most important that the legislation specifies realistic and reasonable standards to be met. That is not just for the integrity of the system but also, equally important, for the public perception. In addition it is also important that the legislation clearly defines, for those who are required to submit returns, details of what precisely is needed. That can be illustrated by reference to two of the roles that commonly apply in and about elections.

A PARTY TREASURER
Each registered political party should be required to have a person registered as the party treasurer. The treasurer should be given the power to delegate specific duties to a limited number of named, designated persons whilst maintaining overall responsibility under the law. It should be the Treasurer's responsibility for each and every of the accounting requirements.

The duties specified for the treasurer should include the keeping of accurate accounting records that are sufficient to show both the party's transactions and to explain them. Such records should be maintained for a period no shorter than five years. A statement of accounts should be prepared for each financial year, approved by the management committee or party leader, as appropriate, before being submitted by the prescribed date to the supervisory body.

AN ELECTION CAMPAIGN OFFICER.
A party can appoint a person as its campaign officer. That officer can, in turn, appoint others, up to a specified number, as deputy campaign officers. No payments should be made or costs incurred, in respect of campaign expenditure, on behalf of a registered party, other than by the party treasurer, deputy party treasurer, campaign officer or deputy campaign officer. In addition all payments above a prescribed amount should be required to be supported by either an invoice or receipt.

It is both common practice and appropriate to set a time limit for the submission of any bills and their payment. That is to enable the party treasure to submit, by the prescribed time, final and complete details of the complete accounts incurred whether paid or not. Any bills not meeting the timetable should not be paid but listed as such in the accounts.

CONCLUDING REMARKS.
Confidence in the process will be lacking, no matter how efficient and effective an electoral system may be, should there be the public perception of the misuse of money to seriously affecting the outcome. The existence of a very active, free and independent media can play an important role as guardians of democracy especially when coupled with strongly developed civil society structures.